SWIMMING WITH THE WHALE

Teachings and Practices of Daskalos

&

The Researchers of Truth

Second Edition

a workbook by Daniel Joseph

Copyright © Daniel Joseph 2014 All Rights Reserved Worldwide

Library of Congress Control Number: 2012912157

ISBN Softcover: 978-1-62890-329-4

ISBN eBook: 978-1-62890-330-0

Cover Design & Photographs by Daniel Joseph

To order the Swimming with the Whale, Diving with the Whale series, please visit:
www.ResearchersofTruth.Net & www.TheWhale.us

No part of this document or the related files may be reproduced or transmitted in any form, by any means (electronic, photocopying, recording, or otherwise) without the prior written permission of the copyright owner.

First Edition: September 2012
Second Edition: January 2014

Contents

Dedication

Foreword

Introduction

Chapter One: A Seven Year Old Master & The 2000 Year Old Lineage of the Researchers of Truth

Chapter Two: A System for the Research of Truth

Chapter Three: A Day in the Life of Daskalos

Chapter Four: Take Aim

Chapter Five: Seven Levels of Consciousness

Chapter Six: Everything Is Mind

Chapter Seven: Three Worlds of Existence

Chapter Eight: Three Vehicles of the Soul

Chapter Nine: The Seven Heavens

Chapter Ten: Human Angels ~ Human Devils

Chapter Eleven: Brick by Brick

Chapter Twelve: I Laugh When I Hear the Fish Is Thirsty

Chapter Thirteen: The Pulse of Life

Chapter Fourteen: The Voice of an Angel

Chapter Fifteen: The Kiss of an Archangel

Chapter Sixteen: Across Time and Space

Chapter Seventeen: Life in the Higher Worlds

Chapter Eighteen: What Changes Is Not Real

Chapter Nineteen: Possibilities, Probabilities & the Divine Plan

Chapter Twenty: Your Brother Lives Again

Chapter Twenty-One: Ascending the Ladder of Relative Truth

Chapter Twenty-Two: The Truth about Myths

Chapter Twenty-Three: The Dead and the Sleeping

Chapter Twenty-Four: Divine Love ~ Human Love

Chapter Twenty-Five: Initiation & Protection

Epilogue: The Great Sun

Glossary: Terms

DEDICATION

The search for truth concerning God, man and the nature of reality is perhaps the greatest undertaking one could ever engage in during their life. It is a calling of many, the duty of some but really it is an underlying necessity for all.

The gentle persuasion to all is to: "Seek the truth and the truth will set you free," because the truth sets us free from our suffering, which is born from an ignorance of the truth. With pleasure I dedicate this book to my family, friends and to all seekers of truth worldwide.   ~ Daniel Joseph

FOREWORD

By Panayiota Theotoki Atteshli, Daskalos' Daughter

Dear Seekers of Truth,

    At the beginning, maybe you will find my father's (Daskalos) teachings difficult to understand, but, slowly, slowly all of you will realize all of these truths are within you. They are God's gift and everyone's rightful inheritance.

    The truths contained in these teachings remain inactive in you for a long time. Now is the time to decide to bring it up again, step by step, and with God's blessings to remember what you already know.

    I will give you some advice, the same advice my father gave to me a long time ago, "Learn to concentrate fully. Observe everything. Nothing must escape your attention. Practice Introspection every night. See your personality's behavior mentally through visualization. See, analyze and correct your personality's mistakes. This will help you meditate deeper and, in time, assimilate your present-day 'personality self' with your real 'self.' What a joy to be able to express your real 'Self', which is love; and to express this pure love through your present-day 'personality self.' Then you will see that it is so easy to proceed to higher levels."

    Daniel has studied and trained with Daskalos since 1989. I am grateful to Daniel for presenting these lessons in a simple and direct way to help you understand and experience the great truths contained in Daskalos' teachings. From the depth of my heart I wish you to fulfill your real aim in this life.

Love Panayiota

Panayiota Th. Atteshli
Strovolos Nicosia,
Cyprus January 24, 2010

INTRODUCTION

Because Daskalos chose not to seek fame but anonymous, selfless service, his time on Earth drew no more worldly attention than a ripple on the surface of the sea. Yet it may well be, that because of the life he chose to live, he will continue to have an ever-growing influence on his fellow man. Such that after he departed, it will one day be realized that there lived in our lifetime, a truly remarkable human being bearing great gifts for us all.

It is not possible to adequately convey the experience of sitting with him. Rather than a limit in Daskalos; I found an ever-expanding horizon of love, wisdom and power. Most human relationships tend to fall into one category or another but, for me, Daskalos assumed them all. He was a brilliant teacher who could describe God, man and the nature of reality in the finest detail and lead you into the direct experience of them. He personified the quintessential grandfather, captivating you with his expert story-telling abilities that underscored the principles of his teaching. At other times his care was like a loving mother watching over you with tenderness. He was a strong, competent father who would confidently advise you when you sought his help. He was an insightful psychologist, an advanced metaphysician, a compassionate confessor, a proficient spiritual co-worker as well as an expert guide to the unseen worlds of Spirit. He was a seeker's most trusted ally and a true brother of mercy. At other times he could make you to laugh so hard your jaw would ache. Even when he felt the need to point out your errors, he did so, not as a stern disciplinarian standing over you, but as a loving brother standing beside you who also offered effective solutions. He is, was and will always be a seeker of truth's best friend.

I wish that these pages open a small door for you to enter into the mystical world of Daskalos and to learn from his teachings and practice how to accelerate your spiritual progress and live happier.

May God's love, wisdom and power inspire your heart, mind and life wherever you are and wherever you go.

Daniel Joseph,

A Researcher of Truth

Chapter One
A SEVEN-YEAR-OLD MASTER
&
THE 2000-YEAR-OLD LINEAGE OF THE RESEARCHERS OF TRUTH

The Truth is a brilliant, many-sided diamond.
The Great Light fills this gem and colors gleam from every side.
Mystics, messengers, sages and teachers of all ages, races, and beliefs have spoken of a different face of this common Eternal Truth. ~ Daskalos

It is not possible for anyone using words from any language, to adequately describe who and what Dr. Stylianos Atteshlis, (aka Daskalos) really is. Nor is it possible for anyone to completely describe the teachings of the Researchers of Truth that poured through him like a mighty river. However, it may be possible to sketch a portrait of Daskalos, the mystic-healer, whose potent works spanned seven decades.

His was a life of healing and teaching that publicly began in 1919 on the Eurasian island of Cyprus at the far eastern end of the Mediterranean Sea -just above Egypt.

At this time, Greek-Christians and Turkish-Muslims living peacefully together populated Cyprus. But historically, Cyprus had seen great conflicts and been occupied by a succession of conquering empires throughout the ages. Layer upon layer of civilizations existed on the island continuously from the Neolithic to the modern age. The capitol of Cyprus, Lefkosia (Nicosia), is one of the world's oldest inhabited cities. The oldest part of the city is a great example of military architecture, enclosed by a moat and massive Venetian stone walls. The now dry moat was once strategically filled with water, channeled down from the mountains, for protection against invasion.

    Invasion, it seemed, was an underlying current of Cyprus history. The Hittites, Egyptians, Persians, Romans, Ottomans, Venetians, English and many others took turns occupying the island, which also had long periods of Greek control. For three hundred years Cyprus and its people were under attack by Arab armies as they raided and looted the island's wealth and terrorized its people. Alexander the Great conquered the island; as did King Richard the Lionhearted (who became the Lord of Cyprus), during the Third Crusade on his way to free the Holy Land from the Muslim King Saladin. One year later, King Richard sold the island of Cyprus to the Knights Templar, who also protected pilgrims on their way to visit the Holy Land and safeguard the pilgrim's cash as they traveled by setting up the first system of Travelers' Checks.

The Knights Templar is of significant interest to the Researchers of Truth, because at this time and location, they kept the ancient teachings on the Symbol of Life. The Symbol of Life was presented by Origen Adamantius (185 – 254 AD), an early spiritual giant, prolific writer, teacher, Christian Bishop, and considered one of the first and greatest Church Fathers. Origen was a strong proponent of the Doctrine of Reincarnation, which was also a solid part of the Church's teachings for the first five centuries AD. Origen taught, "Each Soul enters the world strengthened by the victories or weakened by the defects of its past lives. Its place in this world is determined by past virtues and shortcomings." Origen also presented the term "Absolute Beingness" as a more meaningful description of what people generically refer to as God.

Origen's version of the Symbol of Life and the Jewish Kabbalah both originated from the same ancient Egyptian Symbol of Life used in the old Mystery Schools of Egypt. Using elements of Saint John's Book of Revelations, Origen changed the Egyptian Symbol of Life into a purely Christian work. Earlier in Egypt, Moses, as an Egyptian Prince and High Hierophant in the Mystery Schools, had access to the extremely powerful knowledge associated with this teaching. Moses took the ancient Egyptian Symbol of Life, made changes to it and presented it as a purely Jewish work that is now known as the Kabbalah. The great wonders Moses demonstrated during the Exodus of the Jews from Egypt as told in the Bible were accomplished by his use of this secret knowledge.

Origen had been captured, imprisoned, tortured and had virtually every bone in his body broken at the hands of the Romans during their persecution of the Christians. Upon his release from prison, in the last four years of his life, Origen gave the Symbol of Life to the Essenes. The Essenes were Greek speaking Israelites; Greek was their mother tongue but they also spoke the local Aramaic language. The Essenes in this area are best known for the earlier hiding of their spiritual library from the Romans.

Their library was discovered in a cave by a young shepherd in 1946 and called the Dead Sea Scrolls. The Essenes in turn gave the Symbol of Life to the Knights Templar, where on Cyprus; they guarded its advanced secret science with their lives. Daskalos resurrected the all but lost teachings on the Symbol of Life and trained interested students in its use by giving them the keys to the secret knowledge of this great body of work.

In modern times, the British controlled the island of Cyprus in the early 1900's until it declared its independence from England in 1960. For fourteen years the Greek Christian Cypriots and the Turkish Muslim Cypriots lived under the one flag of the Cyprus Republic until political unrest between the two groups precipitated an invasion by Turkey in 1974. Hundreds of thousands of Greeks were displaced as the invading Turkish army drove them to the southern half of the island. Many were killed and many lost their homes. Daskalos was even shot and wounded during the occupation; he and his family suffered through bombings by the Turkish army.

Eventually the UN had to intervene and set up an armed peacekeeping force with a neutral zone across the entire island, which also ran right through the center of the city of Nicosia where Daskalos lived. To this day walking through old Nicosia, you will see streets with sand bagged and steel drum barricades, barber wire, armed soldiers in lookout posts and bullet holes in the Presidential Palace and other buildings around the neutral zone.

The UN imposed a neutral line (Green Line), which separates the Turkish Muslims on the north from the Greek Christians on the south of the island. But never did the conflict escalate and destroy the city like it did in Beirut, Lebanon just over 100 miles off the coast of Cyprus. Clearly Cyprus, the Island of Love, has historically been a cradle of conflict

It was into this volatile setting that the master Daskalos incarnated once again to continue his work. In 1919, the seven-year-old Daskalos was already able to self-consciously travel to the worlds of the higher dimensions. At this age, he could speak all the languages of his past incarnations, and he consciously communicated with "great intelligences" that guided him from the worlds beyond. His parents knew this and believed in his abilities but warned him not to reveal these gifts to other people. Sometimes his father would try (in vain) to comprehend just who and what his son was. From the beginning of this incarnation Daskalos knew who he was and the purpose of his life on Earth. However, he initially thought everyone could communicate with these higher intelligences that he called "brother guides." What he did not know at age seven, was that all the people around him were not the same as he was. However, he was about to find out just how different he really was.

One day in elementary school, Daskalos' arithmetic teacher called on him to solve a difficult math problem. Unfortunately, Daskalos was not at all prepared and admitted to the teacher that he had not studied this assignment. The teacher insisted that he come to the front of the class and try to solve the problem on the blackboard anyway.

Daskalos approached the black board with no idea how to solve the mathematics problem. The teacher read the problem out loud and Daskalos wrote it on the blackboard. Then, as Daskalos would later describe, "I felt near me one of my brother guides and friend, a Dominican monk who I knew centuries and centuries ago. He told me, 'Give me your hand, we shall solve the problem.'"

Daskalos took the chalk, placed it on the blackboard and his disincarnated guide, took control of his hand and solved the problem.

The surprised mathematics teacher asked him, "Why did you tell me you did not study?"

Daskalos innocently replied, "Sir, it was not me who solved the problem."

The teacher asked incredulously, "Then who was it?"

"It was Father Dominico, the Dominican monk who is standing near me. He got my hand and solved the problem," Daskalos openly answered. Father Dominico was one of Daskalos' mentors in a previous life that continued to assist him from a higher dimension.

The teacher angrily said, "I do not see anyone, and so do you think you are making a fool of me now?"

With the boy in hand the teacher told the principal of the school Daskalos' incredible story and left him with the principal to deal with. Fortunately, as it turned out, the principal was practicing spiritualism in secret. At that time the churchmen of Cyprus prohibited studying spiritualism and it could get you excommunicated from the Church. When the director saw Daskalos' writing on the blackboard he did not think it looked like the handwriting of a seven-year-old and considered Daskalos' explanation more seriously.

On the following Wednesday there was no school in the afternoon and it was arranged with Daskalos' father for Daskalos to come to the principal's office. That day Daskalos came to the principal's office and found a schoolmaster of mathematics, and a schoolmaster teaching Latin waiting for him. They wanted to know more about this little seven-year-old sage and his invisible helper. They planned to test the authenticity of Daskalos and Father Dominico for themselves. First, they tested him on arithmetic problems beyond his level of study. Then, they gave him algebra problems to solve, followed by square roots and logarithms. Each time, Father Dominico guided Daskalos' hand and unerringly solved the difficult problems.

Next, they wanted Daskalos to translate some lines from the works of Ovid (43 BC 17 AD), the Roman poet, whose narrative and linguistic skills are unmatched. Then, the Latin schoolmaster wanted to read the lines in Latin and asked Daskalos to write them down in the Greek language.

"Yes, of course, but in which version do you want it written in -the common spoken Greek or the formal 'pure' Greek?" Daskalos' replied.

The schoolmasters were looking at each other in disbelief. They told him, "Give it to us in both."

Daskalos, with the guidance of Father Dominico, complied and translated two pages of Latin. These astonished educated men challenged him further asking him to translate from a Latin Bible as the Latin teacher read it out loud. Daskalos complied and even corrected a mistake made by the reader whose Latin pronunciation was not so good. Then Daskalos, in full attunement with Father Dominico, began reading the Latin Gospel himself pronouncing the Latin perfectly.

Upon hearing this, the large plump Latin professor became overly excited and embraced Daskalos giving him a big kiss. Like most seven-year-old boys, Daskalos did not like this display of affection and instantly rubbed the kiss off.

Now, it would be a great mistake to think that Daskalos was "channeling" a higher entity called Father Dominico. Daskalos did not channel. Nor did he approve of anyone opening themselves up to unknown entities and unverified energies as a medium. That can be very dangerous and misleading. Instead, Daskalos (by means of attunement and "At-One-Ment") was able to coordinate himself with his old friend and guide. As soon as Daskalos was fully coordinated, whatever Father Dominico was doing with Daskalos' hand or communicating, that knowledge immediately became Daskalos' own knowledge too. Think of "At-One-Ment" between two beings as something similar to bringing two candle flames together. When the two individual candle flames come together, the light gets brighter and the two flames appear as one. Pull the candle flames apart and we see two individual flames again.

Daskalos taught that by developing our latent abilities of attunement, which will lead us to "At-One-Ment", we could assimilate knowledge about anyone or anything directly. Furthermore, the direct knowledge gained from attunement/At-One-

Ment comes much, much faster and more fully than it does by conventional studies. What would take years and years of Earthly learning can be accomplished in moments through "At-One-Ment."

The next time the elementary school director and the other university schoolmasters tested Daskalos, an accident happened. Another boy in the schoolyard was running and fell down on the gravel, which cut his knee open, causing him to bleed badly. The other teachers brought the boy crying into the director's office where Daskalos was.

Father Dominico instructed Daskalos to ask for water to clean the blood and stones from the injured boy's knee. Daskalos removed the stones and cleaned the knee, which continued to bleed profusely.

The director had already sent someone to find the doctor from the local neighborhood, who happened to be the cousin of Daskalos' mother and he knew many things about Daskalos' abilities. He arrived at the director's office and seeing Daskalos cleaning the wound, he told the director to allow Daskalos to continue what he was doing.

At this point, Father Dominico said to Daskalos, "Come, let's cure him," and instructed Daskalos to kneel and hold the boy's knee with both his hands. "Visualize the knee all right," caress it, see it all right and now take your hands away," Father Dominico directed. Daskalos did as he was instructed, removed his hands and there was no longer any blood or wound on the boy's knee – it was completely cured!

When the doctor saw the wound completely healed, he mentioned his family relationship with Daskalos and declared factually, "We are accustomed to these things!"

Sensing the great opportunity presented by this mystic-child-healer, the director made arrangements with Daskalos' father for him to come to the director's house on Friday evenings. Early next Friday, Daskalos arrived at the director's house to find a big sitting room filled with about twenty-five seekers all eager to learn about this amazing boy and his invisible guides.

They asked Daskalos, whom they called by his nickname, Lakis, if they could ask Father Dominico and his other guides certain philosophical questions. Daskalos agreed. They began asking questions and writing down the answers given by Daskalos. Then they started asking questions in different languages. Daskalos answered in perfect pronunciation in the same language as the question asked. The people were astonished. They were wondering how a boy of seven could answer these deep philosophical questions and how could he have learned foreign languages at such a young age.

These meetings went on for three weeks until Father Dominico and another guide, Father Yiohannan, informed Daskalos that these meetings could not continue in this way. Daskalos had been in continual, conscious contact with Yiohannan, his disincarnated mentor, for nearly 2000 years. Yiohannan advised that if the director and his students wanted to continue they must first make Seven Promises.

Yiohannan, guided Daskalos' hand to write down the Seven Promises, which are still used by Daskalos' students to this day – not even a comma has been changed. The Seven Promises are not oaths to any one person, organization or even God. The Seven Promises are promises the individual makes to their own Self, promising to try to live by them in thought, word and deed at all times, and under all circumstances. As Daskalos declared, "The seven promises embody a timeless pledge to the Divine Plan. Taking moral guidance from the promises through daily meditation an aspirant will, in time, attune himself to the Divine Laws of Creation."

On the following Friday, Daskalos announced the requirements for continuing, provided his new class with the Seven Promises and requested that each person make these promises before they continued. The director read the Seven Promises aloud; the other seekers stood reciting them with their hand on their heart, and received initiation from this diminutive master. The young Daskalos sat in a chair with his little feet dangling above the floor, and continued teaching his well-educated audience. So began the teaching and healing work of this seven-year old master on the island of Cyprus in 1919 at a time without, planes, cars, phones or even electricity.

Over the course of the next seventy plus years, Daskalos established more than 100 independent circles of study worldwide and many, many thousands of students have come into these circles and personally experienced profound spiritual awakenings and undeniable healings. So-called "incurable" diseases, such as deadly cancers, were "miraculously" cured in the presence of Daskalos. Daskalos' extraordinary skills empowered by the Holy Spirit, also enabled the "permanently" lame and disabled to walk freely again. Daskalos not only treated physical ailments, but also those whose hearts carried deep and persistent emotional wounds found relief under his loving care. Those who walked in mental darkness, negativity and confusion were led out of the shadows and back into the light by Daskalos. Of course, Daskalos never claimed he healed anyone and stated no person ever healed another person. The Holy Spirit does any healing that takes place. All a person can do in regards to healing is to train to become a fit conduit for the Holy Spirit to do its healing works through.

Daskalos' readiness and ability to train interested seekers of truth in advanced methods of healing and truth-seeking was remarkable. He helped countless seekers raise their consciousness to higher levels. He established a series of studies that revealed deeper teachings to the students as they advanced through the outer circle, inner circle, in-more circle and inmost circle. To those serious researchers who were prepared, he willingly provided more advanced training, in such things as Psycho-Noetical form construction, Exosomatosis (conscious out of body experience – OBE), distant healing and much more.

Daskalos placed the well-named "Golden Keys" to the kingdom of the heavens in our hands and taught us how to use them. We could rightly say that, in 1919, the seven year-old Daskalos established the beginning of the modern day Circles for the Research of Truth and the System for the Research of Truth, which continues to this day. Today, an advanced brother or sister Researcher of Truth heads each of Daskalos' Researchers of Truth Circles. Each circle is independent from the other circles, which means that the leaders and members of one circle do not interfere with the work or members of the other circles.

However, the current expression of the teachings of the Researchers of Truth was originally established over 2000 years ago. Traveling back in time to the beginning of humankind's arrival on the planet, we could also rightly say that the research of the truth began when the first primitive human on Earth began to wonder, "Where am I? Who am I? Where have I come from and what is my purpose?" So the research of truth is not something exclusive to the members of the Researchers of Truth Circles. The research of truth is the real calling and underlying duty of every human being.

The teachings of the Researchers of Truth are not presenting unverified theories to be accepted blindly and without proof. These teachings are the clear reflection of the Truth, the nature of reality and the Soul of each of us. The truth contained in the teachings is to be sincerely investigated and experienced directly by each one of us. The real truth is not something we get from outside ourselves. The real truth is already in us, in our own Divine Nature. Wise, loving brother and sister guides are here to help those who are interested, learn how to research and discover this truth within themselves.

They will not do the work for you but they will help and guide you as you ascend the ladder of relative truth towards the absolute truth. Teachings, teachers and guides show the way, but each one of us must make the effort to walk in this way if we are to reach our aim of self-realization, that is, to realize who and what we really are, have always been and always will be.

THE PRACTICE: OVERVIEW

In order to succeed in raising our consciousness to higher levels we must be honest with our self. The Researchers of Truth make seven promises to the Inner Self. The promises help us clean our personality's consciousness and assimilate it with the Inner Self.

In this regard it does not take great effort. Not to say it is simple to live by these promises, but it is not all that difficult or unpleasant either. All we need is decisive determination; then, in a state of peace and calm, we can begin to practice them. The seven promises are made by an initiate in the Outer Circle of the Researchers of Truth and prepare them for a new way of living. It is a happier life that is calmer, more satisfying and offers a better future. As you slowly start to comprehend the deeper meanings of these promises, you will start to understand many, many things that you cannot possibly understand now.

THE PRACTICE: SEVEN PROMISES OF A RESEARCHER OF TRUTH

I promise to myself:

1. To serve at all times and in all places Absolute Beingness to whom I whole heartedly belong
2. To be ready at all times and in all places to serve the Divine Plan
3. To make good use of the Divine Gifts of thought and word at all times, in all places and under all circumstances
4. To endure patiently, without complaining, all forms of trials and tribulation which the most wise Divine Law may bestow upon me
5. To love and serve my fellow human beings sincerely from the

depths of my heart and Soul no matter what their behavior may be towards me

6. To meditate and to contemplate daily Absolute Beingness, with the objective of total coordination of my thoughts, desires, words and actions with Its Divine Will

7. To investigate and check every night whether all my thoughts, desires, words and actions are in absolute harmony with the Divine Law.

Chapter Two
A SYSTEM FOR THE RESEARCH OF TRUTH

Our system of Esoteric Christianity celebrates the eternal truths known to all great religious traditions, while firmly based in the teachings of the God-Man Joshua Immanuel the Christ and the New Testament. Through directed study, exercises and meditations, we seek the balanced evolution and integration of our entire being. Our approach is methodical, safe and self-evident. ~ Daskalos

THE TEACHING

The official roots of the Researchers of Truth teachings go back over 2000 years. Daskalos organized these teachings into an integrated System for the Research of Truth. Some of these teachings have appeared over the last two millenniums in fragmented parts and are only now presented as a complete whole system. Many of these teachings have been undisclosed to the public until today.

According to the Bible, "When Jesus was born in Bethlehem of Judea in the days of Herod the king, behold, there came three wise men from the east to Jerusalem saying, 'where is he that is born King of the Jews?' For we have seen his star in the east, and have come to worship him."

According to the Akashic records and to the Catholic doctrine, Jesus' mother, Mary, was also born by Immaculate Conception. When Mother Mary was three years old her mother, Hanna, dressed her in all white and presented her to the Essene Temple to be dedicated to God as a White Dove of the Heavens according to the Essene rites. These Essenes were Greek-speaking Israelites living in Palestine and their name meant, "The Pure," and is derived from the Aramaic word "Asa," which means "healer." They were healers. Unlike their brothers the Jews, the Essenes did not believe in an angry and revengeful God, but in a merciful father God just as Christ would come to describe.

As a White Dove of the Heavens, Mary was to live on the temple grounds devoting her life to prayer, service and care of the sick and elderly. Mary was destined to remain a virgin and, at the age of thirteen, her family gave her into a white marriage with a carpenter named Joseph who was a widower. According to the Essene custom, a man could have a traditional marriage but could also have other "White Marriages" at the same time, which were only of pure service and dedicated to protecting and caring for the woman.

At fifteen years of age, Mary was in prayer when the Archangel Gabriel visited her and announced she was chosen to be the vessel for the birth of the Son of God – the Messiah who was predicted to come by the Prophets in the Old Testament. When Joseph found out he became greatly concerned and confused but an Angel also appeared to him in a dream telling him that this was indeed an immaculate conception and Mary would bear a son who would save people from their sins and he would be called in the Aramaic language Joshua, which, in the Greek language, was Jesus. He was called Joshua Immanuel. Immanuel means, "God is with us."

But let's go further back in time to 500 years before the birth of Christ, to the very beginning of our story when a prophecy foretold of Christ's coming. This prophet was no other than the Buddha. About 500 BC, the Buddha's disciple and dearest attendant, Ananda, asked the Buddha, "Are You God?" The Buddha replied, "No, but God himself will be born on Earth in 500 years."

Five centuries later in India there was a mystic-king named Maharajah Ram-Touaivahan who was aware of this prophecy. Through astrology, clairvoyance and Exosomatosis (Conscious out of Body Experience) began to attune and follow the developing events leading up to the birth of Christ. He had followed the life of Mary and determined the time and place in Palestine where she would give birth to the Christ child.

He was so sure of the coming of God that he gave his kingdom to his mother and brother as joint rulers and set out for Palestine, accompanied by his friend and counselor Chekitana. Along the way they passed through Armenia, which in those days was divided into two warring kingdoms, ruled by twin brothers named Gaspar and Dikran. The Maharaja Ram reconciled the brothers' conflict and Gaspar permitted Dikran to rule both kingdoms, so that Gaspar (Kaspar) might join the Maharaja Ram on pilgrimage to pay homage to God incarnated.

Journeying south, they met a Bedouin King and astrologer, the

Shakh Baal-das-Aaussar (his name meant "The Servant of the Egyptian God Osiris"). The Bedouin King Baal-das-Aaussar (Baldassar or Balthazar) asked to accompany them, and, with his two attendants, he also joined the entourage. In time they reached Palestine, These advanced mystic-pilgrims could read the thoughts of Herod, the King of Palestine, and were well aware of the king's evil intent to stop the predicted coming of a Messiah, a savior of mankind. Despite that, Baal-das-Aaussar insisted on visiting Herod in hopes that their visit might change the ruler's crule heart, but it did not.

From there they continued to Bethlehem, where they found the Holy Family. The Maharajah Ram-Touaivahan presented himself and Chekitana to Joseph and Mary. He then presented the Armenian King, Gaspar, and his attendants. The Bedouin King stepped forward introducing himself and his two attendants. Then Maharajah Ram came forward to the Christ child, took off his royal purple robe, and placed it around the manger. Only his white undergarment remained.

Kneeling before the Christ child in the manger, the Maharaja Ram pulled his short sword from its sheaf and broke it in two over his knee. He then laid the two pieces at the foot of the manger saying, "My Lord at your feet is all power and authority."

Looking at the Christ child he exclaimed, "Ham El Khior," which in his language meant "I See God." From then on he was called Ham El Khior, which has been handed down through the ages as Melchior.

Daskalos had a replica of this sword, which he used to initiate members into the different degrees of his Circles for the Research of

Truth. For initiation into the outer circle, a candidate would kneel in front of Daskalos and two inner circle members while pledging his or her service for humanity and other things. Then, with the un-pointed sword, Daskalos touched the candidate initiating them into the outer circle of the System for the Research of Truth.

After the Maharaja Ram broke his sword, the Armenian King Gaspar, or Casper as it has been written in the Bible, knelt before the God-child pressing his forehead to the manger he wept saying, "My Lord and God of Love have mercy upon us. Have mercy on mankind. No more wars, no more bloodshed. Guide us oh Lord to peace."

Then, Balthazar similarly bowed before the Christ Child and glorified the one true God. The Three Kings gave their gifts of gold and incense, as told in the Bible, and advised the Holy family that they would soon need the gold. King Herod of Israel, aware of the prophecy of the birth of the Messiah to be born in Bethlehem, had set out to stop it. Fearing a threat to his Earthly rule, King Herod ordered all boys under the age of two in and around Bethlehem to be killed. The Three Kings warned the Holy family of this and advised them to leave Bethlehem immediately. Then Balthazar gave Mary and Joseph two Bedouin robes to disguise themselves during their escape.

After escaping out of Bethlehem disguised as nomadic Bedouins, they joined a Bedouin caravan in Jerusalem and leaving Israel they traveled along the eastern side of the Dead Sea into Egypt, eventually coming to stay in the Essene community of Heliopolis along the east side of the Nile River. Here they remained until King Herod died eleven years later and they could safely return to Israel.

After this encounter with the Holy Family, the mystic king Ham El Khior (Melchior) began the modern lineage of Researchers of Truth Circles that continue to this day.

These teachings are very deep and broad, so it helps to study and practice them with others as a group. These groups are the Circles for the Research of Truth. An initiated Circle Leader heads them. One can advance very far in the outer circle, even gaining the ability of Exosomatosis. (Exosomatosis is a Greek word meaning "conscious out of body experience.") The Inner circle members wear a long white robe symbolizing Melchior's inner white garment when he removed his worldly outer cloak and draped it on the Christ child's manger. So the Inner Circle members of the Researchers of Truth wear white robes, symbolizing their purity of intent, dedication, and in reverence for that moment.

Each official Circle for the Research of Truth has the whole teaching, "There is enough material in a few lessons to work for hundreds of years," as Daskalos often said. The teaching, the System for the Research of Truth, is complete. As students of this system we do not need more theory, the knowledge is already there in the teachings Daskalos so diligently brought forward. What is needed, however, is for each student to make an honest effort to use these teachings to investigate the truth directly; to find the truth about who and what they are and be liberated from the suffering and illusions woven by egoism.

Daskalos supervised these circles and also considered himself a member of each of the circles. "No successor is needed…When I pass over I will continue to supervise the circles," Daskalos promised. Each one of the advanced brother or sister guides heading an official circle represents Daskalos (as a teacher) to their circle. Likewise, Daskalos represents the teachings of the higher intelligences he is in contact with.

These so-called higher intelligences are not only advanced human beings who serve as disincarnated guides but also the Divine intelligences. These great intelligences express themselves as the Archangels in all the orders known and unknown to man. Daskalos introduced us to these orders and taught us how to come into conscious communication with them. They rejoice in seeing us make our long awaited approach. They welcome us and are ready to reveal their high wisdom to any sincere seeker. Their Divine intelligence is so immense compared to our human intelligence that it is like comparing the intelligence of a great scientist to that of a small child.

Clearly, Daskalos was extremely advanced, as were the teachings he skillfully planted in our hearts and minds. What is most important in the System for the Research of Truth is not the personality of Daskalos or the leader of any circle. The System for the Research of Truth is not a personality cult. Personality-based groups can be very dangerous to both the leader with the charismatic personality as well as to those who follow them. What is important in our system is the teaching, which has been carefully preserved and passed forward for twenty centuries by the brother and sister guides in the System for Research of Truth. The brother and sister guides leading the Researchers of Truth Circles are not accepting praise, adoration, or money for their healing work. They are not expecting or accepting any greater respect than the respect given to each and every circle member.

THE PRACTICE: OVERVIEW

The system for the Research of Truth we are following is free from fanaticism and religious prejudices. What are we researching but the truth? For millennia we have had the persuasion to seek and know the truth. We seek the truth because, when you find the truth, it will set you free. The truth sets us free from our suffering, pain and illusions. Does this mean that other spiritual systems are not good?

Of course there are many other systems, which are very good, but there are also many other systems that are not good. So we must be careful, use reason and observe the effects that any system has upon us and then select one that produces good and tangible results.

The Researchers of Truth are not zealously claiming we are the only ones who found the truth. You can find the truth in all serious religions and spiritual systems. There are many roads that lead to the truth. Our way is good, and encourages the exploration of other traditions and spiritual systems through the framework of our teachings; knowing that it is by comparison that we come closer to the truth. However, there are certain harmful practices we discourage such as, dangerous breathing practices from the east, or any channeling in which a person opens up to unknown sources and energies.

God's first gift to all beings is free will. We respect free will of all and will never take advantage of the financial, emotional or mental autonomy of others. Everyone comes to the truth in his or her own time and in his or her own way. The ultimate aim may be the same for all, but the individual experiences we have along the way will vary from person to person. A Researcher of Truth will not try to get others to accept his or her beliefs. A Researcher will not go out and try to solicit or convert others to these teachings. The Researchers of Truth are not about spreading the teachings, instead they stand ready to embrace those who come to them and help them understand the meaning of the teachings in an ever-deeper way.

The System for the Research of Truth has two legs. One is the Esoteric Teachings, which are very necessary, and suggest a path to follow. The second leg is the Esoteric Practices which, when sincerely practiced, accelerate our movement along this path. The first and foremost qualification a person needs to engage in the teachings and practices is sincerity with oneself and real love for others. The spiritual path that is suggested by our teachings has been tread by advanced Researchers of Truth who have gone before us who take great enjoyment in keeping the path well lit. They aren't keeping it lit for their own progress, but to help you on your way because they have taken an oath that says, "As long as there is pain on the planet, they will not take their final deliverance." They will be the last to reach deliverance. These advanced individuals are real brothers and sisters of mercy.

Some of you will also choose this path, because of your love toward your fellow human beings. You will not make this choice in the belief that you will sacrifice yourself for others. That would be a mistake. Christ said, "It is mercy I want; not sacrifice." If there is even the slightest trace of egoism within you, you might be tempted to think that you are making a sacrifice for others, but it is not really so. Gradually, we will make progress through incarnation in matter, on the cross of the four elements: Earth, Water, Fire and Ether. This is the way towards real life and redemption. This is the way to the real resurrection -living in a fully awakened, Self-Aware state. This is a kind of life that cannot be compared with the life most people are living now in the shadows of their illusions instead of the light. This light will rise from within each of us but, unless you forsake your egoistic self, you should not expect your personality self to be resurrected as the Soul-Self in Self-Realization.

THE PRACTICE: PATTERNED BREATHING

Too many people have developed poor breathing patterns subconsciously and poor health and low energy levels are the result.

We come into this world and immediately draw our first breath of life. Normal breathing provides a certain quantity of energy needed by our material body, but this is virtually done subconsciously. When we start consciously breathing in the proper way, we can greatly increase the quantity of energy we take in and store. There are many good breathing exercises available to us today. However, there are also many bad breathing exercises that can damage your nervous system, over stimulate the energy centers or Chakras and in some cases bring on bouts of insanity. Breathing affects the health of our body as well as our psychological health too, so we must be very careful which ones we adopt.

We recommended a basic breathing technique that has been used for thousands of years that is done in a deep but comfortable rhythmical pattern. Our breath is to be coordinated with our heartbeat simultaneously, which is driven by the Pulse of Life coming from the Holy Spirit. In breathing as with anything in life, steady rhythms create harmony and produce balance, whereas unsteady rhythms bring disorder and imbalance. Start by relaxing your body and dropping all the unnecessary thoughts that race through your mind and then still all of the emotions flooding your heart. Now, inhale for three beats of the heart and then, without pausing, exhale for three beats of the heart. In the beginning you may need to count to yourself as your breathe in and out. Later you will be able to hear your heartbeats as you breathe and not have the need to count.

- Breathe in through the nostrils for three heartbeats
- During the 1st heartbeat, inhale & fill the lower part of your lungs & abdomen
- During the 2nd heartbeat, inhale & fill the middle part of your lungs
- During the 3d heartbeat, inhale & fill the upper part of your lungs & chest fully. Then, immediately begin to exhale through your mouth for three heartbeats
- During the 1st heartbeat exhale to release the air in the lower part of lungs
- During the 2nd heartbeat exhale to release the air in the middle part of your lungs
- During the 3rd heartbeat exhale to release the air in the upper part of your lungs

Repeat this for up to five minutes each day and in time it will become smooth and natural.

    We start this practice with three heartbeats during inhalation and exhalation then we can try with four or six. For those doing healing work and psychotherapy they should practice until they can do the six count breath. Later, one might advance to seven or eight heartbeats. Be warned, forcing the breath or holding the breath between in inhalation and exhalation can cause hemorrhaging in the lungs. We do not perform for five heartbeats because that rhythm can produce undesirable results. Simply find one that you feel is most natural and comfortable for you and develop your skill with that one. Learning this vital patterned breathing will be like building a foundation for all our meditation practices that follow.

Chapter Three
A DAY IN THE LIFE OF DASKALOS

All you need is to practice; to make as part of your life the teaching and to engage yourselves seriously, daily, with the right meditation, learning the concentration, observation, and introspection. You have to work; you have to use your own powers. Everything else, books and brother-instructors are showing the way and helping you, but -you have to toil yourself to find the truth, and to know the truth concerning Life. ~ Daskalos

Traveling from America to Daskalos on the island of Cyprus at the far eastern end of the Mediterranean Sea was a long journey. After the typical 24-hour passage and landing on the coast of Cyprus in Larnaca we would immediately make our way to where Daskalos lived in the capital city of Nicosia at the center of the island. Approaching the city, it is impossible not to notice a huge Turkish Flag in the distance that had been carved in to a mountain range in the Turkish-occupied half of the island; it the largest flag in the world according to the Guinness Book of World Records.

It is a painful reminder of the invasion that drove 40% of the

Greek population from the northern side of the island to the southern. About 200,000 Greeks lost their homes, businesses and (sometimes) family members as they ran for their lives to the southern side of the island. In another carving on a mountain range (in huge Greek letters), the Turks put the words, "The last time you ran, the next time you will swim." This was an ever-present warning of the Turks' desire to drive the Greeks completely off the island.

In those days some of us English-speaking students would often stay in an old style Cypriot hotel called the Averoft Hotel. As mentioned before, the UN created a neutral zone between the Turkish side and the Greek side that divided the capital city of Nicosia. This partition was well-protected by armed Turkish soldiers guarding their side of the division, and then there was about two hundred feet of neutral zone guarded by the UN Soldiers. Then there were armed Greek Soldiers protecting their side of the division. The Alveroft Hotel was a just down the street from this troubling divide. The inside of the hotel featured an old Cypriot style of handcrafted wood; wooden plank walls, balconies, window shutters, and furniture were all made from the same type of wood. Typical of Cypriot structures at that time there were no window screens. Because of the high heat the shutters had to be kept open to let in the night air, which also let in packs of very strategic, aggressive mosquitoes or "Mozzies" as the British students call them.

After a restful night of sleeping (in 100 degree heat with flocks of commando mosquitoes sucking your blood like tiny vampires), we would rise, eat a complimentary breakfast of hard cheese and even harder white toast and head straight to Daskalos' home. Daskalos' home was actually in Strovolos, a suburb of Nicosia. His was a very modest-sized home on a corner lot originally built from stone, but now covered in pastel bluish-green stucco with a clay tile roof in a closely built neighborhood of similar constructions. An iron fence painted an aqua marine color a few yards in front of his home opened to lead to a small terrazzo-tiled porch with long planter boxes containing many plants. Wooden louvered shutters also painted aqua marine covered the windows to block the relentless Cyprus sun. The double entrance doors to his home were painted metal frames with full-length textured glass inserts decorated on the outside with wrought iron designs. If those doors could talk, it would take many books just to contain all the miraculous stories of the people who passed through them.

Opening the door revealed a small living room with simple chairs, couch and a coffee table. On the coffee table was an empty fish bowl covered in purple Smurf stickers that belonged to Daskalos' grandson. Paintings of unusually colorful, bold landscapes hung on every wall, all painted by Daskalos. At this point in time the walls were covered with light tan weave-like wallpaper and the wood trim was painted white. Potted cacti and occasionally fresh flowers and greenery brought by grateful students appointed the room.

Often in the morning Daskalos' daughter, Panayiota would offer a Cyprus Coffee. Cypriots are very hospitable in general and Panayiota is even more so. Cyprus coffee is actually Turkish coffee, but because of the historical problems with the Turks, the Greeks refused to call it Turkish coffee. Cyprus coffee consisted of about a teaspoon of finely ground coffee, a shot glass full of water and what tasted like three teaspoons of sugar all boiled together and served in a little tiny coffee cup. As it cooled, the grounds would sink to the bottom of the cup and you would sip the coffee from the top of the cup so as not to get coffee grounds between your teeth, which I always managed to do anyway.

A typical day in the life of Daskalos in the late 80s, as I observed, started at around 6 AM. He would get up eat and then the local Cypriots would start arriving around 7:30 AM seeking guidance and healing. Around 9:30 the Westerners seeking Daskalos' help would start to stream in. They would come and sit in Daskalos' humble living room waiting their turn to see him privately. When a person's turn came, they would go and sit with Daskalos in a small sitting room adjacent to the living room.

Entering the sitting room revealed simple upholstered furniture, a built-in wooden hutch with shelves filled with various items such as a white eagle carved from marble, pictures, candle sticks, crucifixes, a painting of Christ and other small items; many of which looked like they were gifts given to Daskalos. A large incense burner, like the kind used in the Greek churches, hung from a nail in the wall that was covered in light grey wallpaper with delicate white floral designs. A very large Symbol of Life painting hung on the wall and a loud grandfather clock that sharply ticked as it marked the passing of your precious time with Daskalos. His home was only yards from busy Pericleous Street in Strovolos. Incredibly noisy motorbikes without mufflers often zoomed by drowning out Daskalos' voice from time to time, which never seemed to bother him.

Just sitting with Daskalos alone was an amazing experience at many levels. One thing that was immediately apparent was the degree of care and attention he gave each of us. His deep listening and equally deep replies to your questions brought comfort and insights. He even handled less important curiosity questions with grace and sincerity. He did not always wait to hear you speak your questions before he answered them. He could hear your thoughts perfectly clear, and would often speak to your silent thoughts and questions.

Daskalos' quiet human nature reflected his luminous Divine nature with brilliant simplicity. His full attention, deep gaze, purposeful movement, profound words, and even the gentle touch from his massive hands disclosed the power of one fully established in the Self. At one level, his appearance was that of a common elderly Cypriot. Yet when he taught or healed, the power of something much greater was revealed. What you saw when you were with Daskalos, was seen partially through your own filter of pre-set ideas and partially due to what he allowed you to see. On rare occasion he might slightly lower the veil of the elderly Cypriot. What stood before you then was a being with a strength and radiance impossible to describe.

One day, I took a well-known (but controversial) photo to him for his reading on it. The image in the photo started with a print of the Shroud of Turin. The so-called shroud of Turin purports to have been the fabric they covered Christ with after his crucifixion and allegedly bears the image of the crucified Christ. In 1985, an Australian lady had a printout of the shroud of Turin and took it to Sai Baba, the famous Hindu Swami in India. The lady took the printout of the face on the shroud and handed it to Sai Baba for a blessing. Sai Baba took the printout in his hand and produced from it a sheet of glossy photographic paper that was blank. Sai Baba is well known for his materializations and I had witnessed some myself. So when Sai Baba passed his open palm over the glossy paper a color image of the face of Jesus appeared on it. The resultant image was a more clearly defined face somewhat similar to the face on the shroud with more realistic qualities. Sai Baba announced this is actually how Jesus looked. I had a copy of this photograph and now I had an extraordinary opportunity to ask for verification from Daskalos who, as a Spirit Soul was incarnated with Christ in biblical Palestine.

Daskalos had known the real face of Christ and could remember it as easily as we can remember the face of our dearest loved one. I took this controversial photograph to Daskalos and asked if he knew about the Shroud of Turin. Daskalos replied, "Of course I do, it was created by a Nun." The earliest documented record of the Shroud's appearance occurred in 1350 AD. Interestingly, at the time I handed the photo to Daskalos, three laboratories were each doing independent Carbon Dating tests on the linen shroud. Later they announced from their tests that the shroud was made between 1260 and 1390 AD, further collaborating that it was not possible for the Shroud of Turin to have existed at the time of Christ.

So I asked Daskalos if this image in the Sai Baba materialization was the real face of Jesus. He looked at the image for a bit, which showed Christ with lighter hair than typical, dark brown eyes and a beard. Daskalos announced the face was similar. Then, he started describing the face of Christ from his own experiences. When he spoke, his love for Christ was clearly evident. Daskalos described Christ's eyes as soft green and not brown as shown in this print. He talked about how Christ enjoyed life and always had a sweet smile on his face; and not somber like he has been historically depicted. He said to me, "Christ's hair was not light color," as shown in Sai Baba's image. "Christ hair color was like yours," he said softly and he reached up and pulled on a lock of my brown hair.

After helping as many people as he could in the morning, at 10:30 Daskalos would leave his home and walk a couple of blocks down the street to give the public lesson in the Stoa, with a pack of smiling students happily trailing along with him.

Locals in his neighborhood would sometimes smile at him and give the traditional Greek morning greeting of "Kalimera." Daskalos had some sensitivity with his eyes so he often wore aviator-style dark sunglasses as he walked to the Stoa. In the wintertime, he would drape a long black wool topcoat over his shoulders during this walk and with the sunglasses and his height gave him a very commanding look.

Daskalos gave daily lessons in the Stoa, which was a small freestanding stucco building. Outside the Stoa students would gather in a small pleasant garden area. Typical of Cypriot tradition, the yard had Lemon and Orange trees with Grape vines draped across a trellis. Daskalos loved flowers and cacti and these too were in the garden. At this time maybe 20 to 40 people (young and old) would come for the day's lesson. They were mostly from Germany, Switzerland, and Austria, with the occasional American, Aussie or Brit mixed in. All were eager to hear Daskalos reveal his advanced teaching and perhaps witness a miracle healing.

Inside the Stoa, there were rows of cushioned chairs, paintings of Christ and a Symbol of Life painting by Daskalos hung on the walls. Sunlight filtered into the room through simple wooden shuttered windows. Hanging across the front wall was a golden curtain. Behind it, there was a simple wooden cross, a painting of Christ and other items used in his Inner Circle meetings. Once inside many pulled out their own tape recorders and placed them on a small table next to where Daskalos was to sit. His chair was just like the rest of the ones in the room. He did not sit on a stage but on the same level with us all. There was no special decoration or flowers or guru/disciple like behavior. Daskalos required no special treatment or trappings. It was just Daskalos, his audience, and the high teachings that came through him like a torrent of truth. When Daskalos entered through the doorway a powerful silence fell over the room, the tape recorders were all clicked on and everyone stood for the beginning prayer. Daskalos looked out at his audience, flooding the room with his vibration. He was strong, tall and the energy of his presence gave him a larger than life appearance. His attention to the moment brought focus to us all. Concentrating deeply, fingertips touching with palms apart, Daskalos closed his eyes took a deep breath and spoke the opening prayer. The first part of the opening prayer was the traditional Lord's Prayer.

Our Father in heaven,
hallowed be your name.
Your kingdom come,
your will be done,
on earth, as it is in heaven.
Give us this day our daily bread,
and forgive us our debts,
as we also have forgiven our debtors.
And lead us while in temptation,
but deliver us from evil.

The second part of his opening prayer was:
Absolute Infinite Beingness, God. Everlasting Life, Love and Mercy.
Manifesting Yourself in Yourself as Your Total Wisdom and Your Almightiness.
Enlighten our minds to understand You are the Truth.
Clean our hearts to reflect Your Love towards You and towards all other human beings.
Amen

After the prayer Daskalos sat immediately down and began without hesitation, expressing an un-broken ninety-minute stream of consciousness in words. His word poured from him like a mighty river. He chose his words very purposefully combining them in unique ways to express the lofty concepts of his teachings, all of which he delivered in English with a thick Cypriot accent. It was like spiritual white water rafting. The deep and powerful currents of his thoughts carried the lecture, but it was up to his audience to stay with the flow and catch his meaning. This took steady concentration. Daskalos very often delivered the public lessons starting first with an expansive description of the Absolute Reality. Further into the lessons he would narrow the focus down to finely tuned, practical information concerning our life on the Earth, occasionally seasoned with hilarious personal stories from his own life. Daskalos, like Socrates before him, used a technique in his lectures of asking and then answering his own questions. He did this to draw your attention to very important parts in the teaching and to get you to start your own line of reasoning that would lead you to a fuller understanding of the advanced ideas presented.

From time to time, Daskalos would dive deep into one of the many branches of the teachings, going deeper and deeper. When he sensed he had gone too far and was losing his audience he would stop and say, "I am afraid I have taken you into very, very deep waters now and not all of you are expert swimmers. We must come to shallower waters, to more practical work in order to reach this level of knowledge." Swimming in deep waters was an excellent metaphor; it really was like he was giving us lessons on how to swim through the multi-dimensional ocean of existence. For me, meeting Daskalos was like swimming in a vast ocean and then suddenly and silently having a great whale surface right next to you. The enormity of this spiritual giant completely dwarfed you as a personality. The powerful currents of his massive movements drew you along with him as he plunged deep in to his profound teachings.

My first encounter with him was in 1989 and it was a fortunate time to have met Daskalos. He had purposefully kept a low profile preferring to remain anonymous, but this was about to change. Word of Daskalos, the healer and mystic, was spreading, particularly in Germany, Switzerland and Austria. However, at this moment in time, it was possible to come close to him and get to experience a bit of Daskalos the man too. There were such enjoyable moments just sitting with him in his living room or kitchen quietly. These ordinary times were always extraordinarily rich and pregnant with possibilities

As mentioned in a 2003 issue of Oprah Winfrey's O magazine, "Daskalos was widely regarded as the greatest Christian mystic of modern times." He is not only important in what he revealed, but also in the moment in time he revealed it. Currently, people are living in confusion, fear and under great tension. The overvaluation of the material side of life while underestimating basic spiritual and human values has produced great imbalances individually and globally. Like other enlightened masters have done age after age, Daskalos came to remind this generation of the truth and guide them back to the real Self and its source.

Daskalos explained that, "The teachings of the Researchers of Truth have appeared throughout the centuries but only in fragmented parts." Much of the teachings had been kept in secret; passed on and enriched by successive generations of researchers, while purposely hidden from the public. However, as Daskalos declared, "Times have changed and now it is permissible to reveal much more."

Daskalos and his message are especially important and well suited to the daily concerns and spiritual aspirations of those living within modern culture. Daskalos lived and worked within the framework of society. He held a job, raised a family, paid bills and met all the same worldly challenges most of us do. It is not possible for most people today to adopt a cloistered monastic life or an ascetic life of a yogi in order to develop spiritually. Traditional religious teachings within society have too often stagnated into the dry sands of ritual. They have lost the vital connection to the spiritual reality behind their teachings and thus they are not satisfying the spiritual thirst within humanity. Many alternative groups have risen up to meet this growing spiritual need only to fall prey to the lure of financial reward. Instead of freeing the people of materialism, they often end up fostering a kind of spiritual materialism. Daskalos never charged those who came to him. He even shared his meager pension money anonymously with his neighbors when they were in need.

Today, Daskalos and his teachings are vitally important as they offer both the theoretical framework and experiential methods for each of us to know truth directly for ourselves. Daskalos' spiritual wisdom and knowledge of the worlds beyond was his very own. It did not come from reading books or listening to the dogma of a particular brand of religion or spirituality. His teachings came from his own direct research of God, man and the nature of reality, which confirmed what other masters in the past have revealed. Therefore, what he taught was authentic and verifiable by anyone who wants to make the effort to engage themselves with these teachings. He was an exemplary citizen of two worlds within the same reality: the luminous world of Spirit and the mundane world of matter. Because of this, Daskalos' teachings strike a chord in those who seek a spiritual life while still engaged in family, careers and worldly responsibilities.

Experiencing Daskalos up close revealed a benchmark of the human potential. His way of living and helping revealed what being human really means. Daskalos had two daughters, which he raised after his wife passed over. He also had two granddaughters who tell how when they were young he would tell them lively bedtime stories, complete with sound effects. Daskalos would create a kind of never-ending bedtime story for the granddaughters just like he had done for his daughters. Each night he would tell them a little bit more of the story. First, he would tell part of the story while sitting on the bed of one granddaughter then he would move over and sit on the edge of the bed of the other granddaughter and tell the next part of the story. He made the stories very funny but also with a bit of teaching mixed in.

Daskalos had a grandson, who would often come to his home after school dressed in the compulsory school uniform of black or navy blue paints with a snow white shirt. It was clear that his grandson loved Daskalos very much and Daskalos loved him very, very much. Sometimes his Grandson would sit with a few of the westerners at Daskalos' kitchen table as they discussed the teachings in English. He was very conscious and mature for an eleven-year-old and he sat quietly watching while everyone else did the talking. At the time it was assumed by most visitors that he did not know English, but I think maybe he did know some and understood but chose to keep quiet anyway. One time we were talking about how fast paced and crazy America was and we asked him if he would like to visit America. The question was translated into Greek and his answer was that America sounded so crazy he would not even want to fly over it.

Sometimes after school one of Daskalos' young granddaughters liked to come to the Stoa to see her grandfather after he gave his afternoon Inner Circle lessons. She would come in the Stoa and visit Daskalos and the other Inner Circle members who wore their white robes for these advanced classes. So that the granddaughter would not feel left out, Daskalos had a little white robe made for her to put on when she came to visit them.

This was the kind of gentle loving care Daskalos gave…not only to his family but also to all. Everyone coming to him was treated with respect and loving kindness, which is the sign of a true master.

After the daily Stoa Lesson that ended at noon, Daskalos would walk back down the street to his home for lunch. The street was lined with colorful flowering bushes; with the occasional palm tree and very tall and very narrow Italian Cypress trees that Daskalos often painted into his landscape pictures. The aroma of fresh baked spanakopita accompanied the walk from the bakery across the street from his home. As he walked, the students followed happily along asking him questions and softly talking among themselves about the day's lesson. After the Stoa lesson many of the students went to a small home-style Greek restaurant next door to Daskalos' home for lunch.

After lunch, Daskalos continued seeing students privately for healings and personal guidance. Many felt that the time they spent with Daskalos was some of the most profound moments of their lives. I certainly did. Often he would deliver his helpful messages in the form of a question comprised of a few well-chosen words. His words were designed to get you thinking along the proper way, and come to the truth yourself. It was easy to see that Daskalos really loved his students and most of his students really loved him.

However, every master who tries to reveal the truth at this level has their Judas, because betrayal by those you love is a required experience at some point on the spiritual path. Daskalos' own trial in this regard would be revealed over the next two years. This spiritual test has been referred to as the "Earth Initiation" and is certainly one of the hardest initiations of all. It can put the personality into the so-called Dark Night of the Soul. Of course the Soul is never in darkness but it is like the light of the Soul is eclipsed from the personality's perception for a period of time and as a personality you feel being alone in darkness. This experience is something like when a sun passes in front of a cloud and eclipses the sunlight; the cloud has not affected the Sun in the least, it just blocks the sunlight from the Earth until the dark cloud passes and you can see the Sun again.

Each day Daskalos received letters from all over the world with requests for absent healing. The letters contained photographs of the person needing the healing or guidance and his amazing psychometric abilities could coordinate with the person in the photo, know everything about them. One of his ongoing works was to reply to the letters and send healing energies to those who asked for help. Daskalos would hold the photograph in his hand, attune to the vibrations of that person, make the diagnosis and send the sufferer the appropriate healing energy. Daskalos was very adept at reading vibrations from photos; he could discover an incredible amount of information about the health of a person's material, emotional, mental and spiritual condition. He was so skillful at this he could tell instantly if the person in the photo was living or had passed over. He often detected things that their medical doctors had missed or misdiagnosed.

He would also recommend specific non-traditional treatments that unquestionably produced lasting cures. Sometimes he would recommend conventional medical treatments, as he was not always opposed to modern medicine, but he always sent needed healing energies to the patient. His ability to sense and identify the true cause of a patient's suffering gave him a distinct advantage in prescribing remedies.

I came to experience his incredible sensitivity to vibrations first hand on many occasions. People sought Daskalos' ongoing protection in their lives and I was no different. To meet this need in the people he created talismans. For one type of talisman, Daskalos would place powerful protective energies on a small silver or gold six-pointed star. Long before the Jews called the six-pointed star the Star of David and used it as a symbol of Solomon's seal, it was a used by the High Hierophants in ancient Egypt and called the Sba Saas. Daskalos' version of six-pointed star also had a cross in the middle. For the Researchers of Truth its symbolism is immense.

In brief, the upward pointed triangle of the six-pointed star represents Spirit. The downward pointed triangle represents matter.

So the union of the two triangles represents the perfect balance of Spirit and matter. This six-pointed star symbolizes the human being who has developed these two principles within. The cross at the center of the star did not stand for the Crucifixion. It represented the balancing of the four prime elements: Earth, Fire, Water and Ether. I too had gotten one of these talismans.

Several days later, I traveled to Cairo, Egypt, where I purchased a small pendent of the Egyptian all-seeing eye. It was an image associated with the Archangelic order of the Cherubim. The next time I saw Daskalos I asked if he could bless the image and he agreed. I took the pedant out of a small bag that contained other jewelry items and handed it to him. As he touched it, he instantly replied that he had blessed it before and started to hand it back. I explained that it was impossible as I purchased it in Cairo and just now returned to Cyprus with it. He took it back placed it in the palms of his hand and took a slow deep breath. With full concentration, he blessed it and handed it back to me. Then he added in a more confident tone, "I had already blessed it, it had my vibrations on it!" Not wanting to argue the point, I said nothing and started to put the pendant back when I saw the six-pointed star talisman, which he had blessed, in the same bag.

So the pendant had come into direct contact with the six-pointed star talisman and been charged with his energy. He was so sensitive, that he was able to feel his own vibrations on the pendant that had only been in contact with the talisman for a short time. I pointed this out and he confirmed that was how it had come to have his vibrations on it.

After an afternoon of work, sometimes Daskalos would give an Inner Circle class in Greek in the Stoa and/or go to another city and give a lesson to one of the many independent circles on Cyprus. He would come back and eat dinner and start seeing people again and that would last until sometimes after 10:30 PM, then he would work on the manuscripts for his books. I had seen him writing as late as midnight before. When he found the time he would paint unusual landscapes and imbue them with benevolent energies for people.

He was seventy-six at this time and started his day around 6 AM then healing, teaching and counseling until midnight. By his own admission he saw about 80 people in a day and most of them would be healed of afflictions and helped. One day when I was there he healed five atrophied legs in a single day. Daskalos would flood each person he saw privately and his entire audience during circle lessons with great quantities of etheric energy. Can you imagine how much energy it took to do all that work each day?

How was this possible? Of course he could only do it because he knew how to stay connected to the source of the etheric energy so he was not just using his own personal energy supply. Otherwise, it would not have been possible to do what he did.

Daskalos would typically dedicate one day a week as healing day. Of course, every single day was a healing day with Daskalos. However, on this day instead of a regular lesson in the Stoa he would give a short lesson then devote his attention to helping those who had come seeking healing of one sort or the other.

During the healing sessions we all gathered in the Stoa and one by one those seeking healings would come to up to him. There was a hushed anticipation in the room as Daskalos began his work. When a person approached him, they explained a bit of their problem and then Daskalos would immediately begin working on them. I sometimes positioned myself immediately on Daskalos left side just slightly behind him so I could get a good view of his work without being in the way. Of course, most of what transpired was not visible to material eyes. Nonetheless, what was visible was truly amazing. Many people came forward in these sessions. One day there was a healing of a German woman.

    This lady was on crutches with one leg distorted and shorter than the other leg. Two friends helped her as she awkwardly moved her damaged body to Daskalos. She did not speak English. It did not seem to matter though as Daskalos immediately went to work. He first took a long flat wooden ruler and measured her best leg. Then he measured her distorted shorter leg. Those sitting close to him could see on the ruler the difference of about two inches between the two legs. Daskalos asked her friends to help support her as he lifted her damaged leg up and began to stroke it with a concentrated purpose.

    He rubbed the leg with his hands for a short time and then began pulling on it. He pulled and stroked and pulled again for a few minutes then re-measured the leg. During all this, the lady had a slightly confused look about her. Daskalos set the ruler down and again stroked and pulled her leg for a couple more minutes. "There," he announced assuredly and lowered the newly restored leg to the floor. A wave of exhilaration that felt like warm fizzy bubbles swept through me as I now saw both legs equal and whole. Once more,

Daskalos measured her legs with the ruler verifying to us empirically that her legs were now the same length.

Her friends and those sitting close began talking excitedly as I looked up into her face. I was expecting to see relief, joy or maybe even gratitude. Instead, her face revealed bewilderment as her mind seemed to struggle to understand the healing she just experienced. She left the Stoa whole but looked more confused than when she approached. Her personality simply could not immediately grasp the miraculous transformation that had just occurred in her body.

With faith healing, we hear that a certain degree of belief and faith is a necessary component for a healing to take place. This is true for faith healing. However, Daskalos was not a faith healer and, in this particular case, the lady's personality exhibited more disbelief than faithful belief. Yet, the healing occurred perfectly. Later he explained how he facilitated the healing saying, "You cannot just lengthen only the leg; the tendons, bones and the veins had to be lengthened too, giving them heat and life."

Daskalos said first he would create a strong Elemental, a thought-from, by visualizing the leg whole and healthy. He then visualized the bones, arteries, veins and ligaments just as they should be – perfect.   He would then transfer large quantities of etheric energy into the Elemental to do its work. The visualization has to be very strong, and contain no uncertainty. Then, the healing Elemental will get that perfect form and, if the Holy Spirit permits it, the leg would be restored.

For most who observed a healing with obvious visible evidence, no additional proof was required. There had been others though, who became more scientific about the proof of Daskalos' healings. They had followed the before and after evidence of medical x-rays. X-rays taken a few weeks before Daskalos' intervention would show damaged spines and dislocated bones. After a healing session, new x-rays revealed normal healthy conditions as if there had never been any problem.

As soon as Daskalos would finish working with one person, without a pause he was ready to receive the next. On and on they came, as he worked continuously on all that needed him. It was such a beautiful experience to witness. I could sense the fervent hope for a healing with some people, which would also resonate in me as my own desire to see them whole and healthy. It helps to have others near you that want to help in the healing. We see that in serious cases, Christ was often asking certain disciples to be with him, while sending other disciples and onlookers away. He did that because their ardent wish for the person to be healed and the etheric energy they sub-consciously contributed helped in the healings. Likewise, those around any healing work who have doubts are sub-consciously sending negative energies that work against the healing. So when engaging in healing work do not have people with negative thoughts, instead have friends who you love and who love you and wish to cooperate in the healing.

When there were no more to be treated, Daskalos went back to his home for lunch. Daskalos always declared that it was not he doing the healing and that no person has ever healed another person. It was God's expression as the Holy Spirit that did the actual healing. Even when Christ performed miraculous healings he never took credit and would say it was God the Father that did the work. Daskalos did claim was that it was possible for us to train ourselves to be fit conduits for the Holy Spirit to work through and for physical healings that training included a good working knowledge of the human anatomy as seen in the above atrophied leg case.

When the weekend came, his daughter, Panayiota, would take Daskalos to Governor's Beach on the Mediterranean Sea for seclusion and rest. They made a place where he could rest in the sun without being disturbed by the public. He loved Governor's Beach, where there was an unusual formation of white rocks on the shoreline, which was one of the power spots on the Island.

Many years later, it was here on Governor's Beach that I had my last conversation with him before he passed over. He was sitting alone relaxing in a lounge chair and gazing peacefully out at the Mediterranean Sea. I went over to him and squatted down beside him. We talked and he revealed some things to me that I did not understand at the time but do now. He finished saying what he wanted to tell me, and I thanked him.

As he was lying there relaxing in his chair, he made one last statement. He said one of the things he liked to do that gave him pleasure was to spread his consciousness out over the entire locality at the beach and become one with the wind. In doing this he could know everything going on in that locality and caress the people. This he did by expansion of his consciousness and not by an out of the body experience. Just as he finished telling me that, a gentle breeze washed over us. Daskalos eased back in the lounge chair, closed his eyes and became one with the breeze. I left him to rest and I left

Cyprus soon after, not realizing that was to be our last Earthly conversation.

Diabetes had weakened his circulatory system and later a blood vessel burst causing a brain hemorrhage in 1994 and he could no longer speak. He lived for some months after the stroke, as Panayiota believed, to give his family and students time to prepare for his departure. He refused rehabilitation for his stroke and passed over early in 1995 at the age of 82.

There is a point of view expressed by certain Buddhists regarding death, which says that the person passing over was only "pretending to die." The meaning is that the death of the material body is only a change in conditions and not a final annihilation of the person. Passing over is just a continuation of the self-consciousness but at a higher level of existence. Death of the material body is not even the end of the personality nor could it ever be the end of the Soul-Self.

Daskalos consciously drew his last breath as he passed out of his material body and the Earth plane. As a Spirit Soul the Earth plane and all the planes of existence are always within him. So really, he is still "here" – here with us in the Worlds of Existence. We can contact him anywhere we are. As he told us more than once, "There is so much suffering in the world and as long as there is pain on the planet, I will remain 'here.' As long and there are eyes with tears I will be here with a handkerchief to wipe off the tears."

Daskalos is truly one of the great brothers of mercy. He and others have taken this vow of service and will be the last to take their liberation. Furthermore, for the those sincerely studying and practicing the teachings of the Researchers of Truth, Daskalos made another promise that after he passed over he would remain in faithful contact with each of them and would continue to guide the circles for the Researchers of Truth.

Chapter Four
TAKE AIM

Ascending, ascending and ascending the ladder of evolution. That is Self-Realization. This is the real aim of any Researcher of the Truth, at least of the circles all over the world I am heading. How can we, as human beings, find our real nature? How can the boundless be limited? How can the imperishable become the perishable? It is the Present-Day-Personality that must open up, extend and develop that little self-consciousness to the levels of its real inner nature and reach, what we call, Self-Realization. "Many make the mistake to think that Self-realization means knowing the Present-Day-Personality as it is. They make the mistake to think that their Self is only their personality (the material, emotional and mental bodies). When I say Self-Realization I don't mean that. Of course, you must start from this point -to analyze and know your Present-Day-Personality.

But then, step forward and say, "I am not only that. I am something more." This means -After becoming the master of my material body, the master of my emotions (Psychical Body) and my thoughts (Noetical Body), I must break the mirror in which I see myself reflected and see that I still exist and I still AM -without seeing my image in the mirror. Who am I then? You are making the mistake to consider you are the reflection of yourself in a threefold mirror of matter, emotion and thought where you see your real Self, distorted very much. You have to get rid of the images in the mirror. Then you will find who you are! ~ Daskalos

THE TEACHING

Before engaging our self with the teachings of the Researchers of Truth or any teachings, we should have a clear idea of our aim. Before anyone starts to go anywhere they should have a good idea as to where they are going. It is not wise to head off into the unknown, with no aim or without having something in mind. We should know something about the way we are meant to go and to understand what dangers we may encounter along that way. So where are the Researchers of Truth going? We are going to find that buried treasure, hidden in the field as Christ put it. That treasure is the Inner Self – the Soul-Self Awareness. We as a personality start the search for the buried treasure by investigating who we are as a personality, which leads to the study of what we are: an eternal Spirit being, an offspring of God just as the masters in the past have declared. We can find this most valuable treasure buried in our personality self. Because even without us knowing it, at the very core of the personality is that brilliant ray of our Spirit-Soul Self, which is a true god within the one Absolute God.

There is a direction to our approach. Yet inherent with any aim or direction is an expectation of what is to come. The problem is that our expectations can color and limit our experience of a greater reality that will unfold before us. Historically, the two common approaches to God were a solitary path like a yogi sitting motionless in a cave or by joining an organization like an orthodox religion.

Addressing the problem with these approaches, the 10th century Sufi mystic and poet, Niffari, wrote, "If you cast yourself into the sea [of life], without any guidance, this is full of danger, because man mistakes things which arise within him for things arising elsewhere." This is a danger in approaching the Absolute Infinite

Reality alone and with no real idea of where we are headed.

Niffari continues, "If, on the other hand, you travel on the sea in a ship, this is perilous, because there is danger of attachment to the vehicle." This is a danger in approaching the Absolute Infinite Reality via the vehicle of an orthodox religion or organization. Niffari concludes with, "In the one case, the end is not known, and there is no guidance. In the other case, the means becomes an end, and there is no arriving."

Alternatively, the teachings of the Researchers of Truth offers a system by which each one of us can use to approach and experience Truth directly. This is a system and not an organization you join. In this system rather than a hierarchy of teachers and gurus you will find loving brother and sister guides to help you along your way. These guides never stand between you and God; instead, they stand at your side to assist you on the great, great journey of awakening. Their help never attempts to dominate or limit your free will, which is one of the most important gifts from God. These guides are both on Earth and in the worlds beyond. The service they offer to all human beings in the Worlds of Existence addresses the triadic nature of human existence. These three natures are the physical, emotional and mental.

Initially, as a Researcher of Truth, we learn to work within ourselves to restore and maintain the health of our material body. We work to calm emotional imbalances and to clear our mental confusion. We work to cleanse and harmonize ourselves physically, psychically and noetically. This restores balance and purifies our personality. Balancing ourselves we are then better able to assist those around us and to align with the Soul Self.

The healthy and balanced expressions of body, heart and mind are truly a wonderful achievement. Yet, this is not the ultimate aim of this system. The real aim of our system is Self-Realization. By Self-Realization, we do not mean just realizing our present-day personality, our little self and its transitory expressions in the Worlds of Existence. This is a necessary beginning but not the real aim. By Self Realization, we mean full Soul-Self -Awareness.

So, engaging in the teachings and practices of a Researcher of Truth, what can we expect? First, we come to the preliminary kind of self-consciousness, which is simply becoming aware of our present-day personality self. This is not the full Self-Consciousness we seek, but it is a necessary step. To know who we are as a personality means we know our unique set of thoughts and emotions, strengthens and weaknesses through the practices of Introspection, Observation and safe Meditation. The personality self is like an iceberg; only a small portion of it is visible (conscious). There is another much larger portion, which is not readily visible and remains as what we call sub-consciousness. The fully awaken individual, one we call a master, has no sub-consciousness for he has made his sub-consciousness – conscious.

During this process, we seek to enter the state of consciousness of a keenly aware, but emotionally detached, observer. We want to be a pure witness to our thoughts, desires, words and actions of the day. In doing so, we find places where we could have done better. We learn not to say and do things we should not. We also learn what actions or words would have produced better results and so we resolve to do better in the future and improve the quality of our character as a personality. In other words, we develop the strength and skills to control and change our behaviors, desires, feelings and thoughts. We become masters of our home and of circumstances.

By way of example, let's says a seeker reacted to some unsettling circumstance with strong anger and even ended up speaking harsh words at someone. Maybe at first the seeker feels the urge to defend this behavior and lay the blame at the feet of the other person. In their nightly Introspection they use this unfortunate opportunity to deeply research what really made them act in this unacceptable way and discover the real cause was their egoism feeling offended. The seeker, in a detached analysis, can see a better way he or she could have responded to such a situation and resolve to do so in the future. Maybe that sounds like a small gain but, in truth, it is a big gain, because this means the seeker is conquering his own egoism and becoming the master of his own home.

We first learn to introspect on this day…this year this lifetime and one day even beyond this lifetime to previous incarnations. Practicing introspection over time you will find yourself not just doing Introspection at the end of the day but also during the day after a noteworthy event. As you take this practice further, you will notice that automatically you start doing Introspection in real time as events unfold. This skill of Introspection can and will be transferred to your experiences in the Psycho-Noetical Worlds – either when your material body is asleep or in your life after the death of your material body.

When we discover (through introspection) the causes of

weaknesses and afflictions of our personality self, we can then make steps to clean and correct these limitations and we will be successful at cleaning and thinning the veil that separates our personality self from the Soul-Self. The radiant light of the Soul-Self will shine through our personality self, brighter and brighter, illuminating our way and benefiting those around us. Our personality is like a colored cloth draped over the very bright light of the Soul-Self. Personalities with unhealthy negative thoughts, feelings or desires darken and obscure this brilliant light of the Soul-Self. However, when the personality is freed from negative thoughts, feelings and desires, this Inner Light shines through brightly, lighting their own life and the lives of those around them.

It is at this stage in the process we discover something truly extraordinary and to date un-noticed. We will begin to realize that this mysterious Self of ours is able to change the undesirable expressions found in our personality. This means we have discovered the real Self behind our temporary personality self. In time, we will gradually awaken to the truth that we are much more than the personality we have created. We will examine, learn and be able to transmute the lead of negativity in our personality's heart to the true gold of love in what the mystics call true Alchemy. We will discover the Self behind its phenomenal expressions in the worlds of time, space and place. Self-Realization is the aim of a Researcher of Truth.

THE PRACTICE: OVERVIEW

One practice that Daskalos insisted must be done by the beginner as well as the advanced seekers of truth is Daily

Introspection. Because it is this practice that will produce some of the greatest breakthroughs and results for a sincere spiritual seeker. The result is real freedom from troubles, suffering and illusions. Introspection is one of the basic "Five Golden Keys" to the kingdom of the heavens given in this system.

Daskalos observed, "Today people are living in confusion and I said it is because they don't know the nature of their desires and emotions. They have enslaved their thought to serve their emotions and desires. This is the main reason causing the confusion in people around us today. Anybody has the right to use the Mind as thought and reason in the same way he is using the air and vitality by breathing and living, but why don't people want to use reason? It is because people do not want to come out of their illusions. Researchers of the Truth come out of their illusions by self-analysis and introspection, studying their circumstances with courage, studying the nature of their emotional body, of their desires, seeing that they created weaknesses, hatreds, jealousies, and passions in their personality. Anybody can do this deep work if he or she wishes to and comes to a conclusion to do it. All people, though they admit they are in confusion and in misery, don't want to get out of it. How can you come out of it? That's easy, if you can come to the decision that you have to use the right thinking instead of just following the stupid, torturing desires and emotions. So, there is no excuse."

Introspection cleanses our Sub-Consciousness of harmful combinations of thoughts, emotions and desires. The Sub-Conscious mind has three chambers. One of the chambers is like a warehouse, in which all of our thoughts, emotions and desires reside. This is the chamber where we will work during our introspection exercises. Each day, the thoughts, feelings, desires and events of our life slip below the surface of our conscious mind and rapidly amass in our sub-conscious mind. So in introspection we start to examine, in a detached way, the events of the day. We are not to make excuses of our behavior, and not to condemn ourselves (or others) for less than desirable behaviors.

During introspection, internally we are finding the sources of our mental and emotional behaviors in an effort to consciously structure our personality and its sub-consciousness. This releases us from undesirable, outdated and unnecessary thoughts, emotions and ideas. Introspection is also called self-analysis and looking within. It is not the Soul-Self that needs Introspection or analysis; it is our personality self-awareness that needs this in order to blossom into true Self-Awareness. This is a primary practice of a Researcher of Truth or anyone seeking Self-Realization.

THE PRACTICE: DAILY INTROSPECTION

Each night just prior to sleep (when your subconscious is more permeable) inhale and exhale in a 4:4 pattern and relax completely. (Four beats of the heart during the in breath and 4 beats of the heart during the out breath)

Either lying in bed or sitting up (try not to fall asleep) begin to recall the day from start to finish. Review each event, each encounter; of the day and with full impunity and leniency towards yourself and others ask yourself the following questions:

- What did I think or feel that I should not have thought or felt?
- What did I not think or feel that I should have thought or felt?
- What did I say that I should not have said? What did I not say that I should have said?
- What did I do that I should not have done? What did I not do that I should have done?

The goal is not to blame or to praise yourself or others, but simply to observe your activity and work to correct your behavior. Praise and blame are like two sides of the same coin; they are dualistic. In time you will grow more accomplished at seeing yourself and will find that advancement in your worldly life and spiritual life will accelerate.

Chapter Five
SEVEN LEVELS OF CONSCIOUSNESS

Now, we have spoken about matter and we talked about the vegetable kingdom, the different varieties of luminosity of Light, we spoke about the animal kingdom, again another degree of luminosity of Light, about things in the ethereal and in the Psychical Worlds, and in the Noetical World. So, we have the sensitivity and the sensibility in matter and in the vegetable kingdom. Now, the animal kingdom has the instinct. The human beings have the sub-consciousness and I am telling you that ninety percent of the human beings living on the planet today are living subconsciously. Yet, there is the waking consciousness. How many are expressing this waking consciousness and know what they are doing? How many? Very few! We have to unfold in us, our real Self, which means our real Self-Consciousness. And we should aim to unfold in us, the Self Super-Consciousness. ~ Daskalos

THE TEACHING:

There is a dynamical expression of God, which is called the Holy Spirit in Christianity. It is the "Almightiness"; the Omnipotent characteristic of God. It is the Pan Universal Feminine and the giver of life. We see this Life manifesting in us and in all the living forms around us. There are countless life forms on the Earth, but there is a distinction between The Life and the various forms of life. God as the Holy Spirit is not expressed as a personality, it does not have self-awareness; it does not need it, because it has another boundless expression: the Absolute Super-Consciousness. God as the Logos is the Absolute Self-Super-Consciousness.

From God, the Logos, the Holy Spirit and all the Eternal Spirit

Beings, the Mind Super-Substance emanates and it is used in the creation of all the Worlds of Existence and everything in them. This Mind is not God or the Holy Spirit, yet even this super intelligent medium called Mind is comprised of Divine Principles, Laws and Causes.

As consciousness we are cells in this Absolute Holy-Spiritual Consciousness. As self-awareness, even self-awareness as a personality self, we are cells in the Absolute Logoic Self-Awareness. So we have the two: consciousness and self-awareness. As a Spirit-Soul Self we are also much more than cells, we are The Life, the Everlasting Life.

A human being expresses his or her self in a sub-conscious way too much of the time. To reach the highest level of consciousness we must unfold our sub-consciousness to alert consciousness, and further to Self-Consciousness and one day to the highest level of Self-Super-Consciousness. Not only is this possible for a human being, it is desirable and eventually everyone will reach the state of Self-Super-Consciousness. It is the destiny for all of us. It does not matter if that destiny comes in this lifetime or centuries from now it will come. What will we know in this Self-Super-Conscious state? We will know that we are an immortal Spirit-Being Self. It is not that we have an immortal Self; that is the wrong way to think about it because, as a personality, we do not possess the Spirit-Soul-Self. The right way to think about this is: I am a Spirit-Soul-Self that has a body and a personality.

Now all the degrees of brightness, of the luminosity of the Divine light are manifested as the seven levels of consciousness.

Also each degree of the luminosity of the inexhaustible Divine Life-Light gives us one of the so-called seven heavens. The main difference between these seven heavens is the brightness of this magnificent Divine Light. In each of these higher heavens there is much greater light than can be found in the material plane of existence. If we would compare the brightest day on Earth with the light in the Psychical Worlds it would seem like we were comparing the light in a dungeon with the light of a crisp, clear fall day. As a human being we have the right and the calling to develop our personality to the highest level of consciousness.

This is something the animal life cannot do. They cannot raise their consciousness from their instinctive level to any higher level of consciousness. So we study and develop all the possible stages of human consciousness from sub-consciousness, to fully alert consciousness, to real Self-Consciousness or Soul Self Awareness, to the Self-Super-Consciousness. Then the realization will come, that we are not the expression of consciousness, we are the Self, which can express all the various levels of consciousness.

First Level of Consciousness: Sensitivity

The mineral kingdom is living and expressing a kind of consciousness known as Sensitivity. Iron is consciously sensitive to moisture and will rust. It undergoes change and decomposes. Likewise, silver's sensitivity will cause it to tarnish when exposed to air. Metals also have sensitivity to heat and electricity; and will conduct both in varying degrees. Mineral crystals are living and the pattern of their growth exhibits their consciousness of sensitivity to the force of gravity. Experiments on the Space Shuttle proved to scientists that in zero gravity crystals grow larger and more neatly ordered than on Earth. Pizo-Crystals are sensitive to pressure and under strong pressure they emit electricity. Pyro-Crystals are sensitive to temperature and when heated they also produce electricity. Sensitivity is a level of consciousness and is a characteristic of the mineral kingdom. Throughout the entire natural world we see life expressing different levels of consciousness.

Second Level of Consciousness: Sensibility

The next level of consciousness is called sensibility and it is first found in the plant kingdom. This type of consciousness is particularly noticeable in flowers. Flowers exhibit a great deal of sensibility. They have a remarkable ability to sense the light of the sun. The plant kingdom is very conscious of night and day. Some species like water lilies are so conscious of the sunlight that they open their blossoms when they sense the first rays in the morning and close back up when the sun sets. Some flowers sense the movement of the sun and turn to follow it closely as it moves across the sky.

In temperate climates as the winter gives its place to spring; the amount of sunlight increases and the consciousness of the plant kingdom senses this and comes alive with fresh growth. Within weeks the plants and trees send forth buds, blossoms and leaves in an amazing demonstration of materialization. The Divine Plan calls for an immeasurable abundance of life on Earth. The entire plant kingdom has the second level of consciousness called sensibility, and also has the first level of consciousness called sensitivity. The sensitivity consciousness of plants also senses heat, gravity and chemicals.

Third Level of Consciousness: Instinct

Coming to the animal kingdom we see life expressing sensitivity, sensibility and another higher level of consciousness called instinct. The migration of fish, birds and other animals are prime examples of this inborn instinctual consciousness. Animals instinctively give birth, nurture their offspring; they instinctively seek food and protect their territory. The animal kingdom does not use the mind as thought like humans. Rather they are governed by what have been called the Nature Spirits. These Nature Spirits are the projected angelic Elementals from certain classes of Archangels. Many people have come into conscious contact with these living entities. These Nature Spirits govern the life of an animal (or a plant) and live within them. Observing animals closely we can detect the great wisdom and intelligence ruling all these forms of life as instinctual consciousness. What we are calling instinct is a kind of intelligence behind the animal that gives each animal such protection that it makes us astonished at all this wisdom. Who or what is giving this level of conscious intelligence to the animals?

The animal life also has the first and second levels of consciousness called sensitivity and sensibility. They eat, sleep, wake up, go around searching for food in the wild, give birth and die. That is all they can do. All of them are following their instinct. Every cell in our body has its own kind of instinctive consciousness. Like the animals, the human beings express instinct as well as sensitivity and sensibility. Unlike the animals the consciousness of a human being is not only confined to these lower states.

Fourth Level of Consciousness: Sub-Consciousness

In the human kingdom we see expressed all these three lower levels of consciousness: sensitivity, sensibility and instinct. We also see another type of consciousness in man called sub-consciousness. It is called sub-conscious because it operates in a habitual way just below the surface of our awareness. The average person operates sub-consciously too much of the time. The sub-consciousness is composed in part of all the thoughts, emotions, and desires we experience in our life. These are the Elementals that make up our personality and shape our character. Collectively these form a limited type of self-awareness. This shadow self-awareness is not our real Self-Awareness and thus it is always changing.

Human beings are gods covered in illusions and in a state of amnesia, forgetting not only where they came from but also who they really are. The Elementals cannot be seen with the material eyes but can be seen in their etheric form by a clairvoyant. The Elementals take a form; if you could see some of them you have created that host in your sub-consciousness they would frighten you. Their form is especially disturbing when the Elemental has been created by strong feelings of hatred, jealousy and desires of taking revenge or destroying what others have. In this regards, the sub-consciousness is like an untamed wilderness with some angelic Elementals and with some devilish Elementals. The territory of the Sub-Consciousness is not well known to the average person yet, in our Sub Conscious mind, is all the lessons learned in previous incarnations. At the same time we can find in our Sub-Consciousness the very lessons we need to learn next in order to advance spiritually.

Consciousness, however, is in knowing that we know, while sub-consciousness is all that we have known in the past, which now only exists to us as memories and habits. The habits are a result of having in the past, used our consciousness to train and learn certain actions and skills. So it is the consciousness that is enriching the sub-consciousness. Whatever is coming to our conscious mind gets transferred into our sub-conscious mind. We must not confuse sub-consciousness with unconsciousness. Unconsciousness means that the material brain is not receiving any impression from the outer world through the five senses.

Even the limited self-awareness of our personality has the ability to use the Mind as thought. Animals cannot use the Mind as thought nor do they have self-awareness. They have a consciousness as described above and a governing Angelic Nature Spirit, which expresses its wisdom through that animal. However, human beings are Eternal Spirit Beings and are a separate creation from animal kingdom. Animals, plants and minerals are Holy Spiritual expressions and do not have a Self. Rather they are living creations of Super-Conscious Archangelic orders. It is the Selfhood of a human being that sets us apart from the animal kingdom. Our bodies share common characteristics with the bodies of animals: flesh, hair, bones and blood but not much more than that.

The sub-consciousness is primarily located in the material body's solar plexus, in every cell of the body and at the same time it is found in the Psychical and Noetical Bodies. The sub-consciousness is the base of our personality's egoism. Proportionally, our sub-consciousness is similar to the ocean. The surface of the ocean is like the conscious part of our mind. The sub-conscious portion of the mind is symbolized as everything under the surface. At any time, we can draw to the surface of consciousness as memory what has been stored in our sub-conscious mind. Sometimes these rise to the surface of our consciousness spontaneously or when triggered by an event. We can swim on the surface of the ocean or we can dive to the bottom of the ocean. It is the same ocean, the same water; likewise it is one consciousness whether we call it sub-conscious, conscious or even super-consciousness.

Fifth Level of Consciousness: Consciousness

God has given the human race the great gift of using the Mind. This has afforded humankind the opportunity to raise his or her slumbering sub-consciousness, to fully alert waking consciousness. This is not our ultimate aim of Self-Consciousness.

There is a great range of waking consciousness from somewhat conscious, to more conscious, to more and more conscious. It is this process that gradually replaces sub-conscious thoughts and emotions with more and more alert conscious thoughts and feelings. For the human being, there is only one mind but expressed in the states of sub-consciousness, consciousness, Self-Consciousness and Self-Super-Consciousness.

A Researcher of Truth makes the effort to discover and know what consciousness is as he assimilates with it in order to express it better and better, which is revealing that consciousness is not our self; consciousness is our expression. Slowly, we will unfold spiritually as we increase consciousness until we attain full Self-Super-Consciousness. Teachings and teachers can point the way but they cannot take us there. This cannot be taught by teachers, masters or by reading books; it needs long training. To reach this beautiful and true Reality, we must be the one who climbs the ladder of consciousness, passing through high states of contemplation, meditation, ecstasy and bliss.

In making this climb we will develop our self-consciousness to different degrees. However, know that the Self is something very different from the consciousness that the Self, expresses. Many spiritual systems of study mix up the consciousness and the Self and imagine that they are one thing. Consciousness is the expression of the self through the mind. It is the self that is behind the expression consciousness. This means any person's self-consciousness at any level; it created by how that self uses the Mind. What we think of as human waking consciousness of a personality is very, very limited compared to real Self-Consciousness and Self-Super-Consciousness.

Sixth Level of Consciousness: Self-Consciousness

Raising our consciousness to still higher levels we will one day reach the true Self-Consciousness. This is the real spiritual awakening. Full Self-Consciousness is the total realization of the Soul-Self-Awareness. True Self-Consciousness or Self-Awareness does not have degrees or levels. It is a state of conscious awareness of the Self within the Divine Plan, and it is attained by effort and will power to awaken from the slumber of everyday consciousness into expanded Self-Awareness. This is Self-Realization and it is the real aim of the Researchers of Truth and any sincere spiritual system. Self-Realization means knowledge of the Self. Self-Realization does not mean just knowing our little personality self with its strengths and weaknesses.

Because we have discolored the reflective quality of our personality's consciousness with lesser emotions and thoughts it cannot reflect the light of the Self very well. Just as muddy water cannot reflect the beauty of the natural world immediately next to it, a dull and dirty personality cannot reflect the glorious reality of Soul-Self Awareness. This is also a reason why we do not remember our past lives or experiences of other dimensions. It is not that these things do not exist; it is that we as personalities have allowed our daily consciousness to become soiled by base desires, impure emotions and worldly interests. This has dimmed and limited our ability as personalities to perceive and reflect the light of our true nature. So it falls to the personality to clean up its consciousness and sub-consciousness in order to reflect more and more of this perfect light.

This is how we "raise our consciousness" to higher levels. We begin through the practice of Introspection and then develop our abilities to observe and concentrate in order to discover and remove unclean/unnecessary thoughts and emotions lurking in our subconscious mind.   With great courage we enter our sub-consciousness using the Golden Keys of Introspection, Concentration and Observation. This means we must study our personality self and find the quality of our emotions and thoughts that are composing our sub-consciousness. In the lair of the sub-consciousness you will find a very challenging adversary who is the cause of all our troubles.

However, by cleaning and aligning our personality we can eliminate this enemy and reflect the light of the Soul in much greater measures. An initial result is that we will live a happier and more harmonious life and, eventually, we will realize the true Self-Consciousness.

Seventh Level of Consciousness: Self-Super-Consciousness

Beyond the level of Self-Consciousness there is the Self Super-Consciousness. Self-Super-Consciousness means total awareness within the Worlds of Existence (past and present) as well as total awareness in the realms of Beingness. Self-Super-Consciousness goes beyond the limiting concepts of time, space or place of the three Worlds of Existence. Super-Consciousness is beyond any person's ability to describe in words yet it is the intrinsic characteristic of our Spirit-Soul-Self and the ultimate state of consciousness of every Spirit Being. Super-Consciousness is also called Christ Consciousness and is the highest state of consciousness as it is based on true archetypal ideas. Whereas; the various states of ordinary consciousness are constructed with the relative ideas held in one's mind. The self-consciousness of humanity has a wide range; from deep ignorance with very little light of knowledge, all the way up to the most luminous states of knowledge and wisdom. Self-Super-Consciousness is Total Awareness in both existence and in the state of Beingness. In

Christianity, this is known as "Theosis" and in eastern schools it is known as God Consciousness. It is full At-One-Ment with God the Absolute Infinite Beingness.

It is the long awaited return of the Prodigal Son to his loving father. What lies beyond this is so magnificent that no human being can adequately describe it.

PRACTICE: OVERVIEW

Observation means that we try to notice and understand what we are seeing in our life, in our relationships and in our hearts and minds. Nothing should escape our attention, which means we aim to be fully awake. Observation means attentiveness but it is attention without any tension. Most people go through life with only a vague idea of how things work and have not developed their power of Observation to penetrate deeply into the nature of the reality they find themselves in. The practice of Observation also needs Concentration to go with it. If you cannot concentrate well, you will not be able to observe keenly or fix and hold your attention to meditate properly.   Observation and Concentration enable us to skillfully investigate our inner and outer world; raising our consciousness to the highest levels. These are vital skills needed by a Researcher of Truth.

PRACTICE: WALKING MEDITATION WITH RECOLLECTION

The Buddhists know the benefits of walking meditation very well, and the Researchers of Truth have a similar practice but with the added element of recall. After a walking meditation we sit and meditate to recall the details of our walk. This not only develops the skills of Observation and Meditation while raising our consciousness but it also improves memory. You can do this practice anytime you will not be disturbed. It can be done inside your home or office, but it is especially enjoyable to do it outside in your neighborhood, park or woods.

1. Sit for a few minutes and coordinate your breathing with your heartbeats. Breathe in for four beats of the heart and without a pause, breathe out for four beats of the heart. Do that for a few minutes until you feel a heighten sense of awareness. Then stand up and very slowly start your walk.

2. Notice everything encountered on you walk in as much detail as possible. Notice the size, the colors the textures of the objects you see. Notice any smells or sounds that you may experience. Walk in this alertness for fifteen minutes as you absorb as much of your environment as possible; then return to the place where you started. Repeat this exact same walk for a few days in a row.

3. Then after a few days of this practice add the recollection.

Now when you return to the place where you started sit down and relax completely. In your mind recall all that you have seen in as much detail as possible. Recreate all the details clearly in your mind: the sights, smells and sounds as you experienced them on the walk. This will not be hard because you have been studying all these things for several days.

4. The next day go for the walk again and try to notice those things that escaped your attention on previous walks. When you return sit for ten to fifteen minutes as you recall the walk. Now you will start to observe that the images of the scenes stored in your memory are recalled in much greater detail.

Once you attune to the stored image of the walk in your mind, you will be able to enter it to observe more and more subtleties in this detail rich holographic-like image. In this living image we call a memory; all the details are there and can be relived at any time through recollection. The more you practice this exercise the more and more detail you will start to observe. With increased skills in Observation you can extend your newfound ability into other areas of your life. In time Observation actually becomes a way of life for you.

Chapter Six
EVERYTHING IS MIND

We said that everything existing, everything that existed or will exist, is made of the Super-substance we call the Mind. The Mind is Holy. But, the Mind is not God. Mind is the stuff by which the Holy Spirit and the Holy Archangels (the builders) have created all the universes: The material universe, the so-called Psychical universe, the Noetical universe, and everything in them. Whether you know it or not, you are using the Mind. Sometimes you are making very bad use of it by making yourself the slave of your emotions. Now, it's up to you to change and make new decisions. You can use the Mind. It is our "daily bread" given to us by our Father -God.

Our life on the planet is just to learn the nature of matter and the Mind in all its vibrations (as emotions and thoughts) in order to become masters of matter and of the Mind. This is the aim of life. You may say "Yes, we are living in this material plane, but, oh, there is so much suffering, so much pain, and so much misery." Yes. Maybe these are the necessary conditions to wake us up so that we may understand that our aim in life is just to become masters of matter and Mind. And, I said, the more bitter the experience that comes to us to wake us up, the greater the lesson that is given. ~ Daskalos

THE TEACHING

Once, in Cyprus, Daskalos was giving a lesson on the subject of The Mind. After the day's lesson on The Mind, as the other students were dispersing, I caught up to him and asked a question about an aspect of The Mind. Apparently it was the wrong question.

He seemed to ignore my question and replied in a powerful voice that still reverberates in me today, "Everything is mind." His one sentence answer catapulted me up to a much higher view on the subject than my limited thinking had understood so far. It was as if I was sitting on the low end of a seesaw and a giant foot came down swiftly on the other end. In an instant, I was catapulted a mile higher and now looking down on the subject from a much greater vantage point.

What he was trying to get me to understand was that everything is produced by the Mind and everything is the Mind manifested at different frequencies, different densities of vibration and that what we call physical matter is the Mind made solid. So it is the Mind in different states that is composing the elements, the building blocks of Earth, Water, Fire and Ether. God and the Archangelic Orders in all of creation use mind. In order for God and the Archangels to express themselves in and as creation, they must have a means of expression and this means is the Mind. The Mind was created and is created and will always be created. The Mind is not God or the Holy Spirit, but is a Holy Super-Substance through which God expresses Itself in Itself, which means in Its omnipresence.

The Mind is expressed in many different rates of vibration. At the highest rate of vibration it is the Mind Vitality as formless Super-Substance and at one of its lower rates of vibration it is called the Etheric Vitality. The etheric counterpart of the material universe is the finest version of physical matter. It is invisible to the eye but it is part of the three dimensional physical universes and the vibration of the Etheric Vitality can be lowered still further in the process of the materialization of solid mater.

This is what Christ did when he materialized the loaves and fishes to feed 5000 men. It took a couple of hours to do this and they had a surplus of twelve baskets of food after everyone had eaten their fill. Daskalos and at least one other living Researcher of Truth have also been able to materialize food.

So what is dematerialization? Dematerialization is the raising of the vibrations of solid mater to the rate of vibration of the Ethereal and higher, which makes it disappear from the sight of our material eyes. Daskalos and others have demonstrated this. How did they learn this? In the visualization practices we learn to visualize forms and then dissolve these etheric forms. These are the preliminary steps that after long practice can lead to the skills of materialization and dematerialization. Not that materialization or dematerialization is the aim of our work, it is not. However Daskalos was adamant that such a skill should only be used for healing and not to impress others. Referring to his wonders and miracles Christ explained, "Very truly I tell you, whoever believes in me [which means whoever believes and learns what I know and teach] will do the works I have been doing, and they will do even greater things than these."

Now those builder Spirit Beings, the Archangels of the Elements, use the Mind to create everything. Following the blueprint of the Divine Plan with all its Archetypal Laws, Causes, Principles and Ideas, these Archangels commence their great works. They create all the Worlds of Existence (Noetical, Psychical, material and their etheric counterparts). They create everything existing in these worlds including the plant and animal life. In their creative work, these

Archangels first lower the vibrations of the formless Mind Super-Substance to the frequency of Noetical Substance to build the fifth dimensional Noetical Worlds. It is here in the Noetical Worlds that we first see the appearance of forms -All kinds of living forms.

Lowering the vibrations of the Mind to a slower frequency, these builder Archangels use the Mind now as Psychical-Substance in the creation the Psychical Worlds and all the life forms living in these fourth dimensional worlds. These life forms are like the ones known on Earth and also other life forms that do not exist on Earth.

Lowering the Mind to an even denser vibration these Lords of the Elements create the material universe in a blaze of light. "Let There Be Light" as it is stated in the Bible or as it is called by Science the "Hot Big Bang." The Archangelic orders literally materialize the Mind into Matter in the creation of the entire physical universe. Here the Noetic Laws, Causes, Principles and Ideas, now appear as the laws of physics discovered by the scientist. These laws govern and control the long, long evolution of our physical universe in its progression as it coalesced into all the galaxies, suns, planets, and moons. This physical universe is as dense as the Mind vibrations get.

The Mind is not separate from life. It is not Life, but an expression of life and so the Mind is living. One of the natures of the Mind is called imprinting. It imprints or records everything and nothing is lost. It is like a living memory. We refer to that characteristic as the Cosmic Memory, the Cosmic Consciousness, or the Akashic Records. It is, has and always will be recording everything taking place in the creation of all the universes and everything that happens in these universes. Even the movement of small insects on Earth is recorded. A mystic or advanced Researcher of Truth can develop to the point of being able to contact the Cosmic Consciousness of planet Earth and see in moments what had taken place in centuries. He or she can also connect to the Cosmic Consciousness of our solar system or the Cosmic Consciousness of our Milky Way Galaxy. This is due to the fact that all the planets, suns and galaxies are floating in the Super-Substance of the Mind. The Mind is recording everything occurring in it. This makes the Cosmic Consciousness the most reliable source of information available – at least to those who can access it.

When people read the Cosmic Memory they are not always reporting what they see in the same way. Why? It is like the first explorers who came to America and drew maps of what they saw. None of these early maps are exactly the same. So we see that different explorers can draw different maps of the same place. It is similar with those who can access the Akashic records – the accuracy of their descriptions depends on their powers of observation and concentration. Those who can access the records do not always have the same level of skill. What is needed to see the recordings is not sight, but mind. The Greeks have a saying that, "it is not the eyes that see and the ears that hear it is the person's mind that sees and hears." Many can contact the Cosmic Memory but what are they seeing? Some clairvoyants are honestly describing what they saw there, but what they are really seeing is according to their self-development. If you take a child, a teenager, an adult or an elderly person to a park and leave them there for a while, you find that each person has eyes and can see what is going on in the park. When you come back and ask them what they saw, each will have noticed what interests them and will not have noticed all the things that interested the others. It is the same with readers of the Cosmic Memory.

Sometimes people would say to Daskalos that they wanted to become a clairvoyant. Oftentimes he would laugh and say something like, "What for? Do you want to know the reality of Life or simply catch glimpses here and there that are coming from the Psychical planes and then color it according to the quality of your personality and claim you are seeing the truth? Clairvoyance and clairaudience means nothing if the one who is supposed to use it is not developed."

Many can enter the Cosmic Consciousness, which is everywhere, but what these people are telling us about the Cosmic Memory shows their own level of development as they color what they have seen, which is revealing the quality of their personality. We must not rely much on the descriptions of those who consider themselves a clairvoyant before they are properly developed, first as a healthy balanced personality and then as Soul Self-Consciousness. Before they reach that kind of development they may see recordings in the Cosmic Consciousness, but what they understand about what they see is a different matter.

Again, this formless Super-Substance of the Mind is everywhere outside of you and inside of you. Anyone can learn to use it consciously and once you do use it, you know for sure it exists and no one can make you doubt its reality. Unless we ourselves learn to use the Mind in Observation, Concentration and Meditation, it will not matter how many spiritual books we read, how many spiritual teachers we visit, we will not benefit much. So how do we come to live a happier and more satisfying life by using the Mind?

It is here in the densest of all the Worlds of Existence that we find ourselves as personalities seeking to unfold spiritually. To do this we have to initially sit down, use our mind to think consciously and come to conclusions. Through meditation we will come into the meaning of God, and that of our real Self.

What will be the outcome? By using the Mind as right thinking, by means of concentration and contemplation, we may claim more power. One day, we will reach a point, where we no longer depend on knowledge, which we receive from our environment, from the outside world. We will gain new powers. These are the powers of Concentration, Attunement and eventually At-One-Ment, but first we must use the Mind to clean and purify the personality, to learn how to disentangle our personality from our troubles, illusions and live a better life. Slowly and surely we will free our personality from its misidentifications, its illusions and its intoxication with the material world. As Researchers of Truth, we begin this effort with our own personal reality. We begin by introspecting on our own actions and especially our reactions to the people and conditions around us right now. We research all this by using our latent power of observation to expose incorrect thoughts, negative emotions, enslaving desires, and unhealthy life patterns that seal us off from truth, love and a happier life.

Through this line of research, will discover that our thoughts, emotions, and desires (good or bad) are ours; we are responsible for them and their effects. They are ours but they are not us! They are ours and we can change them, improve them or abandon them completely. So if we are not our body, not our emotions, not out thoughts, then what are we? This is what a seeker must find out. We must discover who and what we really are. In doing so, we learn about our conflicting strengths and weaknesses. We discover something of our Psychical Body, the body of our emotions. This is the body that we will find our self in after the death of our material body. We will also come to know about our Noetical Body, the body of our thoughts. This is the body we will find our self in after the second death as it is called in Revelations, but even the second death is not the end of our life or research; we will continue on to discover and experience what we are beyond our three bodies and what we are even beyond the Human Form. The indescribable experiences that await seekers that do not faint in the face of challenges, trials and tribulations are beyond our comprehension or even our best imagination.

Even with a basic concentration on something simple like a flower, it is possible to become one with the flower and in an instant know everything about the flower. In this way of study we can learn things about the object of our concentration that would have taken years of normal study. This is the power of concentration, leading to attunement and At-One-Ment. So by Observation, Concentration and Meditation a Researcher of Truth can know so much about the life forms all around. Orthodox science is using material instruments to do the same. So both are studying the living forms of life, but can anyone understand these living forms without having a source of that life? Can we understand something living that moves without having a source of energy that causes that movement?

To study means to know by Observation and Concentration what the reality is, that is behind everything we see and experience. Using Observation and Concentration, we start Meditation. We will develop our ability to concentrate in order to hold our attention and continue meditating, otherwise, a swarm of thoughts and feelings will enter to disturb and derail you intended meditation. As a Self-Aware Soul we all can concentrate and study things, but as personality self-awareness our unruly hoard of thoughts, feelings and desires arises to distract us from our intended concentration. We can overcome this disturbance by insisting on concentration. In the beginning, when you do this, the personality will continue to try and distract you -not just a few times but many, many times. You remain undisturbed as the Soul-Self and keep on insisting to hold your concentration and your personality will keep on intervening. Give this repeated intervention no importance, in time it will subside and, in the end, you as a Soul-Self will be able to hold the concentration, calm down the personality and lead it into wisdom. All the answers we seek are held by the Soul-Self, but the personality must enter a state of calm coordination to be able to access these answers.

We all gain knowledge about the world around us in the normal way by concentration on objects and conditions. We perceive something we want to know about as being separated from ourselves and the moment we do that, we are expressing our self. We concentrate on the object or condition and that gives us knowledge about it. Knowledge in the world comes from a concentration by the self on something that can be perceived but not the reality behind the perception. As we advance spiritually, we proceed through the perceptible towards the reality and this eventually gives us knowledge of the reality that has given birth to the perceptible. You cannot reach this point through blind Faith or reading about it. You come to this only though your direct experience.

Developing the skill of Concentration empowers Meditation, but you need to ask yourself, "Who is it that is actually meditating?" Is it your body that meditates? Is it your brain that meditates? The means that you use to meditate is the Mind. We may be tempted to call the Mind intelligence, perception or thought; but these are just the expressions of the Mind. We have to go beyond the expressions to find out what the Mind truly is.

Developing Observation and Concentration skills we also gain powers of Visualization, which leads to real clairvoyance. Sometimes in the beginning of their development researchers may make the error to think that what they see in visualization is really clairvoyance. Daskalos had a student who after some practice said to him, "Daskalos, I can now go to London!"

Daskalos replied, "Seriously? How can you go to London?"

The student said, "Yes I went there many times and got to know it. Now I can close my eyes and move about in the streets of London."

Daskalos asked him, "When were you physically in London the last time?" "Eight years ago," he replied.

"Tell me," Daskalos continued, "what changes have taken place in London in the last eight years? If you cannot detect the changes that have taken place then, my dear, what you see in your visualization is only what you have seen eight years ago. You have brought all that to your mind from your sub-consciousness by your thoughts and you move about in this Elemental image. This is a good visualization but you did not go to London! Why don't you go to Paris or Brussels?"

The student replied, "But I have never been to Pairs or Brussels, so how can I go there in my visualization?"

"You cannot go somewhere in your visualization that you have never been before.

You cannot recall something that you have not placed in your sub-consciousness," Daskalos concluded.

Obviously, the student was not going to London as he thought he was by an out of body experience (OBE) or astral travel as some call it and this is a common mistake; to confuse a good visualization with an OBE. Yet, if that seeker continued with the practices of Observation and Concentration one day he can find himself in London and will be able to see the physical changes that have actually taken place and not just a detail recollection from his memory of London. He will have accomplished this by transporting to London by OBE or what Daskalos called Exosomatosis. The student was satisfied by just moving about in the Elemental of London, the thought-form of London he had in his sub-consciousness. But by doing this, he created an obstacle to his progress and the development of a real out of body experience.

With practice, Concentration and Meditation comes real power that, when mastered, will broaden your life. Once you get this skill you use it for the most needed study of the book of your life. We all have written many pages in the book of our life in the past and every moment we are continuing to write new pages in that book. Study to see what pages you have written in the past and what you should be writing in the future. On these pages we are writing the script for our life and we follow that written script going forward in life. Do not lament badly written pages in the past; those unpleasant things in your past serve as important lessons you needed so as not to write new pages in the future as bad as those.

This line of effort will produce a happier and better way of life for you and those around you. In time you will raise your consciousness from its lower sub-conscious states to more and more conscious states all the way to Self-Consciousness and Self-Super-Consciousness. This means the Seeker of Truth, over the course of time, will be able to assimilate his personality self with his or her real nature: the Spirit-Soul.

By using the Mind we are formulating our thoughts and emotions, which creates Elementals (good or not so good) and these determine the quality of our personality. We do not receive readymade thoughts and emotions. Without understanding what we are doing, we get the Super-Substance of the Mind and form it into thoughts and emotions then empower them to various degrees according to our interests. So we are all in touch sub-consciously with the Super-substance of the Mind. This means everybody has been granted the right to use the Mind, in the same way that everyone is entitled to use the air to breathe. No one has been granted greater privileges to use the Mind than anyone else. There are no limits or prohibitions; it is just a matter of your will, your effort to train and time.

Knowing this, we can start to use the Mind consciously in creating a better life and a personality of a better character without egoism. What is the goal of this work? We will never reach a goal in this effort but what we will do is develop our personality self-consciousness to higher levels as we master our emotions and thoughts. We will continue ascending this evolutionary ladder to reach Self-Realization.

Think of the first cavemen living precariously in a dangerous environment so hostile to their existence that both cavemen and cavewomen were carrying heavy clubs to protect themselves from wild animals. They were using the Mind to protect and express themselves. Later on mankind started using the Mind to express themselves in better and better ways. So the expressions of the Self were better, but the Self was always the Self. Do not confuse the expression with the source. In truth, we are not developing a Self; our Self is a perfect offspring of God, an eternal Spirit-Being, which needs no development. What we are doing is developing the skills of expressing that Self in a better and better way over time. That is why it is called Self-Realization. We are not trying to build and develop a perfect Self. We are trying to wake up from our illusions in order to realize the perfect Spirit-Soul-Self we are, were and will always be.

THE PRACTICE: CONCENTRATING THE MIND

The ability to concentrate the Mind is very necessary for creative thinking, healing and meditation. Success in the spiritual world or the material world depends on our ability to concentrate the

Mind. Thus, it is necessary for us to be able to concentrate all our thoughts on a subject of investigation or contemplation. We can also concentrate on an emotion or thought all by itself. When we choose to focus our undivided attention, we should choose a definite length of time for this concentration and hold the concentration so firmly that nothing can distract us or pull our attention away. There are no limits to how far concentration can take us once it is developed.

Concentration is using the material brain to focus the Mind Super Substance to know more and more about something. Still, it takes practice to get the skill of doing this in the right way. The process is somewhat similar to using a magnifying glass to focus rays of the sun. On a clear day in winter it can be bitter cold but if you take a magnifying glass and concentrate a few sun rays on to a piece of paper at the proper distance it will burst into flames and give you warmth. Similarly when we use our brain to concentrate it becomes like the magnifying glass and focuses rays of the Mind on to the object of our concentration and it gives us knowledge about that we wish to know.

The secret of living happier is in knowing how to use the Mind in the right way as reason, Concentration and Observation instead of the wrong way by enslaving the Mind to unnecessary and uncontrolled desires all the time. By desiring one thing after another, on and on, we are using the Mind to serve only our emotions and we call this life. Just fulfilling one desire after another, year after year is not the kind of thing that makes for a happier life. It is just another form of slavery. Our ardent intent is to become free of this kind of slavery in order to find our real Self.

PRACTICE: ROSE CONCENTRATION

Take a physical red rose and hold it in your material hands. Concentrate your attention on the rose, without feeling any tension in your body or mind. Observe its shape, color, and size as you turn it around in your hands. Feel the velvety petals, notice the subtle colors and hard smooth stem with the sharp thorns. Lift the rose to your nose and inhale its fragrance. Concentrate and take in the full beauty of the rose.

Set the rose down and close your eyes and breathe deeply but comfortably for a few minutes. Now using creative Visualization see yourself holding the rose in your hand. Concentrate and see the rose clearly in your mind's eye. See its shape, color and size. Feel the hard waxy stem and sharp thorns. Feel and see its veined green leaves and is soft velvety red petals. Visualize bringing the rose to your nose and recreate its rosy fragrance. Look into the center of the rose and see how all the petals unfold around this center. Hold the image of this fragrant red rose steady in your mind for a bit and then see yourself giving it to someone you have difficulty with. Offer the red rose to this person with peace and love.

Chapter Seven
THREE WORLDS OF EXISTENCE

Place is a definite condition of the three Worlds of Existence, the material world (which is in space) and of the Psychical World and the Noetical World. They are the Worlds of Existence and of place. When Christ was going to the home of His Father, He said, "In my Father's home there are many mansions. I go to prepare a place for you." He didn't mention space.

So, the Psychical World is exactly the same as the material world. There you can see mountains, seas, lakes, trees, everything. The Psychical World of our planet is exactly the same as our material world, and in it there are many, many things and much, much more than what you can find on the material plane of our planet. And, that's the world we'll some day pass over to and leave behind our material body. ~ Daskalos

THE TEACHING:

The three Worlds of Existence are the Material Plane, the Psychical Planes and the Noetical Planes. They interweave and coexist together just as our material, Psychical and Noetical Bodies do. Our three bodies are the vehicles we use to inhabit these three worlds. It is within these Worlds of Existence that we, as personalities, create our own conditional paradises or hells. We build our paradises or hells in all three worlds simultaneously without really understanding what we are doing. We call these self-created paradises and hells conditional, because our life in the material, Psychical and Noetical worlds is a condition of our conceptions. As such, they are not permanent realities but temporary shells we construct with our thoughts and emotions. Our positive, noble thoughts and loving feelings create our paradises. Our negative, ignoble thoughts and unkind feelings create our hells.

The third century Christian Bishop and mystic, Origen, taught in his schools that the duration of our hell was not eternal. Rather it was temporary, and it was only proportional to the guilt of the personality. Origen also taught that the consequences experienced in these conditions would stop in time and the end effect would be to purify the personality. We must study our personality's conceptions in order to understand them, break free of the illusions and realize the reality of our Inner Self.

Everything in the Three Worlds of Existence is under the phenomenal law of duality. The dual in one and the one in its dual expression: Hot and cold, up and down, good and bad, in and out, etc. All life forms, in all the Worlds of Existence, have the law of duality at work in them and around them. Our material bodies manifest this duality. We have a brain with two lobes. We have two eyes, two nostrils, two ears, and two lungs. Our heart has two upper chambers and two lower chambers. Our body has two hands, two feet and so on. All the forms of life in these worlds have a temporary existence. They are born, they live and then their material form dies. Moreover, while in these worlds, all the forms of life undergo change – constant change.

Spiritually speaking about all the known universes in existence, it is as Daskalos put it, "The universes, as the texture of God, pour forth in Space." So he is saying Space is a Nature of God.

Scientifically speaking, about the composition of the material universe it is as Einstein put it: $E = MC2$. This equation means Energy can be transformed into matter and matter transformed into energy. So Energy and Matter are two sides of the same coin. Energy and Matter are one (as matter is condensed Energy). So to a physical scientist the entire material universe can be considered as comprised of only two things: energy & space. We find this energy, or what we call Mind Vitality, in many different rates of vibration, from lower to higher.

The three Worlds of Existence are the Material World, Psychical Worlds (sometimes called the Astral Worlds), and Noetical Worlds. Connecting these three worlds is the Etheric; each of these three worlds has an Etheric counterpart, which interpenetrates, surrounds and connects these worlds. Within these worlds, our planet has a material existence as well as a psychical and Noetical existence – three states of existence. A rough comparison can be drawn with water, which exists in three physical states as solid ice, liquid water and gaseous vapor. It is just its energetic state, its rate of vibration, which determines if water is in a solid, liquid or gaseous state.

All of the Worlds of Existence are made of Mind in different rates of vibration from the most refined levels to the densest. The Material Plane is the lowest vibration of Mind manifesting as solid matter. Daskalos would emphasis this point repeatedly saying, "Matter is Mind made solid." Vibrating at slightly higher rates; the Mind manifests as the psychical substance used in the creation of the various planes and sub-planes comprising the Psychical Worlds. How does the law of duality manifest in the Psychical Planes? The psychical planes are worlds of emotions, desires and sentiments. So, the law of duality here manifests as attraction and repulsion. Kind, loving feelings create the attraction, whereas hatred and uncaring feelings create repulsion.

The Noetical Worlds are Mind worlds of a still higher dimension but they, too, have a beginning and will eventually come to an end. In the lower Noetical Planes, the law of the dual is still at work. Beyond the lower Noetical Planes, we start to lose the temporal experience of duality as we approach the unity of Beingness in the Eternal Now. Here, evil is experienced as undeveloped good or simply ignorance of the truth as the Hindus teach. Here is where we find the full happiness we have been expectantly seeking in the Worlds of Existence as we enter into states of ecstasy, bliss and beatitude, which have no dualistic counterpoint.

For most of us, our attention is so focused outwardly on our world of the three dimensions that we do not even consider the possibilities of the other dimensions and levels of reality. We also lack the theoretical framework and the personal experience that would adequately provide us a sense of these dimensions. It may be initially difficult to comprehend the worlds of the higher dimensions but everyone understands that we live in a three-dimensional world. In this dimension, we understand relative space in the three dimensions – height, width and length. The Material World is the entire three-dimensional universe and everything existing in it. It is under the limits of both space and time. That is to say, the Material World is under the constraints of measurable distance and the progressive sequence of events as measured by hours, days, weeks and years.

The Psychical and Noetical Worlds (Psycho-Noetical) give us a similar sense of place and have natural landscapes and everything that exists on the material plane. There are also many more beauties there than are present on the Earth. All these planes in all the universes are creating a continuum of worlds. The obvious difference between them is the amount of light experienced in each plane. This gradation of the light and vibration give us the sense of the lower and higher planes in these dimensions. On the material plane, the main characteristic of light is reflection. We see the various material objects around us when light is reflected off them. In the Psycho-Noetical Worlds, light's characteristic is self-illumination; every particle of Psycho-Noetical substance emanates its own light here. The Psychical planes also have different governing laws. The sense of time is also different there and not measured in hours, days or years and yet, in the Psychical Worlds, there is still the sense of time as passing events. The psychical counterpart of Earth interpenetrates our planet and extends thousands of miles around our planet but does not touch the psychical counter parts of the other planets in our solar system. The Noetical counterpart of our planet interpenetrates and extends much further. The Noetical counterpart of Earth is in contact with the Noetical counterpart of other planets and heavenly bodies. Our entire solar system floats within the Noetical.

With training, it is possible to learn to cross into the Psychical plane consciously. However, everyone is crossing into the Psychical planes subconsciously when they sleep. "Dreams do not exist," as Daskalos often declared. "Dreams are experiences you have in the Psychical planes," he further explained, "but you bring back the memories of these experiences to the material brain in a jumbled and fragmented way and so they do not seem real to you."

Often after waking from sleep you may remember a dream and start telling it and say something like, "I was some place…" The Psychical planes are giving us a sense of place. In the Psychical planes, we lose the sense of space but not the sense of place.

Space is different from place. Place is a definite understandable condition. The material universe exists in space; its vastness is beyond our understanding. Within our galaxy there are over 200 billion stars of which our sun is but one. Our Milky Way Galaxy is so large that it would take light 100,000 years just to travel across it. Beyond this, there are billions and billions of galaxies in the material universe.

Our Earth is rotating at over 1000 miles per hour on it axis. In the time it takes you to read this paragraph you will have moved about 50 miles in space due to Earth's rotation alone. Where in space did you really go in those 50 miles? At the same time, the Earth is orbiting around the sun at 67,000 miles per hour and our sun and Earth are rotating around the center of the Milky Way. Furthermore, our galaxy is traveling in space too. At the same time everything in the entire material universe is in a state of outward expansion with every galaxy, star, planet and moon moving farther apart from each other. We are constantly moving vast distances, in a spiraling motion through space, so space itself is not giving us any meaning except the relative space between measurable objects. It is the sense of place that gives us meaning. The Psychical and noetical planes are worlds that give the sense of place.

Just because these are non-physical worlds, we should not think they are abstract or less real than the more familiar material world. They are not. Conditions there can last much longer than on the material plane. In the fourth dimension, the sense of place is determined by rates of vibration. In the third dimension, two objects cannot occupy the same location. However, in the fourth-dimension, many objects can exists in the same location without mixing up. The closest three-dimensional similarity to this occurs with television broadcasts. As we all know, different television stations broadcast different programs, which are all around us in the same locality. All the many programs exist simultaneously in our living room without mixing up. That is because they are transmitted at different frequencies – different rates of vibration. We can tune our television to receive one program and not receive the others co-existing in the same location. Something similar occurs in the fourth dimension and we experience different places of this dimension by our attunement to the specific frequencies of these different places. It is all about attunement. The Esoteric Practices of our system teach us how to raise and lower our vibrations and attune to different frequencies. These exercises provide us with the means for conscious "movement" within the higher dimensional universes.

The three Worlds of Existence are worlds of forms – living forms. The fifth-dimensional Noetical World is where the laws, causes, principles and ideas of the higher Noetic State are first expressed as forms. The forms on Earth are but reflections of the forms found in the Noetical Planes. For something to exist in the third or fourth dimension, it must have a counterpart in the fifth-dimension. Every form existing in the material universe exists in the Psychical Planes and the Noetical Planes.

In the Noetical Planes, time loses its meaning altogether. The Worlds of Existence are realms of condition and perception but are not the ultimate Reality. From this point we advance and penetrate through the perceptions of these worlds to the Reality behind our limited perceptions. We cross the threshold from the time, space and place Worlds of Existence into the Eternal Now -into the time-less, space-less realm of Beingness.

When we say Worlds of Existence we mean these worlds have been created, exist for a time, and in some distant future will cease to exist. All the heavens and everything in them have been created using eternal, immutable Divine Law-Causes. These Divine Laws are permanent but the mundane heavens created from these laws do not last forever. Speaking to this, Joshua Immanuel the Christ declared, "...it is easier for heaven and Earth to pass, than one tittle of the law to fail" (tittle means the smallest part of something). It was these Divine Law-Causes and the Worlds of Existence he was referring to.

The Noetical Worlds are worlds of thought. The Noetical Worlds have seven main planes, and within each plane there are seven sub-planes. So it is an extraordinarily vast reality composed of 49 sub-planes with many localities within each plane. At an even lower frequency we have the Psychical-Substance that is used in the creation of all the 49 sub-planes of the Psychical Worlds. The Psychical Worlds are the places visited by those who can have conscious out of body experiences (OBEs). Again, these are the very same worlds we all visit each night while our body is asleep on our bed but most people lack the ability to bring back these experiences fully to the material brain in the morning. Remembering bits and flashes they believe they had a dream that they consider as totally unreal. These incomplete memories are just jumbled fragments of experiences in the Psychical Worlds of existence.

Upon the death of our material body we will all find ourselves fully residing in these Psychical Worlds with the same feelings, thoughts and interests as we had the moment before the death of our material body. Just like in the Noetical Worlds, colors, sights, sounds and smells in the Psychical Worlds are much richer and broader than we have on Earth. In these worlds, our feelings and desires are much more intense because the Psychical Worlds are worlds of emotion, and the experiences of time and place in these worlds are more fluid, elastic and vivid. The psychical substance composing these worlds is more easily affected by our motivations and intentions. Now we find that the higher Worlds of Existence are exactly like the material world.

They have oceans, mountains, rivers, lakes, trees and all the life forms on Earth. There are also more exotic life forms and many things that are not found on Earth. There is more abundant light the higher you ascend and this light gives nourishment and understanding in the higher worlds. However, while on Earth, unless we tune our consciousness to the frequencies of Psychical and Noetical light, we will not be able to perceive anything of these worlds. That is why most people have no idea they even exist. It is like the radio stations that all concurrently exist around us. We are not able to perceive anything about them unless we tune a receiver to their specific broadcast frequency. The three Worlds of Existence, the Noetical, the Psychical and the Material co-exist and are intermingled with each other. They all exist together but at different rates of vibration like musical octaves and so these worlds do not get jumbled and mixed up.

Think for a minute how much of the Earth we actually inhabit. As you know the Earth is 71% covered by water, but we are not living in the water we live on the dry land. Of the 29% of Earth that is dry land, humans only inhabit about one percent of it. So, proportionally, we live on a tiny part of the Earth and yet that part seems very vast to us. If you compare the inhabited part of Earth to the Psychical Worlds, you would find it to be just a small portion of one of the 49 sub-planes. With training, a Seeker of the Truth can learn to open the portals to self-conscious movement within all these worlds.

THE PRACTICE: OVERVIEW

It is said that our material body is a temple of God. At the same time it is the temple of our Inner Self. The Soul-Self is living in this temple which is most intelligently cared for by the Holy Spirit and it Archangelic emissaries. The Holy Spirit is alive and working in every cell of your material body to maintain its health. We should love our body and give thanks to the Holy Spirit who cares for it in our behalf and so we should cooperate with the Holy Spirit and the Archangels in order to know what is taking place in the body temple. All the forms of Etheric Vitality are controlled by the Holy Spirit and the Logos and perform great work for the building of our material body. By practicing our exercises of Introspection, Concentration and Meditation we are, at the same time, collaborating with the work of the Holy Spirit and Archangels. It gives them joy when they see our personality mature to the point of conscious coordination with them and their work in our body temple.

We also must practice exercises that balance the material body, Psychical Body and our Noetical Body for good health. Each of our three bodies corresponds to one of the three Worlds of Existence and we use these bodies to live in and express ourselves through while being in these worlds. We want all our emotions and thoughts to be under the control of our Inner Self and not under the control or our egoism, which we have mistaken to be our real self. Our practices bring these under the conscious control of our Inner Self. In time you will gain full mastery and can use logical thought to dissolve unreasonable thoughts and emotions. Then you will discover who you really are as the Soul-Self. Balancing our three bodies enables our approach and entrance into the Psychical and Noetical Worlds of Existence.

We can vitalize and balance our three bodies by working in the three main centers of consciousness and self-awareness: The Solar Plexus, the Heart center and the Head Center. In the Solar Plexus it is safe for anyone to concentrate and store energy there.

The Solar Plexus is a storehouse of energy. This energy spread throughout the body. It is the basis of the metabolism and the Holy Spirit performs great work there. In our practices we should not concentrate directly on the material heart, it can cause heart problems, but we can safely concentrate in the entire chest cavity without doing any harm. For the same reason, we want to concentrate in and around the head area.

THE PRACTICE: A PRELIMINARY MEDITATION

Concentrate in your material body and relax every muscle. Feel you are in your whole material body. Your body is a gift from God, sustained and lovingly maintained by the Holy Spirit and Archangels. Simply feel you are in your material body completely relaxed. Even though you know very little about it, you can be the master of your material body.

The Holy Archangels are working in all your organs and in every cell of your body. Thank them for their tireless work. They love you and rejoice when you become conscious of their work and cooperate with them.

Concentrate and feel you are in the toes of your feet. Consciously feel you are fully in your toes. Take a deep, comfortable breath and move your attention up through the calves of your legs. Breathe again and continue this movement up through your thighs. See the snow-white light Etheric Vitality radiating in and around your legs. Feel it in and around your legs.

Move slowly from your legs up and into your Solar Plexus. Breathe deeply, comfortably and rhythmically as you concentrate in this center. Breathe in and see a beautiful sky blue nebula of light radiating from this center. Breathe out and see all darkness and fear leave your body.

Breathe in and see the sky blue light in and around your Solar Plexus become brighter and brighter. Breathe out and see this pure light-energy spread throughout your whole body. Wish calmness to reign in your material body.

Now continue to move your attention up to the chest area. See a luminous rosy light emanating from your Heart Center in and around your chest. Quiet all your emotions and desires and fill this center with love. Feel love for life, feel love for yourself and feel love for all human beings. Especially feel love for those whom you have trouble with and those who have trouble with you. Expand this selfless love to spread out and cover our temporary home; the planet Earth. Wish peace to reign in your heart.

Continue to move your attention up to the head. Feel you are in and around your head. Breathe deeply and see a golden nebula of light in and around the head. Silence your ordinary thoughts. Only creative thoughts are in your mind now. Breathe, deeply, comfortably and rhythmically and see how this luminous nebula of golden light becomes clearer, brighter and stronger with each breath. Wish clarity for your mind.

See how the Etheric Double of your whole material body is glowing and scintillating in pure white light? Say to yourself, "I want perfect health in my material body!"

Chapter Eight
THREE VEHICLES OF THE SOUL

The material body cannot exist without the Psychical and Noetical Bodies. So a human being has at his service three bodies, through which he can express himself in the corresponding material, Psychical and Noetical Worlds. That means he must have Noetical, Psychical and material bodies to express himself in the material world. The material body can be completely aborted as it happens with the phenomenon of death. The human self-aware personality then departs and withdraws with his or her Psychical and Noetical Bodies in to the Psychical World, where he lives in the same manner as he lived in the material world. Most ordinary people are not aware of the difference between the material world and the Psychical World when they pass over. The enlightened ones in past centuries not only knew about the existence of these bodies, they were making good use of them. Saint Paul knew them, used them, and mentioned them in his writings. ~ Daskalos

THE TEACHING

The Material Body, the Psychical Body and the Noetical Body are the vehicles of the Soul used during its journey through the corresponding three Worlds of Existence: Material, Psychical and the Noetical. These bodies are made up of substance corresponding to the world within which a human being lives and express his or her self and we have said that these three bodies and the three worlds have their etheric counterparts, which connect them.

These bodies are not separated but coexist with one another simultaneously. At night when the Psychical and Noetical Bodies withdraw from the material body it goes into the state of sleep. The material body is unusable without the Psychical and Noetical Bodies.

However, when the material body is discarded in the change we call death, the self-aware personality then fully resides in its Psychical Body but, for the Psychical Body to exist, it must also have the Noetical Body with it. Because the Psychical Body and Noetical Body are connected and together we call this the Psycho-Noetical Body. Each and every atom of your material body has a corresponding ethereal, Psychical and a Noetical atom.

The Psychical and Noetical Bodies have the identical form of the material body but are beyond the concept of measurable space. These bodies are like clothing we can temporarily take off and put on or, in the case of future incarnations, our current material, Psychical and Noetical Bodies are replaced with entirely new ones. The bodies are like garments covering the ray of our Spirit-Soul-Self. The clothing is not so important; it is the Self that dresses in the clothing that is important. It is necessary to note the difference between the temporary and the permanent…between the temporary bodies and the Permanent Inner Self that inhabits the bodies for a time.

We find our material body, readymade for our use. All we have to do is feed it, wash it and dress it. Karma permitting, it develops perfectly and naturally under the wisdom of the Holy Spirit. We are shaping and coloring our Psychical and Noetical Bodies all the time. Our Psychical Body is shaped and colored by the quality and quantity of our emotions, desires and motivations. Likewise, our Noetical Body is shaped and colored by our thoughts and intentions. If our emotions and thoughts have negativity, being composed of jealousy anger, anxiety, unhealthy desires and unclean thoughts our Psychical Body and Noetical Bodies are discolored accordingly.

At the same time there is the perfect archetype of the Psychical and Noetical Body, which is kept by our Guarding Archangel. So our work in our spiritual unfoldment is to learn to shape our Psychical and Noetical Body consciously so it matches that of the perfect archetype. Of course Christ and certain enlightened masters in the past have come to show us what that actually looks like.

In spiritually un-awakened people, the Psycho-Noetical Body looks undeveloped. It appears as an unshaped oval mass taking on the colors according to the person's feelings and thoughts. So as we work to purify our emotions and clean our thoughts we automatically shape our Psychical and Noetical Body closer to its perfect archetype.

We are born in this world without any real perception of who we are as a personality until around the age of seven. Up to this point in time, all we know is our name, gender and immediate environment. Yet, Karma permitting, our material body tends develops properly without much effort on our part. Our material body grows from the center of each atom. It is the Etheric Vitality that maintains the body's health and makes it grow. Our bodies are a very precious gift from God and we must love and respect them.

Yet the common person has no idea about the other two higher bodies but the Researcher of Truth knows the higher bodies in two ways. The first way is by theoretical knowledge. You read or hear about them and you understand they exist. The second way is to come to know them is practically, which means you start to use them consciously. So far you have only used them sub-consciously.

When a person is under raging anger, that person has no idea they are using their Psychical Body subconsciously wasting vast quantities of its Etheric Vitality. Often when people get angry their face turns red and they get hot. This happens because they are making a bonfire of their Etheric Vitality but when the anger subsides they feel exhausted and drained. This is evidence of the tremendous loss of energy resulting from uncontrolled anger.

The result of all this is a disturbance in the Divine harmony and laws that wisely governs the health of our bodies; the result of violation of the laws is diseases and illness. When a harmful violation reaches a tipping point, the personality suffers pain and this physical, emotional or mental pain endures until there is a balancing or restoration of the Divine Law has been achieved. Who is really responsible for this pain and suffering? Some people blame God.

An angry woman who had bad ulcers and needed an operation came to Daskalos. She told him, "I believed in God once, but now I do not believe God exists. Because why should I have to suffer this pain in my stomach and go for surgery to have this ulcer removed? Tell me why God has given me such a bad turn?"

Daskalos replied, "This is what made you reach the conclusion that God does not exist? Did God by any chance teach you to live in an angry way to upset your stomach and create this problem? We all know that anxiety, worries and anger create such conditions."

Unfortunately, the lady had taken no responsibility for her own faults and shifted the responsibility of her aliment to God instead. How can we help a person who takes absolutely no responsibility for his or her own actions? First, the person's thinking must be cured in order to stop laying the blame on others, to become aware of the real cause, and to willingly restore balance. If that can be done, then a lasting cure is possible. The doctors were confident surgery was necessary because this lady had a deep ulcer, but Daskalos showed her another way. She changed her attitude, dropped the anger and was cured of the ulcers without surgery. Today she is a different person. No longer does she get angry, waking up in the morning ready to lash out at others, claiming, "They were ruining her nerves." She does not go around looking for a reason to get upset or feel that others are against her – she really changed. Now, the real gain of this healing was more than just curing the dangerous ulcer. The real gain was that she was able to cure herself from an unhealthy personality that created the ulcer. For lasting cures we must treat the cause and not just treat the symptom, which in this case was the ulcer.

We all know we are living in a material body and we have a Psychical Body which some call the astral body. "Astral" comes from the Latin and means star. We have a Noetical Body. Saint Paul called this body the Spiritual Body. In our system we call it the Noetical Body so as not to confuse it with the word Spirit, which is the nature of God and also our own Divine Nature.

These three bodies are independent of each other. An advanced mystic can self-consciously at will, leave his material body and live more fully in a Psychical Body in the Psychical Worlds but this Psychical Body must still have the Noetical Body connected and interwoven with it in order to live. Likewise, a very advanced mystic can self-consciously leave the Psychical Body and even more fully live in just his or her Noetical Body.

Furthermore, a mystic or Researcher of Truth residing only in the Noetical Worlds who expresses as a Soul and not just a personality can re-appear in the Psychical Worlds, such as one who has aborted his material and Psychical Body and now fully dwells in the Noetical Worlds can materialize a material body to use in the material worlds. Through the force of their own will they can be seen, shake hands, converse and provide real physical help.

As human beings we have at our disposal three bodies, which we can use to express ourselves in the corresponding three Worlds of Existence. Do not think that any of these three bodies are your Self. We must understand the difference and learn to separate the Self from the three bodies the Self uses. An advanced Researcher of Truth is a master of these three bodies and can express his Self completely in any of the three Worlds of Existence with a corresponding body. These are known as the Invisible Helpers – the brothers of mercy. They can materialize anywhere on Earth and give physical assistance. Distance is not a limitation for the invisible helpers. They communicate between themselves no matter how many miles apart they are. These are not the average Researches of Truth but the most advanced ones. These are the ones who have succeeded in assimilating their personality-self with the Soul-Self. They have overcome their personality and placed it under the guidance and control of their Inner Self. They know who they are as a personality self and what they are as a Soul Self.

This is Daskalos' ardent wish for all of us. It may be difficult to do but this is not impossible. Others have done it before us and one day we will do it too. What we need is the full intention and the un-conflicted desire to be of service to our fellow human beings. From the instant we express the wish to love and help others; the great intelligences around us rejoice and give us help. So we are never alone in our effort.

We are speaking about our three bodies, but what is the relationship between the material, Psychical and Noetical Bodies? Again if the Psycho-Noetical Body is withdrawn from the material body for an extended period of time the material body dies. This is because the withdrawal of the Psycho-Noetical Body causes the etheric counter part of the material body to withdraw completely. When this happens it deprives the life force from the physical matter composing the body and the body starts to decompose. The etheric counterparts of the bodies are both the space between the bodies as well as the link connecting these bodies.

We can teach about the three bodies, and can show confirmations from other enlightened masters who have found these other bodies. The instructions are given, have always been given and will continue to be given by those who know but this is not enough. This information can point you in the right direction, but everyone has to make his or her own effort to investigate and have his or her own direct experience. Everyone, according the instructions of Christ, should know the truth for himself or herself. We can intellectually accept the truth from a knowing, trustworthy authority but to really "know" the truth and be freed we must have the direct experience of the truth ourselves.

All these enlightened teachers from all times basically said the same thing. It did not matter which time period they were living, or where on the planet they were living, they all found the same truth again and again. A man or a woman in any nation has the truth available but what is needed is to research and investigate that truth.

Someone might say, "I am not interested in that or what does it matter; I do not have time to investigate these things." The response to that attitude is that people need to study these things because too many people are living an unsatisfying life and suffering to some degree. Nobody can take you out of your suffering unless you are open to knowing the truth.

That person may ask, "Am I really in a hell?" Definitely, if they are under the illusion of separateness, having jealousy, animosity and feeling others is their enemies and struggling against them. To come out of such troubles and suffering we have to find the truth. To be free we have wake up to the illusions, which egoism presents as the truth. As you look at people around, you will notice that those who deny the truth are the unhappiest people on the Earth.

Now without understanding it, every night each of you, leaves your material body as it is sleeping on the bed. Each night the self-aware personality along with the Psycho-Noetical Body must withdraw from the material body. The creative ether of the material body always stays with the material body when the other bodies withdraw during sleep. During this time the Holy Spirit uses the creative ether to make repairs and restore health to the material body. Most people do not consciously work to develop their Psychical or Noetical Body. So everyone has these bodies but they are basically inactive. To activate them and develop the Psychical Body we must use the Noetical Body. This means that to control emotions and desires we must use our mind to think in a reasonable way. In doing so, we set into motion the functioning of our Psychical and Noetical Bodies.

Developing our Psychical and Noetical Bodies is similar to the material body. If we do not move our material body it will become atrophied, weak and unusable. A material body simply will not function properly without activity and use. The same is true with the higher Psychical and Noetical Bodies.

Human life requires us to use our three bodies to at least some degree. So an aim of a Researcher of Truth is to learn to distinguish these bodies and use them consciously. Eventually for Researcher of Truth there is no sleeping. Which means, after putting his material body to sleep every night, the researcher withdraws from it and continues living in the Psychical Worlds just as he did in the material world. A very advanced researcher, as self-awareness, does not sleep or dream but enjoys a continuation of consciousness in these higher worlds.

Now the way to reach these high states starts with analyzing your personality self. This is done to reach the honest truth about who you are as a temporary existence and what you are as an eternal being. This is not easy to do because as a personality you cannot immediately understand this space-less reality. The limited time and space-place personality cannot fully understand its own limitless source while still encapsulated in the three bodies. That does not mean we are not able to know something of the truth of it while still living in these three bodies. Of course, all this needs time and practice on the part of the personality to align and attune in order to comprehend its source. It takes effort to be able to discern your Divine Nature from its human expressions. It takes time and effort because we have this temporary human personality with a material body, an emotional body and a mental body, which we have become misidentified with.

This temporary little self with its three bodies is a product of time, space and place. Some people have confused their self with their material body. Not knowing about the Psychical Body many think they are their emotions. Not knowing about the Noetical Body, the mental body, many think they are their thoughts.

Every one of you is at present in a mundane self-consciousness and living in your three bodies. This is common to all of us. The real question is how developed are your three bodies and who are you living in these bodies? Everyone is constantly creating a personality-self that they misidentify as their real Self. The personality is not God, but it has God in it. This you will discover by self-analysis of all three bodies. This means knowing all three bodies, their nature and their expressions. Knowing how to use them properly reveals the self who is learning how to use the bodies.

Suppose a man's material body is destroyed in an explosion. Immediately you will see that man in his Psychical Body on the Psychical planes. After living some time on the Psychical planes he will pass over to the Noetical planes and continue existing in his brilliant, luminous Noetical Body. There is no death, but a continuation of life on higher and higher levels. Christ was pointing to this when he said, "Do not be afraid of those who can kill your body, they can do nothing to the Soul."

We have stated many times, our bodies are ours but we are not our bodies. They are created and maintained for us by the Archangels and we find ourselves living in these bodies as a personality. The bodies are Holy Spiritual in nature. However, even as a personality, we are Logoic.

The teachings and practices of the Researchers of Truth enable you to shift your center of awareness from receiving impressions in the material world, to receiving impression in Psychical and Noetical Worlds. Pay attention to this clue: you shift the center of your awareness from the material world to the Psychical and then to the Noetical Worlds. When you can do this you will be able to distinguish the difference between the various worlds. More importantly, you will be able to distinguish the difference between your life as a personality from your real Self, which is Life itself. This is the Self-Realization we seek.

Once you recognize it, you can live this reality by living in coordination with it. You can assimilate with this great truth, which is within you. This sets us free from our personality with its limited strengths and weaknesses. This lesson is a fundamental part of our teaching and must be studied well because we must be able to differentiate the two states we have spoken of. One is that of the bodies, which are Holy Spiritual in nature. The other is the self-awareness that is expressing through the bodies. This means knowing the difference between the Soul-Self and the clothing (the three bodies) the Soul-Self is dressed in.

This starts with our practice of Introspection. We must know what we are doing and where we are in any of the three Worlds of

Existence. At the same time we feel we are the I-ness that is higher than the three bodies and the worlds they inhabit. We must raise our consciousness to higher levels to view all the different Worlds of Existence from above. To see it all from this perspective as a point of self-awareness, that can move anywhere in these worlds it wants to.

When you reach this state, you will be able to enter into the Super-Conscious Self-Awareness. Then in Super-Conscious Self Awareness you are free to move into the higher spheres beyond the three Worlds of Existence. When you do this, you realize that no happiness found on Earth can compare to the happiness found in the higher realms. The desire for happiness you seek on Earth is constantly moving from one object or experience to another, just like a flame in a wood fire moves from one log to another as it burns. If you chase desires like this, then happiness for you will only be a fleeting moment before you want more happiness.

THE PRACTICE: OVERVIEW

Each and every person is at this moment, living simultaneously in three bodies without knowing it – the material, Psychical and Noetical. How active are they? Everyone is using his or her material body. They are using their Psychical Body, the body of their emotions, but they use it mostly sub-consciously in expressing desires and emotions. These three bodies are constantly undergoing changes. Our three bodies are connected as a whole and we live in them and express ourselves through them in the analogous material, Psychical and Noetical Worlds. One of the practices of a Researcher of Truth is to learn to distinguish, know and properly use these bodies consciously. With our practices we balance and harmonize our three bodies, we energize, restore health and establish complete harmony in our personality self.

THE PRACTICE: THREE SUNS MEDITATION

Breathe deeply and feel your material body. Concentrate and feel the whole abdominal area.

You are in the aesthetic ether of the Etheric Double of your material body.

Now you will use the imprinting ether. See pure light-energy radiating from within your solar plexus, creating a sky-blue sun. The radiation is a movement, made possible by the kinetic ether.

Feel and see the sky-blue nebula within your abdominal area and a Noetical radiation expanding out of your material body in all directions.

You are now the sky-blue sun, which has in its middle point a sky-blue nebula in more intense light. The sky-blue nebula covers the whole abdominal area. It starts from the sternum and continues down to the pelvis. It extends outside the body in the front and in the back.

If you concentrate intensely, you will feel it. Feel that you live consciously in the abdominal area. Wish that absolute health reign in your material body.

Continue to breathe deeply and comfortably. Now a rosy sun starts to radiate from your Heart Center. Slowly, slowly a white-rosy nebula is created in your chest. It is extended outside of the body in front of your chest and in the back.

We have two radiations now, one of sky-blue light and one of rosy light. The centers are a little different, but the radiation looks like a sun with two nebulas, a sky-blue nebula and a white-rosy nebula.

In the Psycho-Noetical Worlds, the color lights are not mixing; they do not assimilate and create a new color light as it happens in the material world.

Breathe deeply and wish that absolute emotional health reign in your personality-self-aware-self. Wish that this sun clean your lower emotions and unreasonable desires.

Now feel that you are in your head center. Golden light starts to radiate, creating a bright sun. A nebula of canary-yellow light surrounds your head.

Remain still, calm and in peace for a while. Now feel that you are in your whole material body. See an egg shaped oval of white light that encloses your whole body and the nebulas of the three suns in the three centers.

The radiations of the three suns pass through the nebula of the egg-shaped oval of white light. Consciously feel yourself in your personality-self-aware-self and wish to be cleaned and purified. Ask for this and it will be given to you. Take your time until you feel that you are again fully in your material body.

Chapter Nine
THE SEVEN HEAVENS

It's not only one Heaven -there are seven Heavens. The enlightened ones in the past found out, described them, and gave us instructions how we ourselves will find these seven Heavens. Is there only seven heavens? Of course, there are many more, but, the human intelligence, no matter what level it reaches, cannot go beyond the seven Heavens. Of course, it is ridiculous just to speak about the seven Heavens without proving their existence and showing how to approach them. But, these things need study, analysis, and time to find it out. Studying and believing blindly means nothing! Studying it, knowing it, and living it means much. ~ Daskalos

THE TEACHING

As a personality we live in a multilayered reality simultaneously. Adepts today and in past times have experienced these higher planes of existence and even gone beyond them. The Christian church has identified these as the seven heavens. The Buddhist teachings in the Tibetan Book of the Dead tell of these states of existence between death and birth, calling them Bardos. Sages in India also teach of seven Lokas (Worlds). The Researches of Truth through their direct experience know the reality of these seven heavens and teach the way to experience them.

What are the seven heavens? From the viewpoint of the worlds of existence these heavens are:

1. The Material Plane which includes our planet, our solar system, all the other solar systems, our galaxy and all the other billions of galaxies in the universe of three-dimensional space.

2. The Etheric Double of the material plane, which is an ethereal counterpart of matter and composed of ethereal substance.

3. The Psychical Planes with their seven divisions, each with its seven sub-divisions. These divisions are distinguishable ranges of vibration and not divisions in the sense of measurable space.

4. The Etheric Double of the Psychical Worlds, is the ethereal counterpart to the Psychical planes and is composed of finer ethereal substance.

5. The Noetical Planes with their seven divisions, each with its seven sub-divisions. These divisions are distinguishable ranges of vibration and not divisions in the sense of measurable space.

6. The Etheric Double of the Noetical Worlds is the ethereal counterparts to the Noetical Planes and composed of even finer ethereal Substance.

These first six are the mundane heavens as they are the temporal Worlds of Existence, which means they are changing all the time. These luminous heavens have been created using the eternal, immutable Divine Laws found in the higher Noetic State. These unerring Divine Laws are permanent but the mundane heavens are not.

7. The Seventh Heaven is different than the other heavens. It is composed of formless Super-Substance. It is Divine – eternal – permanent. The Noetic State of the seventh heaven is the home of the unchangeable Divine Laws, Causes, and Principles. This heaven is beyond dualistic concepts. This heaven transcends the polarity of good and evil completely.

How could even a Self-Realized master ever describe the reality of a heaven of formless Life to those who only understand life as it temporarily exists in living forms? How could a personality confined in the worlds of duality ever meaningfully comprehend a formless world without opposites? It is just not possible.

So the material plane is the first of the seven heavens. The material plane or world encompasses everything existing in the Third Dimension. The first heaven is Mind matter -Mind made solid. Then, from our standpoint, the second heaven is the ethereal counterpart of the entire material plane. This literally means that every material thing has an exact etheric counterpart. For example, Earth has its exact etheric counterpart consisting of mountains, oceans, trees, rivers, lakes, and everything existing on Earth. The ethereal counterpart of our planet is in, on and extends for thousands of miles around the planet. It is the same for any other planet, moon or heavenly body.

The third heaven is what is known as the Psychical planes of existence. The first heaven is Mind-Matter the third heaven is Mind-Emotion. This heaven is in the Earth, on the Earth and extends for thousands of miles around the Earth but exists at a higher rate of vibration. Each planet, moon and all heavenly bodies have their own third heaven and the third heaven of each planet or sun does not touch the third heaven of the other heavenly bodies. This is the same as saying the psychical counter part of any heavenly body does not touch the psychical counterpart of other heavenly bodies.

Like the Earth the third heaven also has its own etheric counterpart. This etheric counterpart of the Psychical Worlds is the fourth heaven. Everything existing in the third heaven of the

Psychical Planes has its etheric counterpart. Now we come to the fifth heaven known as the Noetical Planes. Everything material has its psychical counterpart and likewise everything material and psychical also has its noetical counterpart. This fifth heaven is in the planet, on the planet and around the planet. Our entire solar system floats within the Noetical substance of the fifth heaven. So, unlike the material and Psychical Worlds with their Etheric Doubles, all the heavenly bodies are connected and reside within the Noetical fifth heaven. Of course the Noetical Worlds and everything in them have their etheric counterpart too, which is the sixth heaven. This heaven is also everywhere in the sense of space and place.

That just leaves the seventh heaven. What can anyone say about this high state? The seventh heaven is the spiritual world, the abode of our Spirit our real nature. The masters that have been able to touch this heaven while still on Earth can hardly speak about it. They can say it is beautiful beyond description. You will not find teachings about this heaven in books.

In the Old Testament, God said, "Let Us make man in Our image, according to Our likeness." "Our image" means to the image of all the heavens…to the heavenly worlds: Material World, Psychical Worlds the worlds of emotion and the Noetical Worlds the mental worlds of thought. These worlds correspond to our material body our psychical or emotional body and our noetical or mental body.

"According to our likeness" means that mankind in its Divine Nature is similar to God as the Archangels are. So mankind is in the image of the heavens, but where are these heavens? Christ was clear about that saying, "The kingdom of the heavens is within you." The heavens are within the Divine Nature of the Spirit Soul Self.

Now we will put this all together. As a human being our material body is of the first heaven. Our material body is a vehicle of expression we use while living in the material world and that material body has an Etheric Double, which corresponds to the second heaven. We also have the Psychical Body, which corresponds to the third heaven. Our Psychical Body is a vehicle of expression we use while living in the Psychical Worlds.

This body also has its Etheric Double, which is of the fourth heaven. We then have a Noetical Body, which corresponds to the fifth heaven. Our Noetical Body is a vehicle of expression we use while living in the Noetical Worlds and likewise this body has its own Etheric Double, which corresponds to the sixth heaven. Finally, we have the seventh heaven, which corresponds to the Spirit Body if you can even call it a body at this level. It is the Archetypal Human Form, but it is not really a body.

We have bodies corresponding to the heavens we use when travelling in these heavens. These bodies, like the heavens, are intertwined and co-exist one with the other. In order to visit a higher heaven, we must come out of the lower body. For example, to consciously visit the third heaven, the Psychical planes, we must consciously come out of our material body, passing through its Etheric Double and compose our self-awareness in our Psychical Body on the Psychical planes. This process is called the first Exosomatosis, which means conscious out of body experience. To visit the fifth heaven of the Noetical planes, we then must make the second Exosomatosis and leave the Psychical Body passing through its Etheric Double and compose our self-awareness in our Noetical Body on the Noetical planes of the fifth heaven. To reach this seventh heaven requires a third Exosomatosis, coming out of the Noetical Body passing through its Etheric Double and entering our Noetic form, which is not really a body but a state of Being.

In the higher radiant Noetic World, we find a world of causes and ideas that are defining the forms we first see appear in the Noetical Worlds. The very advanced mystics, who can reach the Noetic, can see anything and everything concerning any form of life. This means such a mystic could see the entire Circle of Possibilities, from beginning to end all at the same time for any form of life.

Again we have come to a limit. It is not possible using words to convey an adequate meaning of the magnificence of this reality. The only way to understand this is through the Self-Super-Consciousness; by the At-One-Ment of our personality with the Spirit-Soul-Self. What is lost and what is gained by reaching the Self-Super Consciousness? Do we lose our identity as a personality and forget our time and place self-awareness? No not at all. Entering the state of Self-Super-Consciousness we will remember everything about out personality including its name. We will even remember our names as well as all the experiences we had in past lives. This means that a single human lifetime begins as a Ray of the Permanent or Soul Personality descends from the seventh heaven of the Noetic State. This Ray of Spirit Life Light descends all the way into the first heaven of the Material World where we begin our new lifetime, dressed in a new material body.

Then, when the material body dies, we as self-awareness pass through the second heaven to continue our life in the third heaven. After a time living in the Psychical planes of the third heaven we undergo a pleasant second death as it is called and we pass through the fourth heaven and enter the fifth heaven of the Noetical Worlds. Here we again continue living our same life, with our same appearance, interest and name but in the higher conditions of the fifth heaven.

After living for a time in the fifth heaven there is a pleasant third death, and as self-awareness, we pass through the sixth heaven to the seventh heaven and in to our real nature in the Noetic State and rest for a time. Here the Soul, with the help of the Archangelic Lords of Karma, design and plan our next incarnation. Then the process begins again as the ray of the personality is again projected, dressed and incarnated as a new personality in a new material body on Earth. What we call reality is much, larger than anyone has told us, and our existence as a personality lasts much longer lasting than we can imagine now.

PRACTICE: OVERVIEW

By cleaning and purifying our personality along with certain meditation practices we can reach beyond the material world and experience the various heavens described. We can and should become good citizens in these higher heavens. We should not neglect planet Earth, our temporary home in the first heaven. Development to raise our consciousness to these higher heavens must proceed in a proportional balanced way to be safe as well as effective. There is so much suffering in our material world and we should not ignore that and only seek our own personal experiences in higher worlds.

In the Worlds of Separateness we live under the powerful forces of duality. In this condition, it is very easy for us to fall into a "Them & Us" mindset and polarize groups or individuals into pairs of opposites. You can see the "Them verses Us" attitude between peers, professions, family members, religions, and between races. Nowhere is this shortsighted view more dangerous than at the national level. When one nation diametrically polarizes against another nation, very strong and dangerous conditions are created.

We have spoken about the creation of destructive Elementals (the so-called negative thought forms), which exist at the personal and family level. Yet even more dangerous Elementals are created by entire nations. These massive group Elementals become very strong as they are empowered by that nation's population. At this moment in time, immense war loving groups of Elementals are being energized with great strength and consistency. The Elementals of war grow more powerful as they build energy that seeks release. This situation is polarizing the world. People are rapidly dividing into opposing ideological groups, and, within each of these groups, further divisions fractionalize hearts and minds with fear, doubt and confusion.

Energizing either side of the polarity of this situation only fuels the problem. The beating of war drums by one side stimulates the other side to rattle their sabers in defiance. Even protests in the streets, which burn flags and effigies in the name of peace release energies that stimulate and feed the very forces of conflict they are protesting against. Illusion creates opposition and division, while truth engenders integration and harmony.

There is a call to all our brothers and sisters around the world to rise above the lure of conflict and create powerful prayers of peace. True peace is not the opposite of war. True peace has no polarized counterpoint. It is a peace that the world itself cannot give. This peace can be invoked in God and in our own true nature. By visualizing while praying for peace we are consciously creating angelic thought-forms full of love and understanding for all humanity. These prayers empower the vibrations of harmony and infuse reason into insane situations. Transcending the "Them verses Us" mentality also restores our personal peace and lead us into the greater realization that there is no "Them" everyone is "Us."

THE PRACTICE: CREATING PEACE

Begin by inhaling comfortable deep breaths. Slowly inhale white light, exhaling any darkness. Your material body is now glowing in bright white light, while it's Etheric Double and aura is turning misty sky-blue.

Your consciousness is becoming lighter and no longer hindered by heavy thoughts and emotions. Begin to expand your consciousness in every direction from where you are sitting. It passes out of the building, above the trees, like a growing bubble, until you can see the town in which you live.

A lovely rose light pours out from your Psycho-Noetical heart blanketing first your neighbor's home then the whole neighborhood and finally the entire town. You feel joy.

Continue to expand to the point where you can see your entire country. Perhaps there is trouble in some part of it. Your heart continues to pour out love for all. The whole country is now covered in this misty rose-colored light.

Next, spread your awareness to encompass first the cloud cover and then the atmosphere. You can see the whole planet. It is a gorgeous paradise of deep blue oceans, vast mountain ranges and lush plains. You know there is fighting in various parts of the world, great unhappiness, and you want to help.

From where you are, there are no boarders marked, no lines separating people. It is one world. All trouble is born of ignorance and misunderstanding. We want to love one another and live in peace.

Now your heart is a river of rose light which floods the areas of trouble on the globe with peace and love. You see millions of smiling faces bathed in the rosy light. You see men laying down their arms and embracing one another in common brotherhood. You see people giving food and clothes to the others in need.

Now you see the planet move towards you and nestle in your heart. Moments ago you were on the planet and now the planet is in you. Keep the planet in your heart.

Now return back to your present-day personality and your material body. Breathe deeply until you feel you have fully returned. Wish peace and harmony to prevail in your area, your country and the world over.

Chapter Ten
HUMAN ANGELS ~ HUMAN DEVILS
THE ELEMENTALS

Though the Elementals are not visible in the material world now (in the other worlds they will be materialized) they are full of energy and we are always under their burden. The whole life of a man or a woman on the material plane, being happy or miserable, depends upon the weight and the nature of these Elementals, which although invisible, are most powerful.

So, we must learn the nature of these Elementals. First, as I said, by understanding our responsibility in dealing with them, how we construct and build them up, how are they affecting us, and also what these Elementals are doing to others around us. Of course, studying this subject on Elementals we also study how one can dis-energize them, make corrections, and how can one construct Elementals shields (protecting Angels), to stop the influence of the negative devilish Elementals, on us and on the others. ~ Daskalos

THE TEACHING

We dress our material body in clothing. When we dress our body, we do not change the nature of the material body itself. Whether our body is dressed in the finest linens and silks of high society or the dirty rags of a homeless person, our body is not affected by its clothing. It is still the same body, two arms, two legs, two lungs, and so on. We also dress our Psychical Body in the emotions, sentiments, and desires we express. Likewise, we dress our Noetical Body in our thoughts, concepts, and intentions. Most people dress themselves with their emotions and thoughts far less consciously than they dress their material body. These psychical and Noetical garments however, do not corrupt the ray of our Spirit-Soul at the core of these bodies. It remains pure Spirit-Life-Light. This brilliant golden ray is like the backbone of every human personality. This is a common point with all men and women. Yet, no two personalities are the same. Why is there a difference? What makes the personalities of even identical twins different?

Again, the ray of the Spirit-Soul is dressed in bodies during an incarnation – the material body, the Psychical Body, and the Noetical Body. How we dress our Psychical and Noetical Bodies by our thoughts and emotions distinguishes our personality from other personalities. It is the quality and quantity of our emotion and thought based Elementals that create the uniqueness of each personality, covering that pure ray of Spirit- Soul.

In a certain stratum of society, there is the notion that you are what you wear. Others say you are what you eat. Some even think they are only their material body. Equally mistaken is the belief that the real Self is what we feel and what we think. Our thoughts and emotions are just passing expressions that constantly change over the course of our life so they are not the real Self.

The quality, quantity and intensity of our emotions affect the transmission of the Spirit-Soul's life-light through our personality. The more loving and kind emotions we express the more that life-light shines through the personality. Consequently the happier and more connected to the Spirit-Soul Self we feel. The more fearful, angry or negative emotions we harbor and express, the less that life-light is able to penetrate our personality and touch the people around us. The same is true with our thoughts and our Noetical Body. Either consciously or sub-consciously, we choose which emotions, desires and thoughts we allow expression. Thus, we are very much responsible for them.

It does not matter how translucent or obscured that light may be within the personality; at its source it is perfect Life-Light. It is this Life-Light that Mother Theresa referred to when she visited the drug addicts, the alcoholics and the homeless in the Bowery of New York City. Looking upon the derelict personalities she said, "All I see in each of you is Christ in a distressing disguise." She was able to see past their disturbing outer conditions and see the ray of the perfect Spirit-Soul.

We are able to cover over this light or unfold it within our personality. If we clean the personality of negative feelings, thoughts, behaviors and unhealthy attitudes; we can replace them with real love, noble intentions and selfless service. Then we create a translucent saintly personality. Alternatively, the personality can be so contaminated by hatred, impure desires, negative thoughts, and deviant behaviors that an obscure devilish kind of egoism is developed. More commonly, a personality in between these two extremes is created. By these individual expressions, our character is formed and our destiny is sown.

What exactly is an emotion and what is thought? What are they made of and where do they come from? Why do some emotions and thoughts have such a powerful influence on us but other emotions and thoughts do not have much influence? Why is it so difficult to free ourselves from the influences of the undesirable harmful feelings? These are the questions of a Researcher of Truth. These questions bring us to one of the most important branches of study within the System for the Research of Truth – the Elementals. Every thought every feeling, every intention creates and transmits an Elemental. Elementals are far more than static units of thought and emotion. They are living, they have a life of their own and their expression has strength and purpose. Other spiritual teachings call Elementals, thought-forms. The Muslim Sufi mystics' teach about these thought-forms calling these entities Muwakkals, which translates as "Elementals." The Sufi mystics also teach how a person gives birth to them; so they have their own life and have a certain purpose to accomplish. When a person gives expression to anger, jealousy and hatred, it is like they are creating an army of enemies all around themselves. In the ancient Sanskrit language of India, they were known as "Vasanas." The Buddhists call some types of Elementals "habit energies" and "mental formations" from our store consciousness (our sub-consciousness). Certain biologists, psychologists and cognitive scientists have also hit upon the existence of these invisible but powerful forces within the personality of man and the society. They are calling some types of Elementals "Memes" and "Mind Viruses." These scientists focus on group Elementals that are shaping the psychology of our culture. They call their decade-long study of these units of cultural transmission Memetics.

Elementals range in quality from angelic to devilish. Christ called certain Elementals "spirits mute and meaningless", "unclean spirits", and still others "evil spirits". "Spirits mute and meaningless" are the pointless distracting feelings and thoughts that clamor for our attention and clutter the shallows of our mind. "Unclean Spirits" are the negative emotions and thoughts that degrade the personality. "Evil Spirits" are the devilish Elementals that are very destructive to both the host personality and those around it.

Make no mistake about it; these are real devils in every sense of the word but the most awful ones people create are human in nature demons but not the true demons. The true demons are the Elementals created by the so-called fallen ones. If the negative Elementals created by humans are continually allowed expression within the personality, they grow in power and number and form large Group Elementals that can come to dominate the personality they host on. They can even gain a temporary possession over the personality. They can influence that personality into horrible behaviors, crimes, and in some cases drive them insane. Christ taught his disciple-healers how to remove the harmful ones from the afflicted personalities they were torturing. Daskalos and the teachings of the Researchers of Truth also teach us how to free our personality of the negative Elementals as well as how to create Angelic Shield Elementals for our loved ones and our self.

To begin to understand just exactly what an Elemental is we must classify them according to their nature and purity. In the broadest sense there are two prime classifications. The most common type by far is the emotion-thought Elemental or desire-thought forms. Human beings project thousands of this type daily. We even project these types of Elementals when we sleep. This type is composed primarily of emotions-desires and feelings and very little thought. The vast majority of the Elementals created or re-energized by humans fall into this category. The emotion-thought type Elementals can range from most despicable to very noble but most are not so noble. Individually, these emotion-thought Elementals are not as powerful as the other type unless they collect and form large group Elementals.

The other classification is the thought-emotion type of Elemental. This type is created by more thought than emotion. In this type, thought is the dominant force and emotion becomes subordinate. These thought-desire Elementals manifest results quicker and more effectively than do the emotional based ones. Elementals, which are consciously created primarily with thought, tend to have a greater longevity and power. The Hierophants of ancient Egypt knew this and developed their ability of creating these living thought-forms into a powerful science.

Once in Cyprus after Daskalos concluded his weekly lessons, a couple of students and I wanted to explore the Great Pyramid in Egypt. At that time, you could still bribe the night watchmen at the pyramid and they would let you in to spend the night. Once you made an awkward crawl/climb well up inside the mountain of stone blocks to the King's chamber they locked the entrance, turned off the lights and left you alone overnight in absolute darkness. As we were leaving I mentioned to Daskalos that we were considering doing this. I asked him what he thought of the idea. He said softly, "You could do it.....but it will not change you. You might be frightened, because there are Guardian Elementals created by the Egyptian Hierophants still living in the pyramids." He very seriously added, "And sometimes they strike you!" Then, he made a striking motion like a snake with his hand and a chill ran up my spine.

The thought of being "struck" in total darkness by a 4500-year-old Guardian Elemental gave us second thoughts about the whole idea. Later Daskalos wrote in his Symbol of Life book, "Many Elementals created as guardians of monuments and graves of Pharaohs in Ancient Egypt, many centuries ago, are still actively guarding those monuments. Many Egyptologists and archeologists have had bitter experiences when attacked by those Guardian Elementals." There are many stories about such attacks and I personally knew of one fellow who suffered this kind of a terrifying attack in the Kings Chamber but the most notable of these stories was Napoleon Bonaparte's experience.

He invaded and took control of Egypt in 1798, and then went to the Great Pyramid on the Giza plateau. Napoleon asked to be left alone in the King's Chamber. When he came back out, he was pale and obviously shaken. One of his aids asked if he had witnessed anything. Napoleon refused to comment and forbid any one to ever mention the episode. Over the years, he kept his experience secret. Only on rare occasion would he allude to having received foreshadowing of his future, which of course did not end well for him. Just before his demise, he was on the verge of revealing his experience to his confidant, Las Cases. However, he stopped short saying, "No what's the use. You would never believe me."

This also reveals how the active life of the Elementals we create can be exceedingly long. We will find them in the Psycho-Noetical Worlds when we pass over and they even travel with us into our future incarnation and either help or hinder our progress. So the advice is often given, "Be careful what you wish for, what you desire!" This is because all our desires, weaknesses, strengths, and our habitual ways of thinking and behaving create or re-energized Elementals. Once an Elemental is created it cannot be destroyed. They continue to be active until they have fulfilled their purpose or until they have been consciously de-energized. The Elemental cannot be destroyed but its power can be destroyed by de-energizing it. The secret in de-energizing an Elemental is in becoming dis-interested in it completely.

Our created Elementals come to form our personality and define our character. It is this personality; full of conflicting ideas, feelings and thoughts that we have mistaken to be our real Self. This personality self is at best a weak shadow of our real Self cast on the unequal ground of duality. In order to really know and experience this truth, we must shift our sense of identity from our shadow-self to our real Spirit-Soul Self. To do this means we must gain mastery over our thoughts and emotions - the Elementals we create and re-energize. Mastering our undesirable emotions and weaknesses does not mean fighting against them and suppressing them with force. Mastering our emotions and desires means gaining control of them, becoming their master and not their slave.

An Elemental has an existence, a life and purpose of its own. For anything to exist it needs a form. When we have a desire for an object, for example a type of car, we are creating an Elemental, which is getting a form. In this example, the form of the Elemental takes the shape and color of the specific car we desire. It first forms in our

Etheric Double at the location of the so-called third eye. At this point before it is projected it is very small in size – like the head of a pin. Yet imprinted in it are all the details we know about the car we desire. After we project it consciously or subconsciously it will get the full size of the object we desire. All this is visible to a well-developed clairvoyant.

These Elementals are created through our Etheric Doubles. They are composed of etheric substance in varying degrees of purity and strength. Once projected out from us they work to achieve their purpose to bring about the conditions to manifest the desired object or effect we consciously or sub-consciously wanted.

When we harbor and express negative emotions such as despair, jealousy, fear or hatred we create Elementals, which get a form. What form are these destructive Elementals getting? These get the shapes of snakes, beasts and other distressing forms. They get this form according to the quality of the desires and thought which created them. Their forms and their colors reveal their natures. It is really merciful that people cannot see the forms of the destructive Elementals as they would terrify them. It may take a clairvoyant to see these forms but anyone can feel them. If you approach a person you know well and they are having strong negative emotions and thoughts about you it is not difficult to feel these bad Elementals. Likewise when we are around a dear friend or a loving companion we can easily sense these good Elementals.

So our good or bad thoughts and emotions are continually creating new Elementals, or re-energizing pre-existing Elementals. It is our choice which ones we attend to and give expression. Thus we are responsible for our own unique set of Elementals and their effect on ourselves and those around us. When an Elemental is created it forms in our Etheric Double and is projected out into the common environment. We literally live in a sea of these good and bad etheric entities.

Joshua Immanuel (Christ) gave a perfect description of what happens when we project negative Elementals in his parable the "Unclean Spirit." Christ said, "When an evil [unclean] spirit comes out of a man, it goes through arid [waterless] places seeking rest and does not find it. Then it says, 'I will return to the house I left.' When it arrives, it finds the house unoccupied [unguarded], and clean [open]. Then it goes and takes with it seven other spirits more wicked than itself, and they go in and live there. The final condition of that man is worse than the first."

Joshua stated that this unclean spirit or Elemental goes out of man, which means that he or she are giving it expression by their feelings, thoughts or actions. It goes out into the common psychical environment -the "arid" or waterless places. That means places without nourishment for it and so the Elemental does not find the energy there it needs to sustain its life. It then returns "home" to the personality of the one who gave it life and expressed it. In his parables Christ referred to the personality as a home or house.

When the negative Elemental returns, it finds the house unoccupied, which means the personality is open and un-guarded. Then the Elemental enters bringing with it seven other similar Elementals more destructive than itself. These Elementals enter through the centers (charkas) and collect as one in our sub-consciousness. Each cycle of expression and re-absorption of negative Elementals greatly increases their numbers and slowly degrades the personality. Repetitive expression over time can form large group Elementals so powerful that they can come to dominate the personality leading to phobias, fixed ideas, obsessive compulsive disorders (OCDs) and in extreme cases insanity and suicide.

However, this very same process also works to our benefit when we send out loving and positive life affirming Elementals. We are thus strengthened and edified by our repeated good expressions. The Law of Repetition in the creation of Elementals can be one of our strongest allies or our worst enemies.

Our Elementals gather within and compose our personality's sub-consciousness. Since most of our Elementals are primarily composed of emotion, they are associated with our Psychical Body and are very active within its Etheric Double. All Elementals have a psychical component, which are our desires, feelings and motivations. All Elementals have a Noetical component, which is our thought and intent. No one can have a thought without some emotion associated with it. Likewise, no one can have an emotion without some thought accompanying it. The Elementals manifest more easily and more intensely in the Psychical Worlds and in the lower Noetical Worlds but these Elementals cannot reach into the higher Noetical or the states beyond the Noetical. Our Elementals, good or bad, are stored within one of the three chambers of our sub-consciousness and exert an influence on our personality. Under certain circumstances they rise to our conscious mind and seek expression. Every time we allow them expression, we strengthen them. Every time we struggle against them we strengthen them; every time we remove our attention from them and do not allow them expression, we weaken them. Herein lies a clue to freeing ourselves of all kinds of undesirable habits, weaknesses, and behaviors corrupting our personality and veiling the light of our own true nature.

Our character is either debased or dignified by our expressions of these Elementals. Negative emotional based Elementals of fear, hatred, jealousy, envy, possessiveness and meanness create conditional hells within our personality. Their influences torture our minds and hearts and in many cases result in illnesses to the material body. They live and thrive on our Etheric Vitality. In cases where their withdrawal is excessive, our material body is deprived of the energy it needs and becomes weakened and illnesses start to appear.

Consider what happens when a person becomes angry and enraged. During these fits of anger, aggressive war loving Elementals gain access to that person's etheric energy. An angry person becomes red in the face, the body temperature goes up and reason goes out the window. Sometimes they shout, threaten, slap and in extreme cases kill. A person under the influence of anger is convinced that they are rightly justified in expressing anger in these ways. When the person eventually calms down again, they feel weak and exhausted clearly revealing the loss of their Etheric Vitality. It is said that sustained outbursts of anger can waste more energy than we get from eating a month's worth of food. This excessive withdrawal of vital energy stresses and weakens the body. The American Heart Association did a study and stated that, "People who are highly anger-prone are nearly three times more likely to have a heart attack."

There is a popular method offered today by psychologists for dealing with anger that is very dangerous and should be abandoned completely. Some psychologists, who do not know about Elementals that drive anger, advise that when you feel anger to go and beat your pillows with your fist or a baseball bat. Beating the pillows you sleep on to discharge feelings of anger may give a momentary release of pressure. However, the process greatly strengthens the aggressive Elementals in your sub-consciousness as well as the habit of expressing them. It also leaves the pillow you sleep on tainted with vibrations of anger. Never express anger in the bedroom where you sleep or when you eat. Hitting pillows is better than hitting people but it is a poor technique when seeking a real and lasting cure.

There are many methods offering healthier ways to deal with angry feelings today. One of the more effective ways is through breathing. By watching your breath and maintaining a calm deep regular breathing rate you gain control of your Etheric Double. In gaining control of your Etheric Double you deprive aggressive Elementals from accessing this vital energy field. Then you can gain control over the violent psychical vibrations known as anger and suffocate it. In gaining control you become the master of these fierce Elementals and not their puppets.

Harmful Elementals are spreading like plagues through all the nations on the planet today. Everywhere, people are in confusion…not because of what God has made of man but what man has made of man. People mistake obstinacy as real will power temptation as opportunity; and our greatest mistake of all is in confusing the real Self with its reflection the personality. Our semiconscious personality is the sum total of all our transient feelings, thoughts, and attitudes we express. These contradictory strengths and weaknesses create a distorted and dim reflection of our real Self.

The life of most personalities is eighty percent subconscious. The common person wakes in the morning and habitually goes about the day dealing with the issues of their existence in a mostly subconscious way. At night they sleep and for a certain period of time the go into a kind of temporary non-exist in deep dreamless sleep. The next day they get up, their personality is recomposed exactly as it was the day before, and the cycle continues. By sleepwalking through our daily patterns; are we really living life? Or is this the life of the living dead?

Everyone is in their divinely appointed place to get their next important life experience. What is asked of us as personalities is to wake from our slumbering and become more and more conscious of what we do, why we do it and what we really are. This leads us from sub-consciousness, to consciousness, to real Self-Consciousness and eventually to Self-Super Consciousness.

First, we need to understand the nature of the Elementals driving our sub-conscious living patterns; by understanding our responsibility in dealing with them and how we build them, how they are affecting us and the people around us. In studying the Elementals we can learn the way we can de-energize the harmful ones and how to construct Shield Elementals, which serve as protecting Angels. Shield Elementals stop the influence of negative Elementals on us and on our loved ones. A parent or anyone who knows the way can create a protecting angel for anyone they love and bring it to life.

PRACTICE: OVERVIEW

Daskalos once rhetorically asked, "What can prayer be? It is the creation of Angelic Elementals, constructive Elementals, praying for the health of others and to help our fellow men. Our whole life is the creation of these Elementals, the greatest art one should learn is to create good Elementals, good thought-forms for himself or herself and for the others in his family and for other people."

Of course every loving feeling, every noble intention and every heart-felt prayer automatically creates an angelic Elemental. However, when created Self-Consciously, understanding what we are doing, these benevolent Elementals gain real power. In creating strong human in nature Angels for those we love it is helpful to be consistent and energize the angelic Elemental repeatedly for some days. Such exercises can be done for about ten minutes each day for a few consecutive days or as many as fifteen days using the Law of Repetition to empower it. It is very important to keep in mind that our motivation and intent must be pure. This creation is to be a humble prayer offered from one human being to another in love.

Never are we allowed to impose our will on others or to manipulate and interfere with their free will. Once you have finished the prayer, forget about it completely until the designated time to repeat it the next day. The angelic Elemental you create must be allowed to do its work. If you keep remembering it, re-thinking it, you hold the Elemental to you and do not release it to fulfill its purpose. It is best if you can do this practice at the same time each day and in the exact same location. Choose someplace where you will not be disturbed. Before beginning any spiritual practice or exercise it is important to be relaxed and calm. This means quieting our mind and silencing our emotions and desires. Then it is good to do some simple breathing to fill yourself with ample Etheric Vitality to empower this prayer. There are many forms this practice can take and you are advised to refer to Esoteric Practices by Daskalos before attempting more advanced ones

PRACTICE: CREATING ANGELIC ELEMENTALS

To create a simple angelic Elemental for a loved one we will use the white light. In a meditative state with eyes closed see your hands with fingers tips touching and palms apart. Breathe deeply and calmly.

See and feel these etheric hands fill with pure white light. With every breath, the snow-white light becomes brighter and brighter.

Continue breathing deeply and comfortably. Now feel and see the white light forming into a ball of light between you palms.

You may feel a tingling sensation, warmth or slight pressure in your hands as the sphere becomes brighter and more substantial.

Breathe again and see the ball of light become brilliant as its light emanates through your fingers and hands.

Now see clearly the face of the loved one you want to help. Send this ball of light to them with the sincere wish that it helps and protects them.

Visualize this sphere of luminous white light going to them wherever they are in the world. See it entering through their head to become a white egg shaped form encompassing their entire body in sparkling white light. End with the affirmation, "Thy Will Be Done!"

Chapter Eleven
BRICK BY BRICK

No two human beings are similar! What's the difference now? Our material bodies are always composed of the same material: water, salts, proteins, and everything else. But, the personality of a man is not the product of his material body. You will find very, very healthy people, yet stupid. And you have also very, very healthy people who are scientists. And you have very ill and weak people sometime who are geniuses. And you also have people who are very weak and sickly, who are stupid. So, the condition of the material body is not responsible for the personality in it.

What about the personality? Is the personality of all men composed of the same substance? It is the same substance -yes, but not the same quality of substance. Now we have many qualities of substance. What is making this quality of substance? We ourselves! The Super-Substance of the Mind is pure. What about when you are using it creating your desires, weaknesses, purposes in life, and misconceptions? So, we will never find two persons with the same character. The composition of those personalities is the sum total of the Elementals composing them. The thought forms. Day and night and every moment; even while sleeping, we are creating Elementals or revitalizing them. ~ Daskalos

THE TEACHING

The first thing a human being does in life is to develop a personality. The personality self-awareness is nothing more than a shadow of their real Soul Self-Awareness that has been cast in time, space and place. So how does this personality get formed? It has been repeated many times that a human being, in its real nature, is an eternal Spirit-Soul. In order to exist in the time, space and place Worlds of Existence we certainly need to develop a healthy personality.

It is easy to see that no two personalities are built exactly the same. Except for the weight and look, every male material body is the same as all other male material bodies; except for the weight and look, all female bodies are like other female bodies. The Holy Archangels are building our material bodies and that building process is perfectly under the control of these highly intelligent brothers of ours. They build up material bodies from the various elements of matter. That is why we call them Archangels of the Elements, because they use the various elements to build our material bodies and the material world we inhabit. The Archangels of the Elements, the builders, are flawlessly expressing the Will and Pleasure of God as well as their own Will-Pleasure: both in groups and individually. They use the Mind perfectly in all its degrees to build up the created Worlds of Existence.   So we have the creation and the creators.

In this lesson we will see what material we ourselves use to build up our own personality. Of course we are using the Mind to create with too, but we do it imperfectly, not understanding exactly what we are doing. In their creation, the Archangels use the almightiness, which means they maintain perfect control over their creative works and nothing escapes their attention.

The human beings attention however is focused on the outer world of separation. Conditions in the outer world are attracting and capturing our attention through the five senses but mostly through sight. This outward attraction is obscuring the greater truth of our own Divine Nature. However, our personality can (with effort) over time assimilate its awareness with the Soul Self-Awareness and reach the highest state of Self-Super-Consciousness. Then there will not be a difference between the Archangels and us, in terms of consciousness.

First, we must learn about our personality, which of course is much more than just our material body. So we start analyzing our personality to understand its composition. We see the material body is part of our personality self and its form is on the material body. Our personality self-awareness is the total collection of our Elementals – all our thoughts, emotions and desires.

Now we have to think, where are all these Elementals coming from that form our personality? We have to understand that we are creating Elementals out of the Mind and the Mind is living. Or we are re-energizing pre-existing Elementals using the Mind. Literally everything existing in all the universes has been created from the Mind and so it is living in its own way. However, when we say everything existing is created from the living Mind, we do not mean that the eternal Spirit Beings were created from the Mind. They have not been created at all and so they will never cease to be. The Archangelic builders have created the universes and everything in them using the Mind and this is done in the Eternal Now. Working in the Eternal Now the Archangels have in them the Divine Plan, the entire Circle of Possibilities and all the points of development on this circle. For example, this means they are working in constant meditation on all points of the development of a tree. They work on its life as a seed, to a sapling, to its full form as a mature tree and all the way to the end of its existence.

They are creating billions and billions of the same forms working on all points of development in that Circle of Possibilities for all the individual trees simultaneously. They are doing that with all the countless forms of life from the smallest to the largest. This is only possible because they enjoy the highest state of consciousness called Super-Consciousness. Just try to conceive of the Total Wisdom and Power of these Archangelic Beings and, when contacted, they are willing to teach sincere seekers things beyond the seeker's wildest imagination.

Now within the Circle of Possibilities for the human beings are all the possibilities of the Archangels too, because the Human Idea Archetype is contained in the Archangelic Archetype. To develop these possibilities to the point of realization, we must study the Human Circle of Possibilities to find our current place in that circle.

The seeker does this by using the Mind consciously. Now we mostly use the Mind sub-consciously in revitalizing pre-existing groups of Elementals, which were created by our predecessors.

Where are these pre-existing Elementals residing? Of course it is the Mind but more accurately, it is that aspect of the Mind called the cosmic and planetary sub-consciousness. Just like a human being has their sub-consciousness, our planet, our solar system our galaxy and the entire Cosmos has a sub-consciousness that records everything that has happened there. In the planetary sub-consciousness there are all of the Elementals of everything human beings have created since their arrival on the planet. Again all these have been created from the living indestructible Mind and so these Elementals are living and indestructible too. They cannot be destroyed but the power in them can be de-energized, and this renders them inactive. Inactive but not annihilated.

The composition of our material body is well known, yet in our material body, our personality has an independent life and a different composition. Our personality is and is not our Real self. At the very heart of it is our Real Self, the ray of our Spirit-Soul Self, but the rest of its composition is not our Real Self. The personality and its material body are living because in them is the Pulse of Life, which comes from the Holy Spirit and the Real Self. However, the unique way each personality is living is different from the way other personalities are living. Life is common but the way we are living our life differs from the way others are living their life. This is because the entire set of our Elementals that compose our personality is different from the Elementals composing other personalities. Our unique set of personal Elementals is not our Real Self. How can we be sure?

Through introspection we can know this for sure. All we really have to do is to think about our personality as a child, a teenager or an adult. The Elementals, our thoughts, emotions and desires, composing our personality at any point in time are never the same.

Your thoughts, emotions and desires as a child are not the same as you have as an adult and they will definitely not be the same as you have as an elderly person. Where did that personality of yours as a small child go?

Our task as a human being is to study and know our personality as it is now. This means studying our thoughts, emotions and desires that are composing our personality. Just as a house is built brick by brick, our personality and thus our character is built Elemental by Elemental. Everything that comes to our attention and we start thinking about it, creates and gives life to an Elemental. Anything that causes vibrations in our Psychical Body as desire for something, or as an aversion to something, empowers the Elemental. Attraction and repulsion are forces in the Psychical Body. This gives us Elementals in different degrees of power.

An Elemental is a living existence and anything existing must have a form. We are the ones giving the form to the Elemental when we create one consciously. When we create one sub-consciously, the Elemental gets a form according to its own nature, which means the nature of the emotions and thoughts that created it. An Elemental has form and power and the power depends on the intensity of our desire, our emotion, and the number of times it is repeated. This is something the Hindus understand and it is what empowers their repetitive mantras. Looking at the power the Elementals have over our personality we see that our personality tends to obey the law of the Elemental. For example we have the law of attraction, of knowing and having. So when you see something that interests you, the already pre-existing Elementals in you exert a force of persuasion in your sub-consciousness. You feel the urge to know more about the subject of your interest and that gives the Elemental strength and energy.

To get existence through you, the Elemental excites your

Psychical Body, the body of your emotions and desires and now you want to have it. The feeling of wanting something is not exactly the same as the desire of possessiveness. The feeling of possessiveness is really negative power. Possessiveness enslaves you to the object of desire and you call that object "mine" and you do not want others to use it. That is possessiveness. Since an Elemental is living it has a self-preserving directive to prolong its own life. So it is an absolute necessity for that Elemental to get more energy from you to continue living and it can be so cunning in this effort.

Remember your personality is composed by the entire set of Elementals you harbor and express. They are stored in your sub-consciousness as well as in the Planetary Sub-Consciousness. However, it is best not to speak much about the sub-consciousness of the planet. We can say that when an Elemental has fulfilled the purpose of its creation it doesn't get destroyed but becomes de-energized and enters the sub-consciousness of the planet, which is a part of the cosmic sub-consciousness. There it remains inactive until someone else comes along who resonates to the same vibration of that Elemental and re-awakens it and the Elemental comes to them.

We have to be extremely careful what Elementals we awaken and revitalize because once we do…they will not automatically de-energize until they fulfill their purpose. We should be especially vigilant with the desires we believe are very important to us today. As Daskalos often warned us, our most important desires today may become serious obstacles to us later in this life or in a future incarnation. Maybe you have had the experience of something coming to you in this life that thwarts and delays you from accomplishing something good you are working to accomplish. Another way of saying this is that all your desires will certainly be fulfilled…but when? They will be fulfilled in what we call the future, the future in this life or in future incarnations. They will be fulfilled, unless you consciously de-energize them before they come to fruition.

All of us have created Elementals with good and bad qualities and these exist in a range of degrees of purity. They can be really bad Elementals, somewhat bad Elementals or slightly bad Elementals. They also can be very good noble Elementals, good Elementals or slightly good Elementals. There is a constant fight between the good and bad Elementals within our personality. When this war gets intense it can make us very unhappy.

An Elemental can be detected in the aura of the material body's Etheric Double. When we give birth to an Elemental it continues to grow and change its appearance. Both the good and bad Elementals take on a coloring. So the color of an Elemental is showing its nature and strength as it expresses itself within a personality. These Elementals have power -the power we give them by our intensity and the number of times we have repeated them.

To detect the powers in us, we need to enter within ourselves, observe and understand the composition of our personality then decide to change what we need to change. For example, say you have a very strong desire in you for having something. We all have desires for something. Desire is not bad in and of itself. Christ was saying we have the right to ask God, for what we need. We should check our desires to see if the object of our desire is something good and needed or if it is not. So we investigate this in order to understand the nature of that desire. The Elementals have their own consciousness and when the Elementals strongly exert an attraction to the object of the desire, they approach you offering some benefit to your personality. If we mistakenly identify our personality to be our real Self, then we are likely to think the offer will truly benefit us and so we accept it.

The Elemental's desire is a force of attraction to that which is of its own nature or quality. That attraction has an influence on us. Elementals can be good or bad advisors to us depending on their nature. An Elemental has its work to do in order to fulfill the purpose for which it was created. However, the Elemental's purpose may or may not be in harmony with your stated purpose in life or with the Divine Plan.

Now we could draw an analogy between a harmful Elemental and a physical tapeworm. A parasitic tapeworm, attaches itself to the intestine and then it secretes a chemical that makes the person crave what is good for the tapeworm. On a continual basis it draws energy from the person it hosts on. In a similar parasitic way, harmful Elementals attach to your Etheric Double and make you crave or desire that which the harmful Elemental was created for. It is drawing energy from you, the Elemental's host.

We all have a mixture of good and bad Elementals. Now both the good and the bad Elementals want to draw the attention of their master, which is you. The good, reasoning Elementals interfere with the negative Elementals and vice versa. Then we have inner conflict or in some cases outright war. Who pays for that war? You do!

It is like you are a storeowner with lots of delicate items for sale. Then two quarreling people come in your store and start a physical fight and as they fight they break thinks and damage your store. Such is the effect of conflicting Elementals in your subconsciousness.

Now when we study our inner conflicts in Introspection who is doing this study? Is it you as a personality or you as the Inner Self? It can be either. When it is you as your Inner Self you will assuredly win the war. If it is you as a personality the war can be horrific.

Yet if you, as a personality, realizing something of your real nature as life, get a decision to end the war and change for the better, that is a step forward. This step forward is toward the assimilation of your personality self with your Inner Self. This assimilation gives true joy – joy to the personality and to your attending Archangels.

Christ stated this when he said, "Joy to your Angels in Heaven for the one who repents." The word repents means a change of heart, mind and action and a return back home to their Divine Nature.

Now we said that the Elementals could be detected in the aura. But do not imagine them sleeping or in a dormant state in your aura. On the contrary, they are very active and affect your personality.

According to their purpose, Elementals make you aware of certain things; they give you knowledge of certain things according to their purposes. Then, there is a reaction in your personality maybe it is mild reaction or a very strong reaction. Pay attention when you have reactions to things – especially the automatic knee-jerk kind of reactions. This happens because there is an influence coming from the Elementals, which causes your Psychical Body to react with emotions and thoughts. Now other kinds of Elementals are drawn in to this process and their impulse in you creates even more Elementals associated with the initial reaction.

Now the newly good or bad Elemental will have many other similar Elementals that come forward and accept it and welcome it in. They give some of their own power to that Elemental, which has a similar vibration. This increases the propagation of Elementals – good or bad Elementals. Pre-existing good or bad Elementals in us will always come forward with their influence and suggestions but, if we are living sub-consciously, we will not notice that. So we must introspect with concentration and observation to notice these influences within our personality. We must stay vigilant in order to understand what is really going on. This means we are using the Mind in a higher rate of vibration in detached observation. Observation means to be on the alert, which is to say: Watch! Christ advised people to watch and pray. We watch and pray so that we do not enter temptation. To watch and pray over our own personality so that it does not become tempted. Actually we are in temptation all the time. So really, we need to watch and pray that we do not succumb to the temptations that are all around us.

The Lord's Prayer has been translated back and forth between different languages and eventually handed down to us with a line in it asking God not to lead us into temptation. Does God really lead human beings into temptation? Or is that the job of others?

According to the Akashic records, Christ gave this part of what is called the Lord's Prayer after materializing food to feed the

5000. His words were, "Lead us while being in temptation." This is a much more accurate way to say this.

This lesson is very important for everyone on the planet because temptation is a part of humankind's life now, just as it was in all past times and will be in the future. Today there is an ever-growing quantity of temptations available to us. Temptation is a condition we undergo, which comes with an ordeal. Unfortunately people too often mistake what are really their temptations to be their opportunities in life and go astray.

To discover how we are tempted we need to first sit down and enter the silence. We need to be quiet and peaceful in order to detect those Elementals that are tempting and misguiding us. In finding them, be careful not to make the mistake of accusing your own personality or take on the unhealthy feeling of guilt for your errors. No need to accuse your personality for its mistakes, just make corrections so the mistakes are not repeated. To feel negative about yourself, and think, "Oh I am a bad person, I did this and that wrong, alas I am a sinner," is a total waste of time and leads nowhere but down.

These are actually the masochistic tendencies of your egoism, which likes to play both sides. Playing both sides feeds the egoism making it feel more alive. It will praise you and blame you. Because, both praise and blame energize the egoism. Which is probably the source of the old saying, "Praise and blame are both the same." Also beware of this dynamic outside yourself. People who are so quick to praise others tend to be just as quick to blame others.

Keep in mind no matter how evil a person's words and actions may be; there are no evil people. Their behavior may be rooted in what you call evil but human beings are created by God and thus cannot be evil. Human beings can be ignorantly misguided and so the harmful outcome of their actions is called evil. Now we come to a very important part in the teachings. Christ advised us not to fight or resist evil. This is because you cannot put out a fire with more fire. You need water to put out a fire. Similarly we cannot extinguish hatred or other evil feelings in people except by love.

Now in our study to make corrections to our personality we have to separate our sense of self from the impulses of our Elementals. We mistake these impulses to be coming from our real Self. So the first thing to do is to break this subconscious impulse-reaction habit by coming to a solid decision not to be in such a hurry to react. Do not just immediately obey to the impulses coming from your pre-existing Elementals. Secondly we can employ the help of pre-existing good Elementals. These are our ally Elementals. They will come to our aid because these Elementals are quite alert and active in us too. The great art we should learn is how to create good ally Elementals; good thought forms for our self, for our family and friends. We also must learn how to consciously de-energize the unwanted Elementals with reason. Then we will see the Elemental is losing it color and power. When any Elemental good or bad has fulfilled its purpose it also loses its color and power and becomes inactive.

When a strong desire type Elemental is not fulfilled or consciously de-energized what happens? The devil of our own egoism increases its obstinacy and comes forward with dangerous sets of whys. Why are my desires not fulfilled? Why do other people get their desire fulfilled and not me? Now the ancient Elemental of jealousy can find a place in you and make you feel even worse. If you continue on this dangerous course of questioning you may ask, "Who is preventing me from having my desire fulfilled." Sometimes it is the people around you who love you that are keeping your desires from being fulfilled. If this is the case, there is a greater danger in starting to resent them and in extreme cases may even find ways to take revenge on them.

Of course, all these lower nature tendencies have to be rejected. If you hold on to these unhealthy feelings coming from your egoism, immediately there is a self-punishment, as they are producing harmful toxins in your bodies. So we must study our inner conditions and impulses. The gain of detecting these egoistic impulses is twofold. One gain is by identifying mistakes and misguidance; we can make corrections to prevent further pain, suffering and trouble. The second gain is that this process will slowly start to reveal your Real Self. Your Real Self is the master of your body, emotions and thoughts and will act as the master if your egoism is not allowed to interfere and take control. Even at the lowest level of our Selfhood (the personality), God's gift of free will is preserved.

There is a great and good by-product of gaining control over the creation of Elementals. Elementals sap our energy in the continuation of their life. When you eliminate the unhealthy and unnecessary ones, you have more energy to empower the good thought-desire Elementals. Thought-desire means the Elemental has more thought than desire, which make them more effective. Now the good creative Elementals will have more energy and power, which means they are able to manifest and bring good results more quickly. By creating fewer Elementals but more powerful ones, you know the way to have what you need sooner, rather than later and, to reach this point, we must go into that part of our sub-consciousness where we store all these Elementals. There we clean and remove the numerous unhealthy and unnecessary Elementals. The mastery of your Elementals will make your life more manageable. This mastery will give you real satisfaction. Whereas before maybe you were more of a slave to these Elementals and a slave enjoys no satisfaction.

Daskalos was always telling us, we must avoid following the impulse of our desires without any reasoning. He taught how there is no end to desiring and punctuated his teaching on this with a personal anecdote. He told us about a childhood friend in school who was extremely poor. Daskalos felt great love for that friend.

Sometime later, after graduation and Daskalos was employed, the fellow came to Daskalos and asked him to help get him a job there. He told Daskalos he was starving and still living with his mother in a little tiny house. His mother was washing clothes just to earn enough money so they both could live. Daskalos helped get him a job where he worked.

At work the fellow seemed absentminded all the time, but he was not really absentminded. He was always concentrating on those dangerous "whys" we were just speaking about. In his mind he was asking, "Why am I so poor?" "Why am I starving?" "Why are some people around me so very, very rich?" "Their children my age and have everything but I have nothing!" He was eighteen at the time and

Daskalos was seventeen. At seventeen, the young Daskalos had been giving these teachings for ten years.

One day he came to Daskalos and asked if he could attend Daskalos' lessons. Daskalos replied, "Why not?" He attended a lesson on the Elementals, which revealed much about visualization.

Then after just this one lesson he thanked Daskalos saying, "I got the golden key."

Daskalos sighed, "Good God what does that mean?"

His friend happily replied, "Now I know how to get everything I want." "Really", Daskalos replied, "but are you sure that what you want is what you should have?"

"Definitely," his friend replied enthusiastically.

Before long, the friend's mother passed over and he was left with her little house. This happened around 1940s and his mother's house must not have even had a proper bathroom because the fellow complained to Daskalos that he did not want to pay rent for that one room house and be dirty.

Daskalos said, "Well, then what do you want."

He said, "I just want a house with three rooms and a bathroom to wash myself." Daskalos asked, "What are you doing to get that kind of house – visualizing it?"

His friend said yes, that he had gotten Daskalos lesson on how to create Elementals self-consciously through visualization and that is what he was doing.

He came to Daskalos some months later and asked him to come to his house for coffee. Daskalos agreed. So one Sunday, Daskalos went to his friend's new address to find he had gotten the house that he had been visualizing. The fellow had his desired house in mind and one day as he was riding his bicycle he saw a house for sale that matched his visualization. So he managed to get a second job in order to make monthly payments for the desired house.

Eventually, the friend left where he and Daskalos worked and he got a better job. One day Daskalos saw him again and the fellow again asked Daskalos to come to his house, this time for lunch. Daskalos said, "Yes, I know where your house is and I will come."

The man corrected Daskalos saying, "No I sold that old house. Now I got a newer house, maybe it is even better than your house."

Daskalos arrived at his friend's new and better house, and he told Daskalos, "I am doing as you teach using my mind to get…"

Daskalos interrupted, "Look here, honestly you are doing stupid things…"

His friend then interrupted Daskalos and said, "No I got this with my work and sweat I remember what you told me."

Years later Daskalos' friend got married to a very beautiful woman who was also very rich. The man got more houses and built multistory apartment buildings in Limassol on the Mediterranean Sea. He started several companies and became even richer.

At this point it had been over 50 years since the friend had come to Daskalos' lesson and got the key of visualization. Again Daskalos meets him and goes with him to see his latest home. He showed Daskalos his apartments and said, "These are mine now."

Daskalos only made an "Um" sound.

His friend questioned Daskalos' lack of enthusiasm for his success saying, "Why are you doing that?"

Daskalos told him that these buildings will never be his and that he was under a false idea of ownership.

His friend protested saying, "No, no I am rich – I own them." He had brought Daskalos to look at his apartments in a very luxurious car.

Daskalos continued to try to help him see beyond his egoistic desires and asked, "Don't you think a cheaper car would do the same work?"

His friend reacted saying, "Do you think I brought you here just so you could tell me that I am a fool?"

Daskalos assured him that he did not call him a fool.

Still his friend proclaimed loudly, "I am not a fool," and then he said to Daskalos, "What do you want me to do?"

Daskalos asked, "When did you go abroad on a vacation with your wife and children?"

"Ooooh I need so much money for that," the fellow moaned.

Daskalos continued dismantling the man's egoism with love and reason saying, "But you have so much money now, when will you start enjoying life"?

"What? Enjoy life", he replied, "I am too busy now to enjoy life."

It was at this point that Daskalos did go ahead and call him a fool…"a miserable fool."

The shaken fellow tried to reinforce his crumbling egoism by again claiming, "No! I am not a fool. I have something else in mind. I want to be an owner in a ship." Now Daskalos started laughing out loud and asked him: "How old are you?"

"Oh stop it, don't remind me of that," he complained.

But Daskalos was unstoppable and continued with, "How will you manage to carry all these material things with you when you pass over?"

His deflated friend was already disturbed by the idea of death and protested, "I did not bring you here just to torture me!"

Then Daskalos kindly delivered his friend a much needed lesson by saying, "Was it not better to continue the lesson on how to improve yourself instead of getting, as you think, that golden key to fulfill your desires?"

Daskalos' point was this: ungratefulness to God and dissatisfaction with life are blasphemes. He also stated that one should be grateful with what God has given and enjoy life. Enjoy life but not in a stupid way like his friend was doing by creating and serving only materialistic desires. Unfortunately, too many people are still following similar sub-conscious patterns of living. They habitually repeat the same mistakes; they make the same missteps today and will tomorrow as they have done yesterday. Often, these are the same people who are complaining and blaming everyone except their own self. Thus, they are not benefiting from their lessons in the schoolhouse of life.

Of course it is good and right to ask God to give us what we need in order to make reasonable advancements in our life. To devote all your time to chasing after riches and not enjoy the life God has given you…well, it is a huge mistake. At the end of the day, this way of living ends up creating an army of desire Elementals that impedes and blocks the ability to enjoy life on Earth.

These particular teachings Daskalos brought forth are really the Science of Life. The Science of Life leads us out of the confusion, the illusions and pain. God has given an abundance of everything humans need to enjoy life and be happy. When it comes to being happy and enjoying life it is not the quantity of things you have, but the disposition of the heart that counts.

PRACTICE: OVERVIEW

Our personality is like a house we live in and express through. A house is built brick by brick and our personality is built Elemental by Elemental. The Elementals are created by every thought, desire, word and action. Our thoughts, desires, words and actions have a range of purity, from very pure to not so pure. Thus the purity and quality of our personality also has this same range. Elementals always return to their creator and become part of their conscious and Sub Conscious mind. All human beings are in a condition of their own creation, which makes each of us responsible for that good or bad condition.

With common materials such as stone, wood, iron and concrete we can build a closed in prison where no light enters. Or with the exact same materials we can build a splendid palace full of beauty, harmony and light. The materials are not important; it is the intention of the builder that determines if the materials are turned into a palace or a prison. In a similar way we ourselves have built up our personality, which can be like a palace, a prison, or a mixture of both. We all have been given the same basic substance to create the building blocks of our personality. From this basic substance we have created the Elementals (thoughts, emotions and desires), which build a radiant palace-like personality full of light, love, wisdom and strength. Or they create an imprisoned personality, darkened by negativity, doubt, fear, and anger. There is nothing wrong with the substance we use as thought, emotion and desire; it is how we use it that makes all the difference.   So from now on our responsibility is to tear down our prison and build up our palace.

PRACTICE: MEDITATION

First completely relax. Start relaxing your material body from your feet. Then relax your knees and thighs.

Relax you solar plexus. Relax your chest completely. Now relax the hands you feel them completely relaxed Breathe deeply and comfortable without any effort.

Silence your emotions and still your thoughts. Let everything standstill. There are no thoughts coming to your mind to disturb you.

You feel completely calm – mentally, emotionally and physically. You are completely relaxed, yet you are you.

Who are you?

Forget your name and your gender.

Ask yourself: I am a living being but what am I as life? I AM I. But I want to know what my I-ness really is.

I find my Divine Nature, my I-ness, is now covered with a name, thoughts, emotions and a body. Now I want to find my I-ness, my real Self, the I AM, which is beyond the Worlds of Existence. Now as a personality I want to feel this I AM. Now complete the circle and say I AM I.

But What am I – this feeling of just Being? Just try to understand what you are at this moment. I feel I am in a material body.

Being in your body you possess something more valuable than anything material around you. Now I feel being in my body from head to toe.

Say to yourself I want this body to be healthy!

This Elemental of a healthy body you are creating will help you restore or maintain good health. Say again: I want my material body to be perfectly healthy always!

I want strength, health and wholeness in my material body. Breathe deeply and feel your Heart Center. Simply feel your heart.

Say silently: I want all my emotions and desires to be under my control. I want all my emotional Elementals composing my personality to calm down.

I want them to calm down so I will be able to shape, control them and use them consciously. I want to create beautiful emotions of love and goodness.

Feel you are in the head now. Say: I want all my thoughts to be under my control and not to serve the emotions. I want to use my thoughts to make a better life for my personality. I want to create thoughts of clarity and wisdom.

Now we make the most important request by sincerely saying: I want to know more about myself as a personality and as a Soul. Say it again: I want to know more about myself as a personality and as a Soul.

I want all the negative thoughts and emotions that disturb me to be under my control. I want all the weaknesses in my egoism causing me trouble to now be under my control.

Now see material body covered in shining white light. From your Heart Center see rays of beautiful rosy light spreading all around you. Now say: No hostile feelings or thoughts from others may enter my personality and affect me!

Chapter Twelve
I LAUGH WHEN I HEAR THE FISH IS THIRSTY

We may see another aspect of the Mind expression of the Almightiness. We can see it as energy, as Etheric Vitality. Where can we see that? We see it in our bodies. That's our daily bread we are asking God to give us, "Give us this day our daily bread" -the Etheric Vitality. How do we get it in our bodies? In three ways. The first is known – eating, drinking and sleep. The second is breathing the Etheric Vitality, and the third and the most important is -breathing spiritually. How can we know that? By training. And, when we know that, what can we do? We can become masters of matter. We can materialize the Etheric Vitality or dematerialize it. We can change the nature of matter. These are not stories or myths but the reality.

On one occasion Joshua Emmanuel the Christ put in a basket five little loaves of bread and two fish. He prayed to the Holy Spirit and the Logos. He was putting both his hands in the basket containing only two fish and five loaves of bread. The left hand came out with a piece of bread and the other one with a fried fish. "Give to each person a loaf of bread." There were only two fish and five loaves of bread in that basket. How did He feed the 5000? He was materializing the Etheric Vitality. That is not a myth.

That was a reality. He has done that many, many times, not only two times. You will find out the existence of the so-called Etheric Double. You have to know this Etheric Double. You have it, of course, but unless you make use of it how will you know that it is there? ~ Daskalos

THE TEACHING

The mystic poet Kabhir writes, "I laugh when I hear that the fish in the water is thirsty." His point being is that fish are constantly in the water so how can they be thirsty. In a similar way our planet and its inhabitants float in a sea of abundant energy that surrounds and imbues the planet and our bodies. So accessing this abundant energy supply is not a matter of locality because it exists everywhere. Yet, like that fish, humankind remains thirsty for energy.

This energy exists in a vast range of more and more refined vibratory patterns. At the lower end of the scale are the radiations from the sun, at the higher end of the scale are the many so-called cosmic rays, some of which appear and disappear everywhere in space as scientist are now discovering. This universal, inexhaustible energy has been known by many names. Names such as Prana, Reiki, Chi, Qigong, Orgone, Vril, Life Force, Lumeniferous Aether, and many other names have been given for this energy. We simply call it Etheric Vitality.

As we said, the Esoteric Teachings suggest a path within our multilayer reality in the Worlds of Existence. However, the Esoteric Practices are like a vehicle we use to move on this path. The energy, the Etheric Vitality is like the fuel we use to power our vehicle along our path. The real power of the teachings is not in just knowing them but it is revealed when we put them into practice and live them but, when we practice, we should not do it sub-consciously as habit. We should make every effort to do it consciously with focused attention but without any tension. We initially practice with the knowledge of what we are doing and the purpose of it. Then, in time, we learn to practice Self–Consciously. This means knowing who we are as the Self and what we are doing in our practice. What exactly are we practicing with in these exercises? What are the means we are using in our practice?

In any practice, there are three components. The first one is the practitioner. The second is the practice itself. The third is the means the practitioner uses in the practice. This means is the Mind. Consider this point carefully. The Mind is not our material brain. The mind is not our thoughts. Actually, we shape and formulate our thoughts (and emotions) from the Mind Super-Substance. All the Worlds of Existence and everything in them is Mind manifested at different rates of vibration.

The Noetical Universes and their Etheric Doubles are Mind in a specific range of frequencies. The Psychical Universes and their Etheric Doubles are Mind at lower frequencies of vibrations. The Material Universe is Mind at its lowest rates of vibration. Matter is Mind that has been solidified. It is the frequencies at which the Mind vibrates that make things seem solid, liquid or gaseous to us. Scientists tell us that what we call solid matter is mostly space and very little matter. An atom of any kind of matter consists of a nucleus with electrons orbiting around it at a certain speed like our planets orbit around our sun. It is not a coincidence that atoms of matter behave in the same way that solar systems do. To give this some meaning consider this: If we were to compare the size of one atom of solid matter to a large sports arena, then the atom's nucleus would be equivalent to a speck of dust at the center of the sports arena. The atom's electron would be the size of a fly orbiting around the outside of the arena. Just imagine all that "empty" space in the arena. All solids, liquids or gases in the material universe are composed of atoms, which are about 99 percent space one percent actual matter. It is the same with a Solar System with one percent solid matter (sun, planets and moons) and 99 percent so-called empty space. Therefore, what we consider solid matter is not really all that solid. It only seems solid to us because our material bodies vibrate at the same rate of vibration with the matter that composes our material universe.

While we are living in a material body, the material universe seems concrete to us. From this vantage point, the psychical and Noetical universes seem abstract and insubstantial. Yet, during Exosomatosis or after the death of our material body when we pass over, then the psychical substance will feel solid to us and solid matter will seem insubstantial to us. For example, once we are free from the material body and our awareness is centered in the Psycho-Noetical Body; then our hand can pass right through solid material objects. Yet, other psychical substance will seem solid to our hand. This is because our Psychical Body vibrates in the same range of vibrations as psychical substance does. The same is true with the Noetical Body and the Noetical substance composing the Noetical Worlds.

Can a master who has left his material body and has composed himself in his Psycho-Noetical Body ever move material objects? The answer is yes, if he knows the way of lowering his vibration back down to the point of materializing a hand or a complete body in the material world. There are many, many accounts of Daskalos and other masters doing this, but only to help people in times of need. The most advanced masters will not show such phenomena just to impress people.

Every particle of material substance, from the minutest particle to the largest planet, sun or galaxy has a field of energy in and around it called the Etheric Double. Every form of life from a single cell amoeba to the largest most complex living organism has its luminous Etheric Double. Every atom of every form of life is built and maintained in the perfect mold of the Etheric Double. Likewise, our Psychical and Noetical Bodies have their incorruptible Etheric Doubles too. As our material body is the sum total of all its atoms; so too the body's Etheric Double is composed of all its etheric atoms. What clairvoyants refer to, as the human Aura is the light radiations emanating from the Etheric Double.

The Etheric Double of our material body contains centers of Etheric Vitality. In the East, these centers of energy are called Chakras. Currents of Etheric Vitality also run through the Etheric Double and distribute needed energy to the material body. Etheric Vitality is a life force, which can either be expanded or concentrated. Living bodily forms cannot exist without an Etheric Double.

Rudolf Steiner referred to the Etheric Double as the Etheric Organization and spoke of how to draw on it with conscious breathing. In the ancient Aramaic language, which was in use about 1000 years before and after Christ, the Etheric Double was called the Tzool-mah. In the Lord's Prayer Christ referred to the Etheric Vitality as "Our Daily Bread," our daily supply of energy. All the so-called energy work techniques and energy based healing techniques draw on Etheric Vitality in varying degrees. It does not make any difference what you call it, Etheric Vitality exists and we can access it consciously and use it for our own well-being and to help others.

Mystics, sages, and healers in India, China and elsewhere have for millennia been describing and using the Etheric Vitality, but what about western man? The ancients described four prime elements of matter: Earth, Air, Fire and Water. In the west it was Plato, who first spoke about the existence of a fifth element he called aether. In his Greek language, the Fifth Element was "pempte ousia," which means fifth substance. Later this became the Latin word, "Quinta Essential," which means fifth essence. This has now become the English word quintessence. The definition of quintessence is: the purest example of something. Certainly, the Etheric counterpart of matter qualifies as the purest example of matter because the etheric counterpart of solid mater vibrates within a higher range of the third dimension and thus is part of the material universe. Ether is invisible like the air but like air its presence can be detected.

We as Researchers of Truth value the work of science. Both the scientist and the mystic are researching the same reality but from different approaches. So what does Orthodox Science say about this fifth element? English physicist, Sir Isaac Newton (1642-1727), considered one of the greatest scientists in history, cited this all-pervading Ether of absolute space in the context of physical laws. Then, in 1803, the English scientific genius and serious techie of the day, Thomas Young, was the first to demonstrate that light traveled in waves, through some unexplained medium. Again, the word Aether, Luminiferous Aether (light bearing ether), was used to label this mysterious medium.

All this scientific theory about Ether initiated a race led by the top brainpower to identify and measure the medium they called Ether. So up until 1887 scientists believed in the existence of this yet unexplained Ether. In 1887, when Albert Michelson and Edward Morley set out to scientifically prove it, they were not able to quantify this ether with the rudimentary instruments of the day and so Orthodox Science dropped the idea. Later notable scientists like Nicola Tesla and Albert Einstein realized that the so-called empty space in the universe was not really empty. They correctly theorized there was an electro-magnetic medium that filled the atmosphere of Earth and outer space, which carried electromagnetic waves. This is the all-pervading Ether. Fortunately, other visionary scientific researchers have carried on in this area and perhaps are about to demonstrate how to tap this all-pervading Ether, which they are now calling Zero Point Energy: the free energy of the Quantum Vacuum.

For a Researcher of Truth, Etheric Vitality is the means known and used in the Esoteric Practices. With training and just a little time anyone who is interested can develop their awareness of and conscious use of three of the states or natures of this ether. There are actually seven different characteristics of the ether, the lower three of which can be used by everyone. The other four are only useable by advanced mystics. Immediately, once we start consciously using the Etheric Vitality in its three lower states, we will not need a scientist or anyone to prove its existence to us. We will know with certainty, because we can use it directly.

Our Psychical Body and our Noetical Body also have their own

Etheric Doubles. The seven different states or properties of the Etheric Vitality carry out different functions in the Etheric Doubles of each of our three bodies. We will not speak about the higher three states of the etheric at this time. We can speak about four of its states: the Kinetic, the Imprinting, the Aesthetic (sometimes called the Sensate) and the Creative. These four distinguishable states are within every etheric atom of all substance. The first three we already use, but we use them subconsciously without knowing it. Daskalos declared and demonstrated that a person who can consciously use all seven states of the Etheric Vitality, "Matter will be a toy in their hands. They will know what is materialization and dematerialization." His mastery over all the various states of ether allowed him to facilitate healings that required dematerializing cancerous tumors and materializing new healthy tissues or nerves.

Just working with the Kinetic, Aesthetic and Imprinting Ether brings forward great powers and abilities that are latent within us all. In India, they call these powers Sidhis. All the common so-called psychic abilities are really etheric abilities, which are made possible by these three states of Etheric Vitality. Real psychical powers are much greater than telepathy, telekinesis, psychometry, clairvoyance and clairaudience, which are phenomena associated with the etheric. Mastery of three lower states of the Etheric, in conjunction with purifying our personality, prepares us to be entrusted with the Creative Ether. After reaching high levels of Self-Consciousness, the serious researcher is shown how to use the Creative Ether. This is not something that can really be explained in written or spoken words. It needs training and direct experience.

Creative Ether

The Creative Ether is the most important one and is currently only under the authority and control of the Holy Spirit. It is used for the creation of living matter. The work of the Creative Etheric is done without it being necessary for the ordinary person to have knowledge of it. The renewal of the cells and healing of the wounds for our material body is evidence of its existence. This ether constructs, maintains life, multiplies and dissolves atoms and cells of gross matter. Through this work it constructs and maintains all the organs of the gross material body.

Through the practices, a Researcher of Truth can become aware of, and coordinate with, the conscious work that the Holy Spirit does in their body. This is done mostly through the sensate ether, and through various centers of energy (Chakras) corresponding to the body's various organs. In the distant past man did use and misuse the Creative Ether, and we can read about that in the Bible and other ancient scriptures, but that ability has mostly been lost. Precious few today have reached that stage where the Holy Spirit has entrusted them with the use of the Creative Ether. In the future, people will again be able to co-create with this life giving vitality. Yet, it is possible (not easy) to use it today and advanced members of the Researchers of Truth have reached this level.

One day you may choose to become a psychotherapist or Noetic therapist and with pure and sincere work, you will be given the right to use the creative ether. However, the word psychotherapist is really not right, because it comes from the word psyche, which means the Soul. The word therapy is a treatment for healing so technically, it is an incorrect word because the Soul of everyone is pure and incorruptible and not in need of any therapeutic treatment for healing. This means there are no misguided, lost or evil Souls; all Souls are forever free and never bound but, since everyone is using this term, psychotherapy to mean the treatment of mental or emotional disorders, we continue to use that term. To be a advanced psychotherapist means to be a co-worker with the Holy Spirit and be entrusted with the creative ether. During sleep or during an out of body experience; the kinetic, aesthetic and imprinting ether transfers with the self-awareness to the Psychical Body. The creative ether stays with the material body. If the Creative Ether is removed from a material body, that body immediately dies. Such is the importance of the Creative Ether.

Kinetic Ether

The Kinetic Ether within the Etheric Double of the material body has a very complicated and diverse role. The Kinetic Ether begins to function in and around the embryo as it develops in the womb. The Kinetic Ether facilitates movement within the body and the movement of the material body itself. Kinetic is from the Greek word kinesis, which means motion. When we start to move our material body, currents of Etheric Energy race through our nervous system like electricity through wires and coordinate the contractions of all the right muscles to accomplish the exact movement needed. Have you ever thought exactly how you make your body move? After you have the thought to get up and stand, what happens next to make your body move?

We are constantly using the Kinetic Ether subconsciously when we move and do anything. Its work in the material body differs from organ to organ. It governs the autonomic functions such as the pulse of the heart, breathing, metabolism etc...as well as the conscious functions such as walking, talking, eye movement, etc...For something to be living in the material world it must have movement and the Kinetic Ether enables all movement.

Skilled artists and musicians develop a fine degree of control over their hands and fingers through the subconscious use of this Kinetic Ether. As they practice they gain greater and greater mastery over the muscles in their hands, but without knowing it they are using the kinetic property of their Etheric Double to do this. Developing our control and mastery of the Etheric Double also brings forward latent non-physical powers within us all, such as telepathy. It is also possible with training to separate some Etheric Vitality from our Etheric Double and consciously send it over great distances to those who need our help in the phenomenon known as Distant Healing. Healers and psychotherapist do this either consciously or subconsciously. This transference is possible because of the Kinetic property of Etheric Vitality. The Researchers of Truth teach the method for distance healing.

The conscious or Sub-Conscious projection of any Elemental, takes place via the kinetic property of ether. The Kinetic property plays a great and very active role in our material body. Yet, in our Psychical Body the Kinetic Ether is not so active. The material world is a world of time and space. During our existence on Earth, we physically need to move from one location to another. In the

Psychical Worlds, the condition of space as we know it on Earth is absent. There, space is replaced by the conditional sense of place. Changing from one circumstantial location to another within the Psychical Worlds occurs by coordination, attunement and At-One-Ment. A simple comparison would be something like tuning a radio in to different stations. You do not need to move the radio itself but simply set the radio to the different frequency of another channel and you will immediately hear a different radio broadcast. Within the Psychical planes, we create the sense of moving from place to place. We can do all those movements we know on Earth such as walking, running and still others such as flying but these are conditional experiences, and we are not really traveling distances in space.

Imprinting Ether

Imprinting Ether enables us to create thoughts from the Mind. This ether is used to imprint the Noetical images on the etheric brain and all our experiences on every cell of the body. When we visualize we are utilizing the Imprinting Ether in shaping Psycho-Noetical substance into forms: thought and emotion forms. This is how we create the Elementals. The Imprinting Ether allows us to not only create these images but also store them in our mind and recall them as well. Mostly we create and store images subconsciously. Developing our abilities to create clear, vivid and stable images using the Imprinting Ether is a necessary skill for a seeker to develop. It enables not only healing work but is helpful in manifesting a good and satisfying life for our family and ourselves. In the practice of introspection, we are also using the Imprinting Ether as we see and study the conditions of our life.

Of course we will not succeed in our effort instantaneously. This is something that has to be learned. Through our mistakes and errors we gain experience. It is not expected that you will make proper use of the imprinting ether immediately in creating Noetical images. At first maybe you will feel in doubt, you won't be able to visualize exactly what you want. Other thoughts will come to distract you. Now you must keep on insisting to visualize clear and steady images until you succeed.

Aesthetic Ether

Aesthetic Ether is the feeling giving ether. It enables physical sensations. It allows us to feel various parts of our material body, the toes, the knees, and anywhere in the body. The role of this Ether is much greater in the Psychical Body than it is in the material body. Our happy, sad, angry and other feelings are psychical vibrations. These are felt and experienced via the Aesthetic Ether of the Etheric Double of the Psychical Body. Our ability to sense sorrow or happiness in others is also due to the Aesthetic Ether of the Etheric Double of our Psychical Body.

In the material body, Aesthetic Ether is giving us the sense of pleasure and pain. The experience of pain is associated with a lack of Kinetic Ether and the intensified activity and the buildup of Aesthetic Ether, the purpose of which is to bring our attention to the affected area. Anesthesia means without feeling. An anesthetic is an agent such as a drug that produces an insensibility to pain.

Daskalos, however, did not need anesthetics to remove pain. In circle meetings, Daskalos has, on certain occasions, demonstrated how to remove the Aesthetic Ether from his or other peoples' Etheric Double. For the demonstration, he would rub his hands briefly over an arm as he removed the feeling giving Aesthetic Ether. Then he would push a large hatpin through his or someone's forearm and there would be no pain. However, this skill of his was dedicated to remove the pain from others, as he performed cures to their material bodies.

Once after a Stoa Lesson, an elderly lady from Europe approached Daskalos for help. She had a lot of pain in her left arm. She could not straighten her arm and held it curled up to her chest. Even small arm movements gave her a great deal of pain. Daskalos touched her arm gently and immediately proclaimed it was due to nerve damage. He said that he would have to create new nerves and reached to straighten her arm to begin his work. She pulled away guarding her damaged arm and protested that it was much too painful and it could not be straightened. Daskalos comforted her and gently said that he would make it so she would not feel any pain.

I was standing on Daskalos' right side and could tell by the lady's face that she did not believe this was possible. He rubbed her arm with his slightly cupped hand and proceeded to straighten the arm, but as he started the lady again reacted and pulled back fearing the pain she knew would come. Daskalos insisted she would not feel pain as he had already removed the Aesthetic Ether and extended her arm anyway. I watched closely as the lady tilted her head back contorting her face bracing for the pain, which never came. As her arm extended the look on her face changed to astonishment. She watched in disbelief as Daskalos deftly worked on her arm for a few minutes rebuilding the damaged nerves.

"There" Daskalos announced as he bent and straightened her arm several times demonstrating the success of his work. The lady seemed unsure at first as she tried to adjust to the new condition of her arm. The healing had happened so fast it was difficult for her mind to grasp. She walked away looking at her arm amazed as she moved it.

Daskalos employed many states of Ether in order to carry out this healing. For the diagnosis, he used the Aesthetic Ether to sense and feel what was going on within the arm. Using the Imprinting Ether, he was able to see the actual conditions of the nerves. He was able to remove the Aesthetic Ether from the arm and thus eliminating her pain. For the actual healing, he used the Kinetic, Aesthetic, Imprinting and the Creative Ether together. Of course, Daskalos was co-creating with the Holy Spirit in this and he would never claim that he personally did the healing. Nevertheless, his co-operation was skillful and Self-Conscious. He did not just blindly flood the person with Etheric Vitality and pray to the Holy Spirit for a healing. He also knew exactly what he was doing. He used the various properties of the Ether in his work as a surgeon would use surgical instruments. He continuously observed his work and maintained Self-Conscious control as he performed it. He also infused this healing Elemental with his ardent prayer that the damage be corrected and the arm restored to perfection.

THE PRACTICE OVERVIEW

In our meditation practices we work with the three lower natures of the Etheric Vitality. Engaging in the Esoteric Practices automatically starts to develop our ability to use the various properties of the Etheric Vitality. These are the practices of Observation, Visualization, Meditation, Introspection, and Concentration.

We have divided the work of the Etheric Double into the four states according to their function to better describe the work of the Etheric Vitality. We are not dividing the actual Etheric Double or the Etheric Vitality. All the states are contained in each and every etheric atom. We need to begin work, not only to understand them theoretically but also practically by using them. Giving a cello to an untrained person, it would be unreasonable to expect them to immediately start playing like the master cellist, Yo Yo Ma. If we give an untrained person a cello and training, that person may practice until he can play as well as Yo Yo Ma. Once a person learns the skill of playing a cello masterfully or gains the skill of using the ethers masterfully, no one can take his or her skills away. If we truly and deeply enter in to the meaning of one of the lessons or an exercise, it is like we gain a year or two of study all at once. For this to happen we must not only read these teachings but also study and practice them well. For the meditations and exercises we not only need to practice them but also observe the effects they have on us. In time by practicing with the Kinetic and Aesthetic Ether you will be able to notice the circulation of your blood and blood cells. You will be able to feel every organ and you will know what is going on in them. It needs dedicated practice. You must practice to be the master of your human body.

Developing the Kinetic and the Aesthetic Ether we are at the same time causing the development of our Psychical Body. Using the Imprinting Ether in our Etheric Double we can come in contact with and at the same time develop our Noetical Body. Our three bodies are connected by their Etheric Doubles and are influencing each other. By learning the art of Visualization you are using the Mind as the Imprinting Ether. In the course of time you'll gain a new power in Visualization called clairvoyance.

At the beginning we use the Imprinting Ether visualizing colors and shapes. Colors are vibrations and the vibrations of certain colors affect the centers of energy (Charkas). We can start by flooding our Etheric Doubles with certain basic colors. Then we can use disks of light moving them around and passing through certain centers. Later, we use colored spheres, moving and passing through the centers.

A warning: On and in the Etheric Double there are centers of energy, which function as whirlpools of Etheric Vitality. Despite what you may have read elsewhere it is very dangerous to concentrate directly on these Chakras or on the material organs associated with these centers. We can safely concentrate on our Solar Plexus, but never concentrate directly on the material heart or any other organ. That constricts the blood vessels and can cause serious problems and physical damage to the organs and your nervous system.

As we proceed; along with the teaching we need to do exercises on and in the Etheric Double of the material body to get the skill in using the ethers consciously. Once we are capable of consciously using the Kinetic, Aesthetic and Imprinting properties of the ether, we will be in a much better position to facilitate healings. More and more information will be given in future lessons about this for those who progress in this branch of study.

THE PRACTICE: WORKING WITH ETHERIC VITALITY

Relax completely. Start from the feet. Breathe deeply and comfortably. Inhaling as your heart makes four beats.

Then immediately exhale again for four beats of the heart. Inhale... Exhale... Do it consciously, rhythmically and comfortably. Inhale... Exhale... Inhale... Exhale...

Now feel the toes of your feet. It is the Aesthetic Ether that gives you this feeling.

You can move them a bit to feel your toes. That is the Kinetic Ether moving the toes. Now feel the bottom of your feet all the way up to you knees.

Now move your sense of feeling from the knees all the way back down to the feet. Now again feel your knees only your knees. Your attention should move via the Kinetic Ether up to the knees.

You at the same time, begin to use the Aesthetic Ether, to feel that you are going up from the whole foot upwards to the knees.

Now, feel from the knees, up through the thighs to the place you are sitting on the chair.

Feel just where you are sitting. You didn't feel that when you were feeling the feet and knees. Now you can feel it.

Now feel the legs from the place you are sitting all the way down into the feet. Feel them. They are yours. You can be in them and feel them using the Aesthetic Ether. When you can use the Aesthetic Ether in this way fully you will be able to remove pain from your body.

Now, feel the area of the solar plexus. Feel being in the solar plexus. Move it. You can move from inside the solar plexus up and feel the sternum. Now, you are feeling the whole abdomen. The organs are not an obstacle to the movement of Kinetic Ether.

You may think that you are feeling and moving in your body but you are actually feeling and moving in the Etheric Double, which is in and slightly outside of your material body.

Now, take deep breaths and feel the chest area. Feel the chest from the thyroid to the toes. You feel the shoulders. Feel the hands. Move the fingers. You can feel inside your body from the thyroid to the toes of your feet.

It is easier for you to concentrate in the chest, because, there are more active centers of energy in the chest.

Breathe deeply and feel in the abdomen and the chest. Now you feel from your toes, feet, legs, solar plexus, the chest, to the thyroid and now up in to the head. It is not difficult to feel in the head.

Now you are using the Aesthetic Ether to feel you are in the whole body: in the head, in the neck, inside the chest, you feel the shoulder blades behind your back, your hands you feel the muscles, you feel the fingers, now you feel the stomach and the belly, you feel the place you are sitting on the chair, you feel the thighs.

Breathe deeply and now with the Imprinting Ether visualize

and see the Etheric Vitality entering in with every breath.

As you are breathing the Etheric Vitality the light is entering your body. The vitality remains and the air goes out. Breathing you charge your Etheric Double with this vitality See it as snow-white light as it enters your lungs and expands everywhere in your material body. Now, see your material body radiating in pure snow-white light.

Love your body. It is yours, it is given to you to live in and express yourself. So, breathe deeply and feel that you are in your material body and -love it.

Breathe deeply and say to yourself, "I want perfect health to be in this material body of mine." Feel being in your material body, in your Etheric Double, and have the wish for this material body to enjoy perfect health.

Chapter Thirteen
THE PULSE OF LIFE

The heart's purpose is the pulse, and the rhythmic beats of the heart are the kinetic ether. We have inhalation and exhalation, blood circulation, the movement of the etheric fluids and the Psycho-Noetical centers, all tasks and the performance is the kinetic ether. Primarily the creative ether, a nature of the Etheric Double, is under the control of the Christ Logos as well as the Holy Spirit. They are the life givers. The creative ether builds, sustains and maintains, but it can't be done without the use of the kinetic ether.

Can we have life without movement? Can you perceive life, the phenomena of life, without movement? For a phenomenon of life to exist there must be movement of blood and of etheric fluids. Movement of some parts of the body isn't entirely necessary but the pulse of the heart is necessary.

What is metabolism other than movement? It is a form of vibration and movement. Therefore, movement is necessary in order to have the phenomena of life, not Life. Life itself is not in need of a condition. But the phenomenon of life, life within a material body by necessity requires movement, the kinetic ether. We will get to know the nature of this ether through our exercises and in time we will become masters of this ability. You must see what life is in a material body. What is Everlasting Life is something else and it needs much thought, meditation, concentration and raising the self-consciousness to very, very, very high levels to understand it. But what is life in a Human Form, in a human being, should be known by everybody, so that he will be able to face his or her problems satisfactorily ~ Daskalos

THE TEACHING

We know that we are alive. We are living in a material body – no one questions this. The feeling that we are living is common to all.

Yet the exact way each of us is living is different from everyone else and it is the way we are living that determines the quality of our life as a personality. So we have two different things, Life and living.

We know from studying various scriptures and teachings that there is something called Eternal Life – the Everlasting Life. God is Life everlasting in eternity. Everlasting Life means Life without a beginning or an end. The Everlasting Life in Its Self-Sufficiency lacks nothing and nothing can be added to it. This Everlasting Life is God's immortal nature and it is our own immortal nature as Spirit-Beings. As Spirit-Beings we are Everlasting Life. Unfortunately, the truth and magnificence of the Everlasting Life as God's nature or as our own Divine Nature is incomprehensible to our human nature - our personality.

We can also know from observing things in the material world that the Eternal Life is expressing Its Life as the various living forms on Earth and in the worlds beyond. We can study the life of all of the forms of life, from the smallest microbe to the largest Whale, and understand something of the Circle of Possibilities for that life form. Within each and every form of life we can see something of the Total Love, Wisdom and Power in expression. All life forms are phenomenal expressions of the Life -they are temporary embodiments of the Everlasting Life.

Absolute Beingness (God) expresses Its Life within Itself

manifesting Its Life as all the phenomena of life we see around us. According to the Will-Pleasure of God, the manifestation of Life initiates as vibration and this vibration is giving all the living forms a Pulse of Life. By the term Pulse of Life, we mean the cause which gives us tremor, vibration in all the different forms of life all around us. The main characteristic of all these forms of life is this Pulse of Life – the balanced movement towards opposite directions. For example: this movement in opposites is the contraction and expansion of a heart as it pumps the blood or the inhalation and exhalation of lungs as they breathe. There is always a well-balanced movement between opposite positions.

Via the Kinetic Ether, this Pulse of Life sparks nodes on our material heart, transferring ethereal/electrical impulses to the heart muscles, causing it to beat and pump blood. This Pulse of Life is easily seen in the breathing as well as in the heartbeats of animals and humans. We see the Pulse of Life causing the rising and falling in the sap and it is in the budding of plants. For those who have seen an Archangel, they will have noticed the Archangels too have pulsation radiations in their form.

The bodies of humans and the bodies of animals are similar in their construction. Both have skin, flesh, bones, blood, nerves and a skull with brains. There is not much difference between the animals and humans in this regard. However, Man can use the Mind directly, which is something animals cannot do. Animals only have the Mind as their instinct. All plants and animals are the materialization of the Pulse of Life as expressions of the Archangelic orders. We can see the wisdom of God and these Archangelic creators in the flowers, the vegetables and animal life. Yet, unlike humans, no animal can use the Mind and change its way of life because a human being is a Spirit-Soul, a god and an animal is not. We cannot exist as a personality without a Soul-Self any more than our body can live without a heart and our heart cannot live without the Pulse of Life in it. The Pulse of Life is an expression of our Divine Nature – the Spirit-Soul-Self.

Now, it is most important to begin to distinguish our Divine Nature as Everlasting Life, from the temporary life of our material body in which we are living. We can say Everlasting Life "is." We can say that this Life exists as the phenomena of life on Earth, in the Psychical Worlds and in the Noetical Worlds. The Material World, the Psychical Worlds and the Noetical Worlds are Worlds of Existence inhabited with living forms. For anything to exist it must have a form. For human beings to exist in these worlds they must have a form which corresponds to these worlds. Everlasting Life is of Beingness and does not require a bodily form, but the phenomena of life only belong to the changing Worlds of Existence and definitely need a form to exist.

Your material body is yours to live in and express your life through, but you are not your body. Your emotions, the emotions and desires you express are yours but they are not you. Your conscious thoughts and the ones that rise from your sub-consciousness are your thoughts, but they are not you. Detach from the misidentification of your Self with the thoughts, emotions and behaviors you express. Seek the real Self behind these expressions. Go deep in your meditation and enter into a state of dynamic stillness. There you can contact the Pulse of Life and can easily feel it in the beating of your heart. You can sense it in the blood coursing through your veins. You can notice it in the energetic pulsations at the tips of your fingers. It is Life.

Now we know we are not our material body, we are not our emotions or our thoughts. These constitute our present-day personality only. So what is the relationship between our Divine Nature as Everlasting Life and our human nature as an ever-changing personality? Our Divine Nature is perfect, whole, changeless, always free and never bound. Yet, our human nature as a personality expresses a conglomeration of conflicting notions, concepts, desires and feelings. All these manifest in the personality as good or bad predispositions, talents, strengths and weaknesses. A single ray of our Divine Nature is the core or backbone on which we build our personality. The personality we build can have a vast range in purity. Collectively our personality is composed of the Elementals created or revitalized, but our personality is not our Real Self. To know that for sure, we must analyze that time and place creation called our personality to distinguish it from the real nature of our Spirit-Soul Self. Remember, the Elementals composing our personality are living. They are not Life; however, they are living in the Worlds of Existence. Yet their existence cannot extend beyond these worlds.

Elementals are not eternal beings but they express a living existence with purpose and power. The negative Elementals torture our personality and the personalities of those around us and degrade the life we are living. The benevolent Elementals are like strong allies to our own life and those around us. Our Elementals have a kind of power or force in them. It is we who have given them that power and we can take it back any time we like -if we know the way. This means that we feed energy into the Elementals from our portion of the Pulse of Life. The Pulse of Life is our inner nature but it is not the inherent nature of an Elemental. This means we can purify and withdraw the energy from the Elementals.

Now in concentrating on the chest, but not directly on the material heart, you can feel the Pulse of Life. The Pulse of Life is in the material heart but the pulse is not the material. Try to feel the Pulse of Life. This Pulse of Life is working perfectly to make your heart beat, your blood flow, and give life to your material body. It is clear that as a personality we do not control this Pulse of Life. Who controls it and who decides when it will withdraw from our material body and end the beating of our heart? Have you ever asked yourself who or what is creating this Pulse of Life that makes my physical heart beat? This question can initiate one of the first approaches to God.

At the very core of our human existence as a personality is the untainted luminous ray of our Spirit-Soul, steadily pulsating life into our bodies. Find this reality behind your temporary personality self. Find this Pulse of Life in your personality self, and trace it until you find the Pulse of Life as your real nature -the Spirit-Soul Self. This is the aim of a Researchers of Truth. To reach that aim we must start somewhere and that somewhere is exactly the current condition we find ourselves in. This means we start with analyzing our personality self in order to find in it, our Real Self, which is the Pulse of Life. What do we find? We find that the Pulse of Life in us has been covered over by the creation of a temporary time and space self that we call our personality and we need to uncover it.

THE PRACTICE: OVERVIEW

With observation we can easily see that the manifestation of the Pulse of Life is not the same in all the different forms of life, yet there is only one Pulse of Life. If there was no Pulse of Life in your personality it would not exits. Notice that everything takes place within life. Life exists everywhere, but the Pulse of Life is exactly proportioned to the purpose of each form of life found in the Worlds of Existence. So we search the different ways the Pulse of Life is expressed in the different living forms.

The main characteristic of the Pulse of Life is the law of balance and order as expressions of the Divine Total Wisdom and Power and Love. For the creation of living forms, the Pulse of Life comes first as cause, and then produces the effect. The effect is the various forms of life. In the Noetic State, the Pulse of Life is giving us the archetypal Ideas, with the laws and causes that initiate and govern all the living forms we see in the Worlds of Existence. From these Archetypal Ideas and laws, the life forms start to be built up in a steady determined way and are manifested by the Pulse of Life as all the living forms we see around us. The Pulse of Life, as cause and effect, is seen in each and every form of life while still being under the complete control of the laws of harmony, balance and order.

THE PRACTICE: A PULSE OF LIFE MEDITATION

First, relax completely. Feel you are in your material body, from your toes to your head. See that you relax the material body completely.

Now and always, your heart is beating within your material body. It started beating before your birth and it will continue beating until the silver cord joining your other bodies with your material body is broken. At one end of the silver cord is your material heart, and the Pulse of life of that silver cord is making your heart beat.

Try to feel the pulse of Life in your body. You are living. Who are you living in the material body? You are your personality, yet having in it the pulse of Life. You are the pulse of Life, and the pulse of Life is your Selfhood. You have to study who you are as a human being, living in your material body. In studying that you will be able to concentrate your attention and observation on the other bodies too. You will develop what we call the Self-Consciousness.

Concentrate on your heart area. Concentrate on the whole chest, but not directly on the heart. Do not concentrate by force but by feeling. Feel your heart and ask yourself, "Who is making my heart work and beat? What is this pulse of life? It is faithfully pulsating. It makes the blood circulate. Yet it is not under my control. Under whose control is it?"

In every temple there is the Holy of holies. Make your heart the Holy of the holies of God. In the Holy of holies, there is also the altar. Make an altar in your heart. The Inextinguishable Light-Life is burning on the altar.

Now, light another lamp of your personality's love to God and to all human beings around you. Don't allow those flames to flicker.

Keep the flames steady and strong. It is a perfect light. Live with these two flames of love on the altar of your heart.

The Holy Archangels are living in your heart. You are living too. Your life is the Pulse of Life.

Chapter Fourteen
THE VOICE OF AN ANGEL

Now, in the bodies, in the Etheric Doubles of the material, the Psychical and the Noetical Bodies there is an archangel near the Thrones [a Metathrone]. This is your Guardian Angel. Every human being has a Guardian Angel. That is not your so-called higher Self. He is an Archangel different from your Spirit-Soul. Out of Love that Guardian Angel is egofied [unified] to you. When you say that nobody can hear or see what you are doing -you are mistaken. The Guardian Angel knows everything and, sometimes, when you overdo it -he interferes. That is what you call the stings of consciousness. Did you ever analyze what are the stings of consciousness that are coming to us sometimes saying, "That's wrong? You shouldn't have done it?" It is his voice.

Now, I will reveal much more. Do you know that you are in dialogue with him all the time without understanding it? He is egofied [unified] with you. You think that you are making this conversation with yourself. Just notice. When you sit in meditation, in silence, you listen to this dialogue. I ask you with whom are you talking with? You think, "It is with myself." It is not with yourself -it is with your Guardian Angel that you are talking. That's why I say listen to your inner voice and consult that super intelligent Archangel who loves you. ~ Daskalos

THE TEACHING

In our lives there are so many voices competing for our attention. Externally there are the voices from our culture with its laws, news, marketing and social statements. There are the voices of our families, friends and co-workers. Simultaneously, our emotions, desires and habitual thoughts are also speaking to us. All this goes on continuously every single day of our lives. At the personality level, we sometimes succeed and sometimes fail by selectively listening to or ignoring these voices.

Coexisting with this flood of voices inundating our awareness, there is another voice within us. This voice however is often drowned out by the other voices and is seldom noticed. This voice is a true voice, one that will never mislead us, never forsake us, or ever stop expressing its perfect love to us. This voice has accompanied us from the moment of our humanization, through all our incarnations, and will accompany us unto Theosis. Theosis is our absolute unity with God at the end of our long journey through many incarnations.

This voice is commonly known as our Guardian Angel. Our Guardian Angel is from an Archangelic order very close to that of human beings. One of these innumerable Archangels, out of his great love joins with the Spirit-Soul of each of us to accompany and guide us. No one is ever alone or unloved. The Guardian joins with us in complete At-One-Ment, and yet he never loses his own Archangelic nature. He is the perfect guide and flawless teacher. We often seek externally for teachers, gurus and masters to help awaken us and lead us spiritually. All the while, our ever-present Guardian stands ready in his Super-Conscious capacity to serve in this very way. Many have contemplated and wished to be close to a wise master who could help them as they faced their life's challenges. How long has our faithful guardian been waiting for us to become aware of him and engage in conscious communion with him? No Earthly teacher could be closer or know better what you need than your Guardian

Archangel.

Be advised, none of the Archangels give petty advice, or speak of insignificant material things. So we must always use reason to distinguish if we are hearing the "voice" of an Archangel or the sound of our own Elementals (pre-existing thoughts and feelings coming from our own sub-consciousness). Really, this is not as difficult as it may sound, because communications from an Archangel ring with authority, truth and love. Using the golden key of Introspection, you will be able to know the difference for sure. Being able to control and silence your own thoughts and emotions makes it easier to distinguish the guardian's voice but, if you are not able to raise your consciousness higher than the level of your mundane thoughts and emotions, you cannot be so sure you are not mistaking the false, mimicking expressions of your own egoism to be the voice of an Archangel.

Daskalos compared this near and dear relationship with our Guardian Angel with an example we all have seen. Take two lit candles and place their flames together and they appear as one flame, pull them apart and you can see they are two flames. This unity of flames is similar to our union with the Guardian Angel. His unification with us was born, not out of his sacrifice, but out of his great love for us. This unification continues unbroken from the point of our humanization trough all our incarnations until we return home in At-One-Ment with God. At which point we will no longer need a guardian.

Unfortunately, our Earthly lives capture so much of our attention that we are unaware of his presence within us. So we must quiet our emotions and still our thoughts enough to attune to his communiqués. The voice of our Guardian Angel comes not in a litany of words but as complete, universal ideas, which communicate his messages very succinctly.   When we look to our Guardian Archangel for guidance and listen openly, he will reply. We can develop this dialogue and become increasingly aware of his presence and wise guidance. Of course, the Archangels are not male or female, but the term "he" is used as a convenient pronoun.

    Our Guardian Archangel is ready and willing to communicate his wisdom to us. Our Guardian experiences a kind of sadness when we go badly astray. When we fall to the temptations of gossiping, anger, hatred, negativity, blaming others and acting like a victim, it is disturbing your Guardian Angel. Know that during such times, it is like the Archangels are distancing from you and step back until you calm down and they can approach again. On the other hand, they experience joy when we cooperate with them. Christ said, "Joy to your Angels in heaven for one who repents." To repent means turning one's heart, mind and actions away from illusionary temptations and returning back to their Divine Nature.

    Our Guardian is in constant communion with us. His work in our evolution is very important. His voice is not confused, conflicted or complex. His voice does not express complicated mental constructs or vague notions. Instead his voice expresses the language of real Love. It may initially appear this voice is small or weak compared to the other voices demanding our attention. In reality, there is nothing weak or small about it. It is only weak to our personality and that is due to the degree of our awareness.

Knowledge of the Guardian Archangel and other Archangels that are working in our bodies must not remain as hypothetical. This knowledge only becomes practical by our own direct experiences with these radiant beings of light. Individually or collectively, we cannot continue to let our material development race ahead of the development of our spiritual awareness and understanding. It is not wise and it definitely is not without consequence. These brothers of Spirit welcome our approach and our conscious engagement in their great work.

It is written in the Bible that when God said, "let us create man in our likeness and image." It was at that moment, which is eternal, the Spirit Beings destined to become human beings project a single ray to become humanized. At the same instant, a ray from an Archangel of the highest orders, unifies with our ray of Spirit and joins with us on our journeys through the incarnational cycles.

Not for just one incarnation but all of our incarnations we have the same Guardian Archangel, loving and guiding us. So in this way we again see a dual nature. Our own Being and the Being of the unified Guardian Archangel, which has also become one with our Self because of its unification. At the same time this Archangel keeps his own perfect purity. He never detaches from the oneness of God while in unification with us. It happens this way because of the Will and Pleasure of God. The Guardian is fully unified with you out of his perfect unconditional love for you.

Everything concerning our humanization is in the Divine Plan as Archetypes but now they are under the authority of our Guardian. The Archangels of the Elements start their work, building on the

Archetype of the Human Idea.   They are building on these blueprint-like plans, which are held by our Guardian. Now, at one point in his life, Daskalos had the question: Where do the Archangels get this Human Form to work with on our behalf? An Archangel gave him the answer saying, "My love, you always hide it in you, even being in oneness with God." What the Archangel was revealing is that the Human Form was always within us as a Spirit Being, and that we always had the nature to become humanized. We will never lose our Human Form even when we return back to our Divine Nature and the incarnation process stops completely. At which point we can reformulate our Human Form and enter it again anytime we like. We can enter in it at our pleasure and not as a karmic obligation.

Sometimes, when your personality engages in wrong behavior and goes too far, your Guardian will interfere. This interference is his disapproval of your behavior, not of you. It is the so-called sting of consciousness, which is not a punishment but a wakeup call. When this occurs we have to really think about it and use Introspection to check ourselves to find our mistake. During introspection you will find the truth and the cause of this trouble. But a warning, it is at this very point your egoism will jump in and justify wrong behavior trying to excuse it and lay the blame at the feet of other people. Your own egoism is much more dangerous than you realize. So look sharp and be aware of this misleading dynamic within you. On one side of this duality we are trying to study the personality's self-awareness to learn and know it. On the other side, the egoism is hiding, excusing, covering and protecting itself. With time and sincerity, you will discover you are not the egoism and will be able to correct and master it thus avoiding so much trouble and needless suffering.

The work of the Guardian Archangel is not in building and maintaining our bodies. That is the work of the Archangels of the Elements. The Guardian's work is in caring for your personality. The Guardian Archangel is tolerant and very patient with us. Our Guardian Archangel is not only egofied (unified) with the Spirit-Soul-Self, but also with our personality self. When you contact your Guardian Archangel and if you are a clairvoyant you can see him, but you'll think you are looking at yourself in a mirror. Being unified, with you he takes on your name and appearance. Yet, he absolutely does not have your weaknesses and illusions. One part of him is unified with you while the other part stays fully in his Archangelic Super Conscious state.

The Guardian acts as a perfectly clear mirror, reflecting everything about us. When a mirror reflects a beautiful floral arrangement or a pile of rotting garbage it does not affect the mirror in the least. This is how it works with our Guardian. He reflects our good and bad desires, thoughts, words and deeds without being affected or influenced by what is reflected, so any crimes or faults of ours may be reflected in that mirror so that we can see them and correct them, but we have to take notice of that reflection.

This reflection does not stop at the death of our material body. When a person's material body dies they cross over to the Psychical planes of existence. That person then sees his good or bad behaviors, his emotions and thoughts reflected very clearly in the mirror of his own Guardian Archangel. However, the departed may not see the Archangel directly, just their own refection. People with harsh, negative emotions and thoughts are terror stricken when they see an ugly monster in this mirror and wonder what is this monster that I see? At which point their Guardian replies to the departed saying, "That reflection is your refection not mine. I am the mirror; you are the monster, change so you will reflect a better Self." So our Guardian's work is also to reflect our thoughts, desires, words and actions back to us in such a way for us to understand them better and make the necessary corrections.

Unfortunately, when we incarnate in the Worlds of Existence, we all undergo a kind of amnesia, lose sight of our Divine Nature, and become identified with only our limited human nature. Partially to ease the pain of this conditional separation, this Guardian accompanies and guards us during our journey through time, space and place. He eventually helps lead us to the recognition of our real Self and its source; awakening us from our amnesia.

So despite our feelings of separateness, we are never abandoned or un-cared for. We should not let the Elementals of loneliness build within our personality to the point of eclipsing the love and help of our brother Guardian. As the Guardian's presence in our life begins to dawn on us, we realize that he is not a concoction from our own imagination. We understand that he is not some distant entity apathetically overseeing our life. His presence will reveal that the prime teaching he has come to give is how to really love. He shows us how to help others by the way he helps us. His help does not condemn, criticize, and blame us or anyone else even when there are serious mistakes. His love and help is unconditional, patient, kind, enduring, and non-interfering.   We will soon realize that his guidance and protection are not vague or subjective, but quite practical and effective.

For example, there was a serial killer who was preying on female real estate agents in America.   His pattern was to set up an appointment with a female agent to see an empty house she had for sale. Once inside he would rape the agent at gunpoint, take her to an ATM to withdraw her money and then kill her. On one of these attempts after he had raped the agent and was about to abduct her, he made a small mistake. He exited the empty house first with the terrified agent immediately behind him. At that very instant her Guardian spoke loud and clear saying, "Step back in the house and lock the door." Without hesitation she did as instructed and was saved in an instant. The killer had no choice but to flee. So you can see how infinitely intelligent and utterly effective the Guardian's help is and there are many stories like this, perhaps you have one yourself.

Of course the Guardian's protection will not protect us from a necessary life lesson, slated by the Lords of Karma but he can and does brilliantly come to our aid, especially when we cultivate a conscious connection with him and consciously cooperate with his guidance. All of us have experienced, to some degree, communications from our Guardian Angel but we do not always understand exactly what is occurring. Observation and Introspection are needed to accuratcly distinguish the difference between the authentic voice of our Guardian from the echo of our own thoughts/emotions that rise from our sub-conscious mind.

What the Guardian says to each of us, and many have heard this same message, is, "I am always with you, I have always been with you and I will remain with until the very end of your journey and you no longer need me." What a beautiful and unbreakable vow of love!

THE PRACTICE: OVERVIEW

Every man, woman and child is attended by his or her Guardian Archangel throughout the day. At night you are sleeping and dreaming but your Guardian Archangel is not. He is watching over you like a loving mother tenderly caring for her beloved child.

Since the Guardian Archangel is unified with you, there is never a time when you are apart from him. To be in communion with your Guardian it is not a matter of going anywhere, for wherever you go he is there. So it is only a matter of becoming aware of his presence.

Sometimes during introspection or in a meditation you may have some thoughts, remembrances or visions that come to the surface of your mind. These may be pleasing, displeasing or threatening. When this happens do not do anything – just observe what is coming to the surface. After a while you may notice and internal dialog, an exchange of ideas taking place that contains suggestions for you. Who are you having that dialogue with? Slowly in this way you will begin to have conscious contact with your Guardian Archangel.

Your real guide, your Guardian Archangel, is within you. That guide is helping you to reason. So, learn to seek and rely more and more on your Guardian Archangel's most reasonable guidance. When people feel inspired, where is that inspiration coming from? Often writers, musicians and artist say a Muse inspires them. The word Muse is from the Greek language and was a reference to a goddess who was the source of knowledge that inspired poets, and artist of every kind. Most of the time inspiration is coming from your wise brother guide, you own Guardian Archangel, but it can come from other intelligences that also follow and assist in your development. So, if you need guidance, you can have it, either by your Guardian Archangel or by others engaged in the same line of work as you.

Now when you need help, specifically call on your Guardian Angel, expect an answer, and wait for his well-timed reply. The reply may not come the very moment you ask but it will come. In order to hear that reply you must stay receptive, open and attentive enough to recognize the answer when it does come. So ask, watch and pray.

THE PRACTICE: OPENING A DIALOG WITH YOUR GUARDIAN ANGEL

Relax completely and feel you are in your material body the Temple of God. Breathe deeply and quiet your emotions and still your thoughts.

Now ask yourself this question, "I am breathing. I take deep breaths and I can do that. I am feeling I am living in this material body. But, after all, who am I? What am I?

I answer to a name, male or female, but am I that? Or, am I something more than that? Who am I? What am I?" Seriously ask yourself that question. Don't try to give an answer yourself. Who will give you the answer? Your Guardian Archangel will give you the answer some time when he finds that you'll understand him.

In time the Guardian Archangel will answer you through intuition and enlightenment. But you must ask that question! Christ promised, "Ask and it will be given to you. Knock and it will be opened to you." So ask yourself and your Guardian Angel, "Who am I, what am I? When he feels it is the best moment for you to understand, you will get the reply from your Guardian Angel who will say to you, "My love, you are a god. We are gods. Wake up."

Go deeper into this dialog and ask, "Should I be afraid of the death of my material body? Does that mean that my Self will cease to exist with the death of my martial body?" The answer you get is that each and every night when you think and feel you are entering nothingness in deep dreamless sleep, for a time you seem to cease to exist. Yet each and every morning you recompose yourself and re-enter your material body. Just contemplate that.

Take deep comfortable breaths and slowly start feeling you are in your material body again.

Chapter Fifteen
THE KISS OF AN ARCHANGEL

Now, what is the difference among all the Archangelic orders having an Archangelic Self different from the self-consciousness of the human beings? There is a great difference, of course. The Archangelic orders have an Archangelic Self. Billions of Michaels are composing the order of the Michaels, the Lords of Fire and Light. And billions of Gabriels are composing the Archangelic order of the Gabriels. And billions and billions of Raphaels are composing the order of Raphaels. And each of these has its Archangelic Self-consciousness. But, the one does not differ from the other. They are feeling the same. Knowing one Archangel of any order you know all the Archangels of that order. The Archangel's consciousness is united. So, one Gabriel represents all the Gabriels, and one Michael represents all the Michaels. But, no man represents any other man (as a personality). ~ Daskalos

THE TEACHING

As the Guardian Angel watches over and cares for our personality, other orders called the Archangels of the Elements, care for our bodies. You can see evidence of their care in the healing of wounds and mending of bones. You can feel their presence in your body as warmth, health and vitality. You can even feel their pulsations as the beats of your heart and the involuntary flow of your breath.

In the 13th century, Saint, Thomas Aquinas declared, "Angels transcend every religion, every philosophy, and every creed. In fact Angels have no religion as we know it. Their existence precedes every religious system that has ever existed on Earth." Archangels are not theoretical abstractions from some antiquated mythology; they are ever-present Spirit Beings who love and care for each one of us. For Daskalos and the Researchers of Truth, they are real brothers of Spirit who are well known and well loved. The seven Archangelic orders working in our bodies are called the Archangels of the Elements. They are so named because they are using the elements Earth, Fire, Water and the Ethers in building and maintaining our bodies as well as all the universes. Some of these orders are more approachable than others.

The Archangels never come out of their oneness with God and experience separateness in the Worlds of Existence as the human race does. In the process of our humanization, a ray of our Eternal Spirit Being Self is projected into the Worlds of Separation. We say "our' Spirit Being Self, which is not perfectly accurate because as a personality self, neither the Spirit nor Soul belongs to the personality – it is the other way around. Now this projection creates a temporary expression…an existence in time, space and place. This is our human nature and it is this human in nature personality-self that we mistakenly think is our Real Self.

While a human being is in the Worlds of Separation, The Archangels of the Elements serve them unceasingly. They serve according to how the Archangels are using the Mind Super-Substance in their work.

The ones that are most approachable are:
- Archangel Michael, who's primary element is the fire element.

Michael vibrates light, fire, and all the shades of the red color. Fire is the heat of the sun and the heart of the planet. In our body Michael provides warm red blood.

- Archangel Gabriel is the Soul of the Earth. This Archangelic order rules over the element of liquids such as water, which covers about 75% of the surface of our material planet and the 75% of the water composing our material body. Gabriel also helps bring peace and harmony to our Psychical Body. His color is sky-blue.

- Archangel Raphael is the result of the cooperation between Gabriel and Michael. His color is violet; he is the governor of Etheric Vitality and its electro-magnetic force. Etheric Vitality is Raphael's element. He supplies our bodies with power and strength.

- Archangel Uriel coordinates the work of all the Archangels of the Elements. He vibrates silvery-white light. Uriel keeps order and harmony within each of our bodies and between them. Macrocosmically and microcosmically he is the Great Balancer.

These four Archangels appear in the scriptures of the Christians, Muslims, Jews, and in the pre-existing Persian and Egyptian Cultures. "Arch" is from the Greek word meaning principal or chief, so the word Archangel means chief angel. It is important to note that man did not name these Archangels. Their names are the actual sounds their vibration make, as reported by those who have come into direct contact with them. For example, the ancient Egyptians knew Archangel Raphael as Ra-Fa-El. In their language, Ra was the Sun, Fa was vibration and El meant God as it does to the Hebrews and other ancient cultures. Thus, Ra-Fa-El means the Sun vibration God. He is the lord of the Etheric Vitality giving us energy and power.

The Archangels of any order constitute one whole system whereas the Human Beings are a race of billions of individuals. The Greek Orthodox Church still mentions this in their services, but how many people on Earth really know what that means? It means that as a system, each one of these Archangelic Beings is identical to every other one in their class. They have the exact same range of vibration. The countless numbers of Michaels are alike in every way. The myriads of Gabriels are all the same; there is no distinction between them.

Some Archangels, on occasion, take the Human Form and manifest themselves physically on Earth. You can find accounts of this in the Catholic Bible and in the scriptures from other traditions. They have always done this, they are doing it today and they will continue to do so in order to serve man and the Divine Plan. For those who have seen them, they typically appear as very handsome young men without any feathery wings. "They are not birds," Daskalos often quipped. What they do have is streams of radiant light coming off and up from their shoulders, which have often been depicted by artists as wings.

Once in a Stoa Lesson Daskalos said, "If you study other serious religions, you will see that most have mentioned the

Archangels and Angels but they are not telling much about them or their work in the Creation. Maybe the other masters did not dare to reveal it. Nevertheless, it is now time for the people to know the whole truth."

Daskalos paused slightly as his eyes scanned his audience and in a soft voice said, "A human being is from an Archangelic order."

Then as if challenging himself, he spoke very firmly stating, "How do I know this? By reading it in a book? No, it is by coming in contact with them and knowing them directly."

Wanting to give more meaning to his revealing lesson on the Archangelic orders, Daskalos interjected; "Let me give you an example, you have the colorless white light. As it passes through a prism, the white light becomes the colors of the spectrum. The light becomes the reds, blues yellows and so on. In the same way these Spirit Beings are passing through the Logos and classify themselves to their Archangelic orders according to the Divine Plan."

The word spectrum is from the Latin language and literally means "appearance." So we see the seven colors of light appear from within the white light by means of a prism. The prism did not create the seven colors. The prism only causes the inherent colors within the white light to appear. Similarly, rays of Life-Light stream forth from Spirit Beings pass through the prism of God's Will-Pleasure and the seven Archangelic orders appear. Like the colored light of the spectrum, these glorious Archangelic orders have not been created. They appear when these luminous rays pass through the Archangelic Archetypes within the Divine Plan.

The Archangels are Holy Spiritual Beings who project

themselves into the universes that they build and govern without losing their At-One-Ment with God. The Archangels are of the Eternal Now, so they do not really understand what time is in the way we do. Conversely, other Eternal Spirit Beings extend a ray of their Eternal Self from the realms of Beingness to become humanized and incarnate in the time, space and place Worlds of Existence. As human beings, we have a sense of being separate from God whereas the Archangels do not. Upon the completion of our human incarnations, we return to the Realms of Beingness enriched by our experiences during all our incarnations in a way Archangels cannot comprehend. Coming from an Archangelic order makes humankind a real brother with the other Archangels.

Now, imagine two children who are brothers. They were born and have always lived in a room full of light. Yet, in this condition they cannot really understand what light is. Without the experience of darkness, they cannot fully comprehend the light in which they dwell. Now, take one child out of the light temporarily and show him the dark of night. Now that child will understand light much better than his brother who has never seen darkness.

Something similar occurs with the Archangels and man. The Archangels never leave the realms of light to enter into duality and experience the phenomena of darkness. They never feel separated from God as humans in existence do. Yet, human beings have a distinct advantage upon their return to the realms of light in Beingness. Because, they have gained a more complete understanding of the created Worlds of Existence by experience than the Archangels. Throughout all our incarnations, the Archangels are, were, and always will be our caring companions and guides. It brings them joy when we cooperate with their work and guidance. It is time we come to understand and know them better.

No one can say for sure how many Archangelic orders there are but we do know what other advanced masters have found in all past times by raising their consciousness to high enough levels to contact the Holy Archangels, and we can know them through our own direct experiences. What is knowable to the human intelligence is that there are different orders of these Archangelic Beings. The Archangels get key positions according to the work they do. Others are getting secondary and tertiary positions according to the work they carry out.

Human beings know very little about the highest orders because they stay within Absolute Beingness, God, without changing their nature. They do not work in the manifestation but in the Laws and Causes behind the manifestation.

Christ said, "You are gods - sons and daughters of the Almighty." So we are not inferior to the Archangels as Spirit-Beings. These super intelligent brothers will help us understand what the Selfhood really is. A Spirit-Soul-Self is a god and is not just a limited personality composed of conflicting strengths and weakness. Where are the Archangels of the Elementals performing their great works? Everywhere! They have the Archangelic Super-Consciousness, which allows them to work completely outside the conception of time, space and place. This is not so understandable to humans unless we can free ourselves from our bodies by making the three Exosomatosis and enter that same state of Super-Consciousness as the Archangels.

As we said, our Guardian Archangel is always in a state of attunement and At-One-Ment with us. The other Archangels are not in At-One-Ment with us but we can approach and attune to them. Approaching the Archangel Michael, we feel his warmth. Approaching the Archangel Gabriel, we feel his sweetness. Archangel Raphael is more expressive so as soon as we start to approach him, he immediately responds and we may feel a shiver or rush of energy.

Sometimes the Archangels kiss us. When they kiss us they are embracing us. This means that they enter in our Etheric Double and we feel the warmth of their love and light radiating within us. How does this happen? The Archangels have their Archangelic form, but they can take any form they like. Sometimes they like to take the Human Form. The Human Form they take does not need an organ like the brain or heart though, in these same areas of their form, there are centers of pulsating radiations. So when they enter our Etheric Double and embrace us, the pulsing radiations from their Heart Center comes into harmony with our Heart Center. This is their kiss of love for us. When this happens to you, maybe you will feel like you are like butter melting in the hot sun and you know nothing else but love. This pure selfless love is dissolving everything else in you but love. If you allow yourself to surrender totally into it, you may experience what Daskalos called a "sweet slumber." This is their kiss of perfect love for you.

THE PRACTICE: OVERVIEW

Those that are sincere enough in their research of these things and are willing to undergo the discipline of training, can come in conscious contact with the Archangels. By Attuning to them we can reach them and they will teach us. If we silence our emotions and still our thoughts enough we can attune to them. We make our approach through different levels of attunement. To learn this powerful skill we start by attuning to what we want to know. At first we attune to simple things and then to higher things and then to the Holy Archangels. To attune to the Archangels we must raise our vibrations and thus our consciousness to their level. Do not expect them to come to you. Coming in contact with them they are willing and wanting to teach us the secrets of their own elements: Fire, Water, and Energy.

We have to qualify ourselves before they will teach us. Then they can and will teach you so many things that even an Earthly master is not allowed to tell you, but you must approach them first by tuning into them, entering their aura through the vibrations of their colors and enjoy their wisdom – this is attunement. So we practice visualization with colors sometimes as light, sometimes as flames and sometimes with their full Archangelic Form. In order to contact them we need to be able to reproduce the colors and hues in visualization. Otherwise we cannot know the various ranks of the Archangels and Angels. There are many exercises and meditations to help us develop awareness of the Archangelic Orders and our ability to cooperate, which are found in the Esoteric Practices and Gates to the Light books.

Many of the exercises are done, in a visualized pyramid, which is like our workshop for certain meditations. Within the four-sided pyramid, which we construct with Psycho-Noetical light, we come into intimate contact with these Divine Beings. When standing upright within the pyramid Archangel Michael appears on our right side, while on the left side Raphael manifests, and behind us Gabriel comes forth. Uriel, who remains formless, is experienced as silvery white light looking like a misty cloud on the floor of the pyramid. The triangle facing you is the space for God the Father, Christ Logos, and the Holy Spirit.

After Attunement it is possible with training to go further in At-One-Ment with them. At-One-Ment means to be one with them, which is the assimilation of your self-consciousness to their Self Consciousness. Really the only thing keeping us apart from our brothers, the Archangels, is our own ignorance, and it is our research of the truth that burns away the foggy shrouds of ignorance.

THE PRACTICE: INTRODUCTORY ARCHANGEL MEDITATION

Relax completely your body. The Holy Archangels allow you to call it yours, although it is theirs, not yours. Call it yours. You are living in it. Now breathe and feel you are in your material body, from the toes of your feet to your forehead.

You feel you are in the material body, yet you don't know who you are. The only thing you are feeling is that you are living in your gross material body. It is under the care of the Holy Archangels of the Elements. All the hairs on your body are numbered. The Archangels are making each one of them grow. You don't know that but the Holy Archangels do. They are working for you in your gross material body. They give you the right to use it as your own.

At this moment the Holy Archangels are working in you, loving you, making all the organs in your material bodies function properly for you. They are providing health in the eyes so that you may see. Mentally, send them thanks. They will understand it and they will feel pleased.

The Holy Archangels are living in your heart. Here you will have contact with the great intelligences called he Archangels of the Elements. They work tirelessly in your bodies-loving you. What do you offer them? Nothing! What do they offer you? Everything! They are always loving us and waiting for us to join them.

Chapter Sixteen
ACROSS TIME AND SPACE

Everything that has existed, was conceived, thought of and that has lived on the planet is in what we call the Cosmic Consciousness of the planet, the Planetary Cosmic Consciousness, which is not, of course, the Solar Cosmic Consciousness of the whole solar system. Then more and more to the Cosmic Consciousness of the universes. So, you have the individual and the common Cosmic Consciousness in every human being, but you have at the same time everything registered in the planetary Cosmic Consciousness. Why do we call it cosmic? Because it is the Absolute Super substance of the Mind.

What did those enlightened ones in the past see in that Cosmic Consciousness? They saw the planet and its conditions in various times. At the beginning volcanos, the unfriendly atmosphere, difficult things in life. One can see all that. One can see different phenomena of life on the planet suitable for that time: huge serpentine beasts going here and there attacking each other, and things like that. Then, we can see the human beings in the caves, holding just a club in their hands to protect themselves from the wild animals around them, and killing smaller animals for themselves to eat. ~ Daskalos

THE TEACHING:

To understand Daskalos' description of the creation of the material universe it is important to know where and how he did his research. Daskalos frequently emphasized in his lessons that the best and most reliable source of information on anything was in the Cosmic Consciousness, the Universal Memory - the so-called Akashic

Records.

Today and in past time, mystics who have raised their consciousness to very high levels have been able to access the Cosmic Consciousness. We might think of it like the memory of God, and God remembers everything. Literally everything that has happened to us, or on Earth, or in the solar system, or in the galaxy and beyond is recorded in perfect accuracy in the Divine Memory of the Cosmic Consciousness. What is recorded there is not only from the material universe but also in the Psychical and Noetical Worlds of Existence. So a mystic or sincere Researcher of Truth can attune to and come in contact with the Cosmic Consciousness and perform research.

In this Divine archive, one can see anything that has ever happened in the past as living scenes. Not two-dimensional scenes like on a flat movie screen but the mystic will experience himself directly in a living three-dimensional like scene watching events unfold. The scenes contain every detail associated with that event. You can see people moving, working and talking; you can see any birds or animals that were present in the event and even insects. If another mystic were to access that same recorded scene, they could only see the exact same recording, because that is what it is – a recording. So everyone's actions, thoughts, emotions, desires and words are impeccably preserved in this recording. We are constantly contributing to the quality of the Cosmic Consciousness according to thoughts, desires and emotions we harbor and express.

Every human being has what is called in psychology, a sub-consciousness or sub-conscious mind. Here permanently recorded and mostly inaccessible to the common person is everything that we have seen, said, heard, felt, thought, or done throughout our whole life. Even those things we saw but gave no attention to are recorded in perfect accuracy. All of our good and not so good thoughts and feelings simultaneously record in both the Cosmic Consciousness and our own sub-consciousness. It does not matter if a desire or thought became an action or not it is still very real. So it has been actualized in the heart and mind and recorded faithfully for all time.

From the ancient times, mystics, yogis, sages and masters have spoken of the incredible recording capacity of the Cosmic Consciousness. It is here in this Cosmic Memory that the record of the entire creation lies perfectly preserved. It is the imprinting quality of the Mind, which does this recording in the Cosmic Memory, just like it does in our memory.

Each of our incarnations stays forever in the Cosmic Memory as a living record. Recorded there is every detail of every past incarnation of everyone. Nevertheless, similar to any recording, a master who contacts it cannot change the original imprinted recording. We all create a new recording in each new lifetime. Ideally, the quality of what we are recording will improve in each new incarnation, but no one can alter any recording already stored in the Universal Memory. So those stories created by fiction writers about going back in time and changing events in the past to alter the future are just that - fiction.

Now, to witness what occurred with the creation of our solar system billions of years ago, a mystic must enter the Cosmic Consciousness, which is everywhere. So it is not a matter of going anywhere to reach this Universal Memory, it is a matter of raising one's consciousness to high enough levels to contact it and, even then, such a researcher has to be able to scroll back in time to the point of its original occurrence. A Master with powerful concentration can enter the records of distant past civilizations and see everything that has occurred.

The entire material universe is within the Super-Substance of the Mind, which constantly records all that transpires. Daskalos' explanation of Creation comes from his reading of the Universal Memory directly. This he does in a state of Super-Consciousness. However, Daskalos qualified that in order to find the records of the distant past one must develop the ability to, "Play with time - To see in a few minutes what has occurred in centuries." A mystic can see all the things from the past, because even the past is in the Eternal Present. Reading what has taken place over thousands of centuries and recorded in the Cosmic Consciousness can be seen in minutes.

One of the prime characteristics of God in expression is motion, vibration. In the creation of the material universe, Daskalos first describes the Mind Super-Substance in motion. In his reading, he sees a mass of Mind Super-Substance rotating around itself manifesting first as the element of firelight. This is the beginning of the material universe and all the galaxies, solar systems and planets. It is the point where the material universe begins its sudden outward expansion.

This enormous sphere of firelight has unimaginable force and spins on its axis. As it spins it is hurling off many, many other fiery balls of light in all directions. These become the central suns or nucleus of the billions of galaxies in the three-dimensional universe. Again, these fiery central suns repeat the same process; rotating and casting off massive quantities of smaller fiery balls spinning at incredible speeds, which become the hundreds of billions of suns of all the individual solar systems composing a single galaxy. Our sun is one of these. Again, these fiery suns in turn are whirling around on their axis too and are ejecting other still smaller fiery balls that over the course of thousands of centuries are destined to become the planets. These too cast off one, or more, smaller fiery balls, which cool down to become a planet's moons. All of these heavenly bodies are stabilizing at a certain distance from the fiery sphere that ejected them. Each one is finding just the proper orbit based on its size, speed and mass. All are obeying the physical laws of centripetal and centrifugal force according to the universal laws of balance and order.

In the ancient Hindu creation myth, Brahma the creator God breathes out and manifests all of creation in the process. In this story, the universe continues to expand out until Brahma stops his exhalation and begins his in breath, drawing this expanding universe back to its origin. Drawn back in by his inhalation the universe is destroyed. Then Brahma once again breathes out and re-manifests the universe. This creation and destruction of the universe continually repeats over enormous epochs of time. This mythological account of creation is thousands of years old and yet the basic dynamics of it coincide with that of the current scientific explanation.

Now compare Daskalos' account and the mythological Hindu creation story with the conventional view held by orthodox science. Stephen Hawkins (British theoretical physicist and mathematician) describes a very similar scenario as the Hindu myth, called

the Hot Big Bang. The Big Bang theory states in the beginning, plasma (supper heated gas) was concentrated into a very small volume. The gravitational compaction of this plasma in a small space produced unimaginably high temperature. This super condensed hot gaseous state; full of energy caused an enormous explosion that science calls the Hot Big Bang. From this one enormous fiery explosion the galaxies, suns and planets eventually coalesced over eons of time. Beginning with the initial big bang the universe began expanding. Currently it is still expanding and the distance between all the galaxies and everything in the galaxies is increasing as the universe is cooling.

This parallels what Daskalos and others mystics are saying from their research. This should not be a surprise. Scientific research often comes to prove empirically what mystical research has previously stated. Hundreds of years before science discovered the circulatory and nervous systems the mystics in India, China and elsewhere described them in detail.

Orthodox science also theorizes that this expanding universe will one day reach a limit and loose its momentum outward and will begin to collapse slowly back on itself. They speculate that the planets, suns and galaxies in the universe will draw back toward their origin. In Hinduism, this would correspond to the metaphorical in breath of Brahma. As all the matter of the universe, returns to its point of origin a gravitational field of unimaginable strength will compress all matter so much that it will initiate another Hot Big Bang. Again, a new material universe will begin its outward expansion once again only to reach a limit and begin collapsing again. This scientific theory of the creation follows surprisingly close to the ancient mythologized Hindu creation story.

Returning to Daskalos' account, initially these blazing spheres of light are only manifesting the element of fire. Yet, within the firelight all the other elements are contained in a yet un-manifested state. One of the fiery balls that spin off from our solar system's sun is thrust outward spiraling in the absolute zero temperature of space, and cools over eons of time to become our temporary home - planet Earth. It finds its place of balance, orbiting just a certain distance from its source our sun. Over thousands of centuries, the surface of this fiery ball begins to cool. As the surface cools it forms a crust, which cracks back open releasing molten lava, cooling down, crusting over, and then cracking open again releasing more lava and suffocating clouds of gases. There were literally millions and millions of active volcanoes during this period.

This process continues for hundreds of centuries. Gases released during this process are held by gravity around the newly formed planet. So the water element is seen forming in rings of clouds with the smoke from the volcanoes. Seven of these cloud rings were created, covering about a third of the planet. These massive cloudbanks were moving and together created a shroud covering the entire planet that was so thick, the sun light could not penetrated it. The crust of the Earth was very hot at this time; but it was cooling as the clouds heavily laden with water vapor hung thousands of miles above the planet. These gases formed a primitive atmosphere in the space between the Earth and the clouds.

Eventually the water vapors in the clouds precipitated out in a series of many deluges, raining down on the hot Earth. This created new conditions on the planet. The rains hit the hot surface of the planet cooling the planet more and releasing steamy water vapors, which returned to the atmosphere and rained back down on the planet repeatedly. This cycle continued for ages and ages. This process created oceans, lakes, rivers and the necessary chemistry and conditions developed over time to support life forms on the planet. By the time the last deluge of rain had fallen, there was a new environment created. The orbital distance of the newly formed Earth varies 93 to 95 million miles from the sun. This the perfect distance to support life. A slight variation in this distance and the planet would be inhabitable.

Now the human beings found themselves on Earth in a solid body after coming from a more refined state called Eden in the Bible. As the story in the Old Testament states; Archangel Michael with a whirling sword of fire kicks Adam and Eve out of the Garden of Eden for disobeying God. Regarding this mythological story of the Fall of Man as a means to explain man's arrival on the planet Daskalos firmly declared, "Nonsense! It is the Divine Plan. There is no such a thing as the Fall. That is a Jewish invention. No! This is the Divine Plan."

We read in the Bible that after Archangel Michael exiles Adam and Eve from Eden they were dressed in "Tunics of Skin," which is a symbolic way of saying they incarnated on Earth in solid bodies with skin. In the entire physical universe with all the hundreds of billions of galaxies each with hundreds of billions of solar systems and each solar system with many planets it is myopically egocentric to think that only our planet has the human and animal life. This same story is repeated throughout the three dimensional universe.

So in the Cosmic Consciousness, creation is seen first manifesting as the element of fire and then the other elements manifested from it. The ancient Greek philosopher, Heraclitus (540? - 475? BC) considered the founder of Greek metaphysics, also taught that fire is the primordial source of all matter. We also know that the fire element is also expressed as heat and light. What exactly is light? What we call light is only a small range of etheric vibrations, electromagnetic radiations that are detectable by our material eyes. All light that is above and below that range is what we call darkness, which is really just an imperceptible condition. We learn in school that frequencies of light in a slightly lower range than our eyes can see is called infra-red and the frequency slightly higher is called ultra violet. It is black to us yet in reality it is light. We also understand that the same is true of sound; the human ear can detect a relative narrow range of frequencies (110 to 880 Hz). Sound vibrations lower or higher than the material ear can register we call silence. Likewise, what we call solid matter is also only a narrow range of vibrations detectable by the human body's sense of touch. We understand material substance as solid by touching it. If it vibrates at the same range of vibration as our hand, then to us it is solid. The Psychical and Noetical substance composing the Psychical and Noetical Worlds vibrates in a higher range of frequencies than our material body and so remains undetectable by our material body's sense of touch.

As seen from another point of view, the highest frequencies of the light give us understanding. The Mind is light and this light is different from the light at lower states, which humans interpret as emotions and feelings. These give us the sense of being attracted or repelled. In still lower states we have the Light in the world of matter as etheric vibrations emanating from a fire or the sun, and even at this level there is a big difference in the light. We have the light coming from a burning log. Is that the same light as the light coming from the thermo nuclear furnace we call our sun? Is everything either light or darkness? There is no real darkness. Everything is the Mind and this Mind Super-Substance is the light. This means that everything created by the Mind is light manifesting at different rates of vibration. Every plane of existence, the Noetical Planes, The Psychical Planes and the Material Plane and their Etheric Doubles exists because there is light in them. As a Spirit-Soul we are the Divine Everlasting Light, but as a human being entering the Worlds of Existence what we experience as darkness is light in a range that is imperceptible to us. So we misidentify the light that is beyond the range of perception to our eye as darkness.

Light can be classified into seven degrees of intensity or luminosities. As we have these seven degrees of luminosity of the light, we have the seven veils or shadows of the light. To have any shadow we first must have the light, which is the reality. Then you must have a surface on which the shadow falls, which means there must be something in between the light and the surface that is casting a shadow. Darkness and shadows are not real. For example, in the Valley of the Kings in Egypt, there are many tombs that have been sealed shut long ago. For thousands of years, the interior of these tombs have not seen the light of the sun. The walls and roof of the tombs blocked the light and the tombs remained in "darkness," all the while the brilliance of the desert sun was blazing around the tomb. The moment the tombs were opened by archeologists and exposed to the light from the sun, the darkness was dispelled. If darkness and shadows were a reality where did they go when the tomb was opened and the light entered? Darkness and shadows are not real. What is real is the light and the in between thing that cast the shadow.

There have been many in the past and current times that have reached beyond the shadows and attained the light of Self-Realization. The vast majority of people however are still concentrated on their personality-self that is but a shadow of their radiant Spirit-Soul Self cast in time, space and place. Today and in all past times, people have fallen under the illusion to think they are only the expressions (thoughts, feelings, desires and behaviors) of this shadow of their real Self. As a Spirit-Soul, we are the Life-Light that is casting the shadow.

What are the effects of light? If you are in the darkest of a moonless night you cannot see what is all around you. There is not enough light to stimulate the sense of sight in your material eyes, but when the sun comes with its abundant visible light then you will say you "see" what is around you. Exactly how is this light making sight possible? The material light rays coming from the sun take about thirteen minutes to reach the Earth but they cannot penetrate solid objects, so the light only strikes the surface of the objects and is reflected off the front of that surface in all directions. The light reflected off the object carries the imprint of the shape, the texture and color of that object. Now, these reflected light rays carry a miniature imprint of the details of the object that enters the pupils of our eyes and strikes on the optic nerve and creates an irritation. Up to this point the light coming from the sun, striking the object and irritating the optic nerve has been visible material light. This irritation is transferred to the brain and interpreted as the sense of seeing and feeling that we are in the environment with all the objects we see. The irritation coming from the optic nerve to the brain is only a vibration. There is no visible material light passing through the optic nerve or in the brain and yet we experience these non-visible vibrations as the sense of seeing objects illuminated by the sun.

Since there is no visible light in our brain, what kind of light is making us see? It is the ethereal vibrations that are passed to the brain that we are interpreting as seeing. With your eyes closed, you may recall images you have seen with your eyes open. You can recall an object's shape, texture, color and its relationship to other objects all of which appears to you as if you were seeing images in the material light. We call this memory.

Again, there is no light in your brain, so in what light are we seeing the memorized images? There are the illuminated images you see in a dream when your body is totally asleep. Are those images real? Are the images you recall in memory with your eyes closed real? Or is it only the images you see with your eyes open real? There is no light in your brain, so any images you see with your eyes open or closed are real and all interpretations of ethereal vibrations. The real question is, "who is interpreting these etheric vibrations?" It takes deep contemplation and meditation to enter into the meaning of light, shadows and sight.

The Cosmic Consciousness is everywhere, which means we are in it and it is in each of us. Not only can we see the development of our planet recorded in the Cosmic Consciousness, our own long development through all our successive incarnations is also recorded there. We can consider each of our past incarnations a book we have written. In this lifetime we are writing in the new book of our current incarnation and this is what captures all our attention now. We do not remember the good or bad pages we have written in our books during past incarnations and yet it is all there recorded in the Cosmic Consciousness.

Who or what specifically is doing all this writing? The writing is done by the elements we are creating and expressing all the time.

Our past thoughts, feelings, and behaviors are Elementals and they are accurately chronicled and retained as living memories within the Cosmic Consciousness. Therein are recorded the total of all our experiences and this recording is living because it is made of the Mind vitality, which itself is living. When your personality self is assimilated with your Inner Self you will gain access to all the books that you have written in the past. So in this regard we could metaphorically say; the Cosmic Consciousness is like a library, with shelves containing all the many books of past incarnations that you have written.

When you reach this level, there is no one and nothing

preventing you from picking up a book of a past incarnation and looking at it. By reading your book on any past incarnation you can experience again what was enjoyable. What about the very painful parts in your past incarnation when you suffered? Do those parts now give you the experience of pain? By the time you reach this level of consciousness where you can access the past records, these parts will not give you pain, because you have removed the vices that give you things like guilt and shame.

So when you reach the highest level of consciousness you realize you have not lost anything. You will not even lose the short-lived personalities you cherished so much in your past incarnations. You will find all these books of past incarnations perfectly preserved. So there is no loss in achieving Self-Realization there is only gaining. In this state you can attune to any past incarnation and know it. If you want to you can by means of At-One-Ment enter that living Elemental of a past incarnated personality. But in reaching the glorious liberation of Self-Realization why would you want to enter the limited shell of your old personality?

PRACTICE: OVERVIEW

On the spiritual journey, our passage from the shadows to the light, many people read many books on the subject from many different sources. There is nothing wrong with comparative study like this. At some point you may ask yourself, "What am I truly gaining by reading a lot of books about spirituality?" Of course you can gain a considerable amount of knowledge, but if you cannot put it to use what good is it? If you learn to put this knowledge to use; that is good and it will produce lasting results. That is the whole point: it is absolutely necessary that we learn how to make use of the spiritual information we gather. It has to be planted and cultivated in the soil of your own life; otherwise it remains like a beautiful pressed flower. A pressed flower between the pages of a book is lovely to look it but does not have the beauty and vitality that a living flower has.

Simply claiming that you are a mystic because you know something of the mystical teachings will not produce deep and lasting results. A long time ago on Cyprus, a person came to Daskalos claiming he was an advanced mystic; because he believed he had achieved a very high level of spirituality by studying the mystical teachings of the Rosicrucian, the Arcane and the Theosophist schools. However, as Daskalos pointed out, "The only thing he had achieved out of all this knowledge was an inflated egoism." Because he believed he knew everything about the mystical teachings and the people who did not know about spiritual matters seemed like inferior insects to him. This is a very self-destructive belief because, in truth, as you really advance in the research of truth, you will not feel more proud and superior. You feel more and more humble.

The man had told Daskalos that he had passed all the levels of the Rosicrucian school. The Rosicrucian, Theosophical and Arcane schools have truth in their teachings so it is not their fault this man's studies made him feel so superior to others. This older man had been studying since Daskalos was a small child and had a lot of theoretical knowledge about the Chakras, the Kundalini energy and told Daskalos about it.

Daskalos asked him, "Have you succeeded in having

Exosomatosis, a conscious out of body experience?" The man said he did some exercises once and felt he was out of his body but he got scared and returned to his body and never tried it again.

During conversations with people Daskalos always tried to give a needed lesson and sometimes he would test you by throwing out bait for your egoism; just to reveal to you how active your egoism was. So as the man revealed what he thought was right, Daskalos feigned a reaction to what the man believed. Immediately the man lost all his self-control and spoke down to Daskalos saying, "What a pity, that people think you are something great." Then he swore at Daskalos and called him "worthless." In absolute kindness, Daskalos replied, "Let's see, my friend, you lost control, got angry and swore.

Did you really learn anything from all those years of study?" At another point in the conversation the man complained and accused his workers of stealing and backstabbing him. Again Daskalos delivered his lesson saying, "My friend, your knowledge has not helped you at all."

Daskalos' point was that real spiritual advancement comes by implementing the knowledge we study. Killing anger is the first labor a Researcher of Truth undertakes. From the start a researcher must put this knowledge to use and continue to integrate it more and more in to their life as he or she progresses. So parallel to the theoretical knowledge we must have the practical use of it. We must practice and live what we learn. Beware of those who gain powers but do not or cannot use them for good. Even in the system for the Research of Truth, there have been few that progressed but misused their newfound powers. The advanced teachers in this system are aware of such things and unhappily will block these people's powers.   This speaks to the importance of developing a pure and loving heart simultaneously as we gain knowledge and power. Because, without love and compassion what will people use their mystical knowledge and powers for?

There is a connection between our sub-consciousness and the Cosmic Consciousness, but it is not wise to try to prematurely enter the mansion of Cosmic Consciousness before putting the house of our own sub-consciousness in order. So we must establish the habit of checking what impressions come to our attention through the five senses, how we interpret or misinterpret them and store them in our sub-consciousness. We have to find out what these impressions and interactions are creating in our personality: Anger? Peace? Dissatisfaction? Satisfaction? All our experiences either give us degrees of pleasing impressions or degrees of painful impressions. As we study those experiences that give us pain and those experiences that give us pleasure it reveals much about the interests of our personality and the quality of our character. When classifying our experiences in the degrees of pain it caused or in the degrees of pleasure it caused, we also must ask why. Why does a certain experience give you pleasure and others give you pain? Why does a certain experience that gave you pain in the past, today not give you any pain? Why have certain pleasurable experiences in the past, no longer give you pleasure when you experience them today? Which leads to a larger question: What is pain and what is pleasure?

We must keep the question "why?" in mind as we bravely examine our sub-conscious, conscious behaviors and reactions to the experiences in our life. In order to know the truth, we must be the ones that answer all the "whys." We make this kind of self-analysis not only to know how we are being influenced by our life experiences, but the real aim is to disassociate our sense of Self from these reactions in order to find the Soul-Self and enjoy its tranquil nature. By investigating what has been stored in our subconsciousness we can bring to the surface of our memory a disagreeable experience with another person, look at it dispassionately and make any corrections in our attitude. We can then send the appropriate energies to that person and bring down the tensions between you without having to say anything to that person. This is a way for anyone, highly educated or not, to face such difficulties, and silently work to dissolve conflicts.

THE PRACTICE: AN EXERCISE

Start by concentrating in your whole material body. Feel every muscle completely relaxed. Feel being in your whole body from your tips of your toes to the top of your head.

You are feeling in the whole material body but who are you who can feel living in your material body? You are a personality living in a material body. Now recompose this personality with the feelings, desires and thoughts.

That is you as a personality, an entity that is now concentrating in the material body and feeling it is yours. Now ask yourself these questions:

Who am I living in this material body and concentrate in it and feel being in it?

How can I develop my self-consciousness to be able to feel being in my Psychical and Noetical Body?

How can I control my emotions, desires and master my reactions to life experiences? How can I control my thoughts to become a master of the Mind?

Now bring to your consciousness a person you had difficulty with. Maybe you have negativity or hatred in your sub-consciousness for this person and maybe they have the same for you.

But both of you are human beings with weaknesses and faults. Visualize this person in your mind's eye.

Do not see them as angry but clearly visualize that person happy and smiling.

Breathe deeply and comfortably and make your Heart Center a sun of clear rosy light. See this rosy sun in your Heart Center radiating rays of light in all directions.

Now, you see that person's face washed in the brilliant rosy light that is radiating from your heart and see them smiling.

Mentally tell that person that you love them. Never mind the difficult moments you had with them. The difficulties are personality issues. While in reality, the Inner Self of both of you is a god.

Appeal to that god in them and not to their personality. Work from a higher level.

Send that person your love and see them happy and de-energize any negativity in you about them. This brings balance and if you do not want to be in contact, ok, bless them to go their way in peace. If you do want to be in contact with that person, let it be on much better terms in the future.

Our family, friends, acquaintances and especially those who think they are our enemies are in need of our love not our complaints and hatreds. Complaints and hatreds are very strong toxins poisoning our hearts, minds and even our material bodies.

Chapter Seventeen
LIFE IN THE HIGHER WORLDS

The material world is Mind matter. Mind solid is matter. In the Psychical World we have Mind substance. The substance of the Mind can be formulated much more easily by thought of a man or an Archangel than the material we have on the material plane. Of course, we can formulate matter. We can take stones, Earth, water, and create (according to our mind) our constructions. But, it is not very easy to do so using the mind, the thought, the hands, or the machinery to make what we want. In the Psychical planes everything is much easier. Thought creates!

You'll find out and you will see when you develop your self-consciousness in the Psychical Body, that the Psychical Worlds are more real than the material world, because you can use concentration and observation there in a much better way than you do through the material brain. So, in the Psychical Worlds we have the environment created by the Holly Archangels, which is very, very lovely. Even the places we call hells. What are hells? They are very similar to the hells we have on the material plane. Instead of having a very lovely landscape men poison it. It is the same with a man being closed up in his thoughts, in a hell of his own. ~ *Daskalos*

THE TEACHING

Coming to the natural completion of our Circle of Possibilities on Earth our material body dies. When this happens to someone we know and love, we have the feeling we have lost our loved one. Do we actually know anything about our loved ones, children, or parents? What do we know of the real entity that lived in a material body? Likewise, what do you know about what you are in reality? We see the material body but when it dies we do not see the body anymore and many think the loved one has been lost and mistake them to be only the material body.

So we think we are losing our loved ones when they leave their material body, but they are leaving their material body every night during sleep just as you are. The next morning they come back and enter their material body again. This happens to all of us every twenty-four hours. When you return to the material body, you do not retain much or anything of what has happened to you in the Psychical Worlds while you were asleep. If you do, you only remember some impressions from your dream states. This is because there is a gap between your material brain and your Psychical Body and so you wake in the morning not knowing what happened and yet your personality is exactly like it was before going to sleep. You have the same way of living, thinking and feeling.

When you start practicing certain exercises you will come to know for sure that you are not the material body. Archangels are taking care of our body; while we often work against their work by the way we live. Who are you? If I ask you who are you, you will give me your name. It is a name given to you by the whim of your parents. You present yourself to others with your given name but you are not your name or the material body you are living in. When you pass over your personality will remain exactly as it was before you passed over. Your personality as you created it remains intact after the death of the material body. The only thing you lose in the change called death is your material body. It is all right; you have another better body, you have a Psychical Body that corresponds to the Psychical Worlds it inhabits and that body has the same appearance as your material body. If you had a scar on your arm in the material world, you will see it also on your Psycho-Noetical Body, which is the form of the personality. So when you pass over you retain your personality and its appearance.

Are you the personality? Many people make the mistake to think they are their material body and in the same way virtually everyone makes the mistake to think they are their personality.

Eventually you will discover you are not the personality but, for now, after passing over, you will continue your way of living in the Psychical Worlds. On Earth you live in a material body that has in it the personality, which is composed of your Psychical Body and Noetical Body. Now we all know something about how life works in the material world living in a material body. We move about in space, we see the light, trees, lakes, mountains and understand our environment. We use materials from the material plane to build houses and other constructions. The Psychical planes are the Psychical Body of the planet. Just as we have a Psychical and a Noetical Body, the Earth has a Psychical and a Noetical Body. The Earth is living and breathing; it is not a dead thing.

So after passing over people are recomposing themselves in the Psychical planes and those who live self-consciously there know it. Just as we can study and enjoy the environment on Earth, we can study and know the psychical environment. The psychical environment has everything we have on the material plane, and even more exists there. Those who know the physical planes know there are seven main planes each with seven sub-planes – 49 in all. All of these planes are in the planet, on the surface of the planet and thousands of miles around the Earth. So the Psychical planes are a whole lot bigger than the physical planet. Plus the conditions of this fourth dimension reality make these worlds even more unlimited. In the Psychical planes we continue our Circle of Possibilities where our life might be very short or much, much longer than our life on Earth.

What makes our life there shorter or longer has to do with our life lessons that we have to assimilate. In the Psychical planes there are houses, so people continue to live in houses there. How do we get these houses? In the material world we may inherit a house from our parents or relatives who passed over. Or we have them built for us. So after passing over it is the same, we find ourselves with our loved ones and family who have already passed over and are living in houses on the other side.

Typically after passing over the departed do not immediately leave the physical environment of the planet. They may find themselves living in the same house they own or rent now. A person knows the house they live in on Earth, they know what is in that house and so after the death of the material body they simply find themselves in that house. If someone wants a better house and knows how to build with thought using the art of visualization; they will be in that house they built with their thought.

Everything you have and use in the material world is also a product of thought. Look around you, everything you see started as an idea and has been built up by thought. Houses, cars, computers, smart phones and all that are the outcome of thoughts. It takes time, money and hard work to build on a thought to bring it into a three dimensional reality here on Earth. This not the way it is in the Psychical Worlds; there clear, strong thought creates -immediately. This is because in the Psychical Worlds the psychical substance is more malleable to our thoughts. I will tell you a corresponding experience I had in the Psychical Worlds.

In the early eighties, I designed a solar Earth sheltered home of a unique design but it was never built. I loved this design very much and always wanted to build it. So I was retaining the desire to create it. Sometime later when I was in the Psychical planes, I decided to build that house. So I started concentrating, visualizing that home and it immediately began to take form. It was a big construction, so I had to hold my concentration very steadily on the design without any distraction for it to take shape.

This reveals something else. Our unfulfilled desires we hold on to go with us to the Psychical Worlds at night and when we pass over. So if you had a strong desire to be a builder, an artist, a dancer, or anything; and you were not able to accomplish it on Earth. That desire will go with you when you enter the Psychical Worlds. In the higher worlds it will be much easier for you to achieve such a desire. Again, this is because the psychical substance takes form more easily by thought. You must have the skill of visualization. Now most people have not developed this skill consciously while on Earth.

Daskalos had an advanced student that he never met in person on Earth. The fellow passed over and one time Daskalos went to see him in the Psychical Worlds. The man had built a beautiful mansion on the other side; I believe Daskalos said it was built from fine marble. The student announced it was Daskalos' home he had built it for him to live in when he passed over. Daskalos laughed and said he was not in need of any house to live in on the other side. Daskalos did not need a house to live in the Psycho-Noetical Worlds, but the common person still feels this need.

So what happens when a common person passes over? Do they immediately have the skill of visualization? Can they build their own homes? No of course not, it takes training. On the other side there are people there that teach the departed the skills of visualization. Just like there are people here on Earth who teach other people how to work as a carpenter, a computer programmer or a scientist, there are personalities there who teach the new arrivals the art of visualization if they are interested. They teach them how to visualize and formulate psychical substance into whatever they want and need.

The Psychical planes are very nice places to live, even in the lower sub planes where there is less light. In the 49 sub planes there are varying degrees of light and some find it more comfortable in less light, others prefer being in environments with more light. God in its absolute wisdom cares for everything and everyone. In the sub planes we call hells the light is similar to the light on Earth just after sunset. In all the planes and sub planes there is light, beautiful light, peaceful light; blue light, emerald green light and golden light. As you ascend from the lower sub planes to higher ones it gets lighter and brighter. In the paradises the light is full and complete.

As we have said many times there are many hells and many

paradises in the worlds beyond Earth. We also have conditional hells and paradises that exist on Earth too. These continue on the other side. No one will be placed into any hell or paradise they are not already experiencing on Earth. This is because we build these conditional hells and paradises all the time with our thoughts and emotions here and in the worlds beyond. There is no judgment on us by God or an Archangel that puts us in a certain sub plane of the Psychical Worlds. The departed automatically just find themselves in an environment of one of the sub planes that is most suitable and comfortable for them to live. It is our conditions, our emotions, thoughts and desires that places us in the proper place in the worlds beyond. There is no obligation to stay on a lower sub plane if one wants to leave.

The work of the Invisible Helpers in these worlds is to show people in their hells the difference between two places, two conditions of life so they can compare. They are shown a much better place and way of living than the current conditions they are in; then they must choose. Unfortunately, very few decide to change because they get accustom to their hell and do not want to leave it. Since there are no boundaries between hells and paradises, the hell of one person can be the paradise of another.

That is the way it is here on Earth; some people enjoy living in the back bayous and swamps; this is their paradise. Take that swamp person to a formal White House dinner and it would be a hell for them. Take a high level official from a formal White House dinner and make him live in an inhospitable, snake-ridden swamp and that would be a hell for them.

As we said, there are helpers in the Psychical Worlds who try to aid the new arrivals by teaching them about the conditions of life there. Initially many people who cross over are in confusion. As long as they remain on the material plane in their Psychical Body, they might find themselves in their real material home and this puts them in great confusion. Being in a Psychical Body, which has higher more refined vibrations, they are now passing through the doors of their material house without opening them. They cannot open them because the vibrations of their psychical hand and body are much higher than the vibrations of physical materials and this confuses them. Because most people have not made an effort to study all these things, they have no basis to understand what is really happening. Happily the Lords of Mercy try to take the departed away from the material world that is causing them this anxiety.

There is nothing in the material world that does not have a psychical and Noetical counterpart and so going away from the material plane fully into the Psychical planes, they find there everything they left behind. That is because they have it in them, in their heart and mind. Concerning our material possessions, we often hear the old saying, "You can't take it with you." That is true, but we don't really have to, because it will automatically be there.

Now, that psychical house has everything in it as they knew on Earth and so it is more real for them. It has the same solidity as their Psychical Body. So they cannot pass through doors and walls. Now they have to open the doors to go between rooms. If they really understood the reality of their new conditions in the Psychical Worlds they could pass through the walls if they wanted to but, because they do not know the difference between the material plane and the physical planes and its new conditions, they don't even consider this a possibility.

They never studied these things before so they are just functioning in the Psychical Worlds in the same exact way as they knew on Earth. Someone who knows they are on the psychical planes and has developed the skill of raising and lowering their vibrations can make the vibrations of their Psychical Body rarer and pass through the doors and walls should they want to, but everyone cannot do it. The Researchers of Truth in our system who have done a lot of training can do it.

An Invisible Helper, who goes to the psychical planes, will see beautiful environments in all the sub planes of the Psychical Worlds. They see people living in their shells. So to help, the Invisible Helper has to enter the shell of someone they want to help and then they will see different things. The Invisible Helper will see the exact environment that person has made for himself or herself. It may be a hellish or heavenly environment or a bit of both. Sometimes their shell environment correctly corresponds to the psychical environment around them. Sometimes their shell environment does not correspond at all.

A common person in the psychical planes lives in his own world, his own version of the psychical planes. Since that person has no understanding of conditions in the Psychical Worlds they think they are in the material world. He still thinks water will drown him; if he wants to eat he creates everything he needs. Without knowing how, he is creating his food with his thoughts and intentions. If he has trouble focusing his thought enough to do that, there are Archangels that help him do it. These are the same Archangels that were working in his material body when he was on Earth, and so these Archangels stay with him in the psychical planes, working in his Psychical Body and providing things for him.

You can even see people in the lower psychical planes killing animals, cooking them and eating them. These animals are just their Elementals of animals as they knew them on Earth; which can now become manifested more easily in the Psychical Worlds. People there are just enjoying their life as they did on Earth, but all of this is only occurring in their shells. We have spoken about these conditional shells many times. Have you ever wondered, "How big are those shells?" They are boundless!

On the psychical planes can a person in one shell visit with other people who are in their own shell? By other people I do not mean an Elemental of other people they carry with them, which can appear to them. Yes, they can bring a person into their shell in the same way as you invite a person into your home. A person in one shell can accept a person in their shell if they both vibrate at a similar rate of vibration. This is true whether they knew each other on Earth or not. We get new acquaintances in the Psychical Worlds as we do in the material world. We find those we vibrate in harmony with and can connect with them.

Because people only know the material world they think this is the real world and the Psychical Worlds are abstract and less substantial, but the opposite is true. The Psychical Worlds are more durable than the material world. This is because in the material world things change more quickly than they do in the Psychical Worlds. In the material world if you take a flower and put it in a vase, it can only last for less than a week, and then it withers, but in the Psychical Worlds you can have a cut flower in a vase and it will remain fresh and beautiful for an indefinite period of time. This makes the Psychical Worlds more real than the material world.

As a child Daskalos was able to self-consciously travel to the Psychical Worlds, he had friends there he loved and they loved him.

Daskalos also loved weaving personal accounts into the lessons to accent the teachings. We all loved to hear his stories too. He was a master storyteller bringing these teachings to life with great enthusiasm.

"I had an experience", he began once as he eased backward in his chair, "of which I will tell you. It is my own experience. I was six years of age and I was as self-conscious in the psychical plane as I was in the gross material plane. I had a friend there, a Dominican monk." The monk showed the boy Daskalos, a beautiful monastery and took him to a room, which was about twice the size of the Stoa.

It had arches and stained glass windows like in the churches of Europe. There was a crucifix over the bed with an altar in front of the bed. His friend, the monk, told Daskalos this is your place, when you come here you can rest here if you like.

Daskalos had noticed that outside of the monastery there were beautiful fragrant Madonna Lilies, these are the six petal lilies we have at Eastertime. He asked the monk if it would be ok to cut one and put it in the vase on the altar in front of the Crucifix. The monk started laughing and said, "If you want to do that you can, no one will stop you. They belong as much to you as the others." So Daskalos got the lily and asked for a vase.

The monk manifested a nice emerald green vase full of water for him. He did this because this was what Daskalos was accustomed to on Earth. So Daskalos put the flowers in the vase. Now when Daskalos was telling this story he was seventy-six years old and announced he had gone to this room in the monastery recently. He reported that flower is still there in perfect condition after 70 years. Changes in the Psychical Worlds occur when your disposition changes. Life in the worlds beyond is very easy for those that want to live that kind of life. There is no need for eating because the light there is what nourishes and feeds you. You have as much light as you need according to your conditions.

So, you breathe the light; you do not need air to breath in the higher worlds. You can imagine you are breathing air if you want but it is not necessary. Actually, it is the light you are breathing but you think it is air. In time you will realize it is not necessary to breathe. This means that if you want to go to the bottom of a lake to see what is there, you can do it and stay there as long as you like. You can do this only if you do not manifest the fear that you will be drowned.

There are no lungs in your Psychical Body unless you want them but if you imagine your Psychical Body has lungs they will be there, because you create them by your thought. It is the same with the heart or any other organ. There is no heart mechanically pumping blood, but if you feel you need to have it, you will have it. If a common person imagines they have a cut on their arm and expects to see blood coming out, they will see blood coming out.

To move on Earth we have to walk, take some form of ground transportation or fly if you want to travel a long distance. However, all that is not necessary for travel in the Psychical Worlds. Does that mean there are no cars in the Psychical Worlds? Yes, there are wonderful cars in the Psychical Worlds if you want them or need them. Some still need cars because they do not know how to travel without them and in the lower sub planes you can see people driving cars. You do not need them, however, because by clear and steady concentration on a place you want to go or a person you want to see, you are there...or maybe we should say they appear.

Most people who cross over just recreate what they knew on Earth, which seems natural to them. When you get accustom to the new conditions in these worlds you find out that planes, trains and automobiles are not needed, and travel by concentrating on the place you want to go will then seem more natural. This is because in the fourth-dimensional world, the sense of measurable space does not exist like on Earth. These are worlds of place and not space, so to travel we concentrate on the place we want to be.

So place is the condition you think you are living in. Everything there is created by your thought. Now maybe you can see why we stress the importance of visualization. When you achieve good skills of being able to visualize clearly and steadily, you do not realize it yet, but it is like you are becoming wealthy. In the worlds beyond, visualization means having. So it is best to learn it now before crossing over. Virtually everyone on Earth would have preferred to be born into a very wealthy family. If you pass over to the higher worlds with a developed skill of visualization skill, it is like being born wealthy there.

Being able to visualize means you are mastering the light. You need practice over time. Truly the benefit of being able to visualize well is greater than getting any amount of money. Material wealth does not mean a lot because you have no need of currency when you pass over. But the skill of visualization travels with you in to all the Worlds of existence. It becomes yours; once you get it, no person or thing can take it away like can happen with material things. So it is very important for our life on Earth and in the worlds beyond that we learn to visualize.

To develop the skill of visualization it is fundamental that you are able concentrate your mind well. Then you need to learn the right meditations, which develop good visualization skills. With meditation and visualization you enter into the reality of things and not just your imagination or dreams. With the skill of visualization we are able to use the Mind in a higher way, as Creative Thought, which is very powerful. Thought is more powerful in the worlds beyond and visualization is the way we can harness the power of thought. It is important that we learn how to visualize the colored lights, which are specific frequencies of energies. So visualization gives us a means of using these energies to help ourselves and other people.

Learning visualizations of light, colors and forms also leads you towards Self-Realization. This is because, we first do it sub-consciously, then Self-Consciously and one day Super-Consciously. In the beginning you sub-consciously start to wonder who I am that can do these visualizations and in time that line of investigation leads to Self-Realization. Self-Realization means to find your Self not just as a personality but as the Soul-Self and then as the Spirit-Soul Self.

In the beginning many feel the Psychical Worlds is not real. One of Daskalos' Invisible Helpers told him one day that the Psychical Worlds did not seem as real to him as Earth. He said the conditions and laws governing these worlds were so different than on Earth. Daskalos explained that if he had not known the conditions on Earth first and only known the conditions in the psychical planes, then he would find the conditions on Earth unreal and the Psychical Worlds real. So it is that people are so acclimated to the conditions on Earth, it makes them think the conditions in the Psychical Worlds are less real.

After passing over after the death of the material body you will find yourself in the Psychical Worlds without the need of working to make money to live. None of the needs of the material body are required for the Psychical Body. You do not need to care for your Psychical Body by feeding it, washing it or taking it to the doctor. Your Psychical Body does not get dirty unless you have dirty emotions. So the work needed on the Psychical Body is only to clean it from impure emotions. You can meet people there who feel unhappy that they are not working. So what keeps people on the psychical planes busy? They stay busy with their interests, their desires and emotions. The Psychical Worlds are worlds of emotions. The emotions are not characteristics of the material world but of the Psychical Worlds, and so the personality of a man or a woman feels more at home in the worlds of the emotions.

Whether a person knows it or not, they live in the Psychical Worlds according to their interests and way of understanding. We have to re-train our self, to think in a new way in the Psychical Worlds; in order to live in harmony under the conditions and laws governing this new level of reality.

Now you may have noticed this yourself. When you have a dream most people just take what happens in the dream without really thinking about it...they just accept it. This also happens for people when their material body dies and they pass over. While sleeping you may dream you are flying just with your body. You do not stop and think; how can my material body fly? Nor do you think, oh since I am flying that means I am dreaming. You do not become alert enough to make the connection that if you feel you are flying just with your body, you are no longer in the material world. Of course most people consider dreams as unreal. However, dreams are real experiences you have in the Psychical Worlds; most of which is a phenomena associated with your Psycho-Noetical shell formed by your pre-existing thoughts, desires and emotions.

Yet sometime you may have a nightmare and wake up shaken from what you have seen; that unsettling experience you consider as unreal can linger and affect you for days. Whereas virtually all your experiences you have when you are awake will not have such lasting powerful effects. So which world is more real? On Earth as we mature into an adult we have to train ourselves to use our mind to correctly interpret the impressions coming to us through our five senses and be able to use them to accomplish things. In the Psychical Worlds, you have to train yourself in a similar way. In the Psychical Worlds you have more than five senses. There you can more easily develop the so-called sixth sense of clairvoyance or second sight.

Even the common person, over the course of time, gets accustom to the new conditions there and finds it more comfortable than on Earth and feels much happier. Gradually they are feeling more at home. Your life in the psychical planes can be longer or shorter than the life you lived on Earth depending on how quickly you assimilate your lessons and come out of your illusions. Earth life is a world of shadows. Life in the psychical planes has much more radiant light and yet it is still a world of shadows. Still higher in the Noetical Worlds the light is even more glorious, but it too is a world of shadows. We have to go beyond these worlds to find the light of the Spirit-Soul Self, which causes all these shadows to be cast. Then you will have passed through the worlds of shadows and illusions to the reality behind them.

Comparing your personality-self as it is today with the reality of the Spirit-Soul Self is like comparing a toddler to a rocket scientist. There is a great, great difference. Just as we grow in the material body, we have to grow in consciousness too until we come to the Soul-Self-Consciousness then to the Spirit-Soul-Self-Consciousness.

So we have to develop our consciousness to these higher states. Talking about these higher worlds you might get the idea that they are so different it is like they are some distant planet, but they are not. All these worlds exist in and around the Earth. The reality is that the material, the Psychical and Noetical Worlds are like different rooms in the same house. All are Worlds of Existence but you have to get out of this multi-room house in existence one day and enter the limitless realm of Beingness. Then you will find out we do not need this multi-room house; all you need is your real Self.

THE PRACTICE OVERVIEW

The intention of a Researcher of Truth is to engage in meditations using the Mind in a proper way that produces self-evident results. The ultimate aim of this is to continually raise their consciousness to greater and greater heights; one day reaching Self-Realization. Reaching this level we now know for certain we are not what we thought we were. That is to say we are not our aging material body. We are not our personality with its Psychical Body composed of our emotions, reactions and desires; we are not the Noetical Body composed of thoughts.

How will we know that? We know that for sure because we can check our emotions, thoughts; change them and master them. By examining how we use the Mind in creating certain desires, we can see that way too much of the time we are being a slave to our desires, emotions and flawed conceptions. Once you start cleaning and removing your lower and unnecessary emotions and thoughts; it starts to dawn on you that you are not these, because you are the one who changes and removes them. Even though you are creating this entity you call your personality it is not you. So what then are you? Reaching Self-Realization, are you still the personality? We can express our self as the personality but we can also express as the Soul. We will not destroy our personality by becoming Self-Realized.

The personality is treasured by the Soul and cares for it, lovingly, patiently guiding it through all our incarnations until it is able to unite with the Soul-Self. Examining what takes place in your Sub Consciousness composing these higher bodies you can see what is happening, know it, work on it and use it for your spiritual unfoldment and, in doing that, you are automatically raising your personality's consciousness to be able to know and enjoy these higher worlds. Just as you can know and enjoy the natural world on Earth, we can enjoy and know what the worlds of the higher dimensions are like. The builders, the Archangels of the Elements have built all the worlds; the material, Psychical and Noetical. In the worlds beyond Earth you will be able to enjoy their creation better. There you can better understand how they are working because you will come into self-conscious contact with them.

THE PRACTICE: WORKING IN THE HIGHER BODIES

Take deep and comfortable breaths.

Feel complete calmness in your material body and total peace in your personality-self. See sky-blue light shining all around you.

The light is not absolutely sky-blue but it is not completely white.

Do not try to give this light a certain color of blue, just see it as it is. It is more white than sky-blue, but not exactly white.

Breathe in this radiant light and slowly see your body filled with this beautiful light.

We are now more in our Psychical Body and less in our material body.

This sky-blue-white light tends to calm down the psychical substance and makes it a good instrument in the hands of our personality-self. Wish that while you are in this light, you will slowly grow calmer and calmer.

Thousands of unnecessary thoughts are turned over in your mind. Cast these thoughts off and clean your mind.

Feel that you are alone in this light. Pay attention to this detail.

Feel that you are alone in this light, without any disturbing thoughts or emotions. Take deep breaths and mentally wish that peace reign in your Psychical Body.

The blessings of the Beloved Christ are with you, your family and the whole world.

Slow down your vibration and slowly-slowly start to feel your material body again.

Chapter Eighteen
WHAT CHANGES IS NOT REAL

In studying Life we have to see two things -the Everlasting Life, which is the Absolute Infinite Be-ness and, also, Life manifested, becoming the Absolute Infinite Beingness. So, now I have Life manifested. What the Absolute Infinite Life is, no human intelligence can understand, except that it is everlasting. That is the only thing we can know. Though, we as the Life, as Spirit-Beings, we understand ourselves by reflection, by the image we are casting in the mirrors in the Worlds of Existence. So, as human beings we belong to the Worlds of Existence. As Divine Gods, we are in the Absolute Infinite Be-ness as a Spirit-Being. We are in the Absolute Infinite Beingness as a Soul reflecting a shadow on the Worlds of Existence, which is the human being. ~ Daskalos

THE TEACHING

In truth, what changes is not real and what is real does not change. Absolute Beingness, God has within Itself a multiplicity of changeless, eternal Spirit Beings, like individual cells in one body. A way to think about the plurality of God as the Absolute Infinite Reality is in a comparison to the ocean. If we consider God to be like the ocean, then all the phenomena of life (plants, insects, animals) are like drops in that ocean. Life is everything and there is no part of the universes that does not have life. Likewise there is no part in existence that is not the Absolute Beingness. This is the Omnipresence of God. Absolute Beingness is Life and so we see life in all parts of Absolute Beingness -God. These parts we are calling the phenomena of life and they can be found in different dimensions but always in a form. We all see the phenomena of life on Earth in the plants, animals and trees, but many more phenomena of life exist in the higher planes of reality that are invisible to us now. They exist in all the Psychical Worlds and up to the lower Noetical Worlds. These are worlds of living forms too, but take notice…it is not the form that brings forth the phenomena of life, it is Life itself that brings forth all the countless phenomena of life. All these forms of life are expressions of love, energy and movement in a specific form.

All life forms are expressions of the Archetypal Ideas, which are in the Divine Plan of the Absolute Be-ness -God. The Human Form is one of those archetypes.

Seven billion people live on Earth now, and the bodies of these people all have the same composition. All these bodies have movements in the muscular system and in the nervous system. The organs in our body all have very harmonious movement serving an important purpose. We see it in the circulation of the blood, the movement of the air in and out of the lungs.

There is an advanced meditation called The Divine Symphony where Daskalos relays a teaching from an Archangel on this subject. In this meditation, the Archangel speaks of how beautiful it is to see the harmonious movements of our breathing and the circulation of our blood and that we cannot conceive of beauty without harmony. So we have harmony and movement within all the organs of our human body. The form of the human body is in the Archetypal Idea – the Idea of Man. Our body is under the care of the Holy Spirit and it has a life of its own. Now we see another expression in the material body and this is the personality. As we said before, our personality is a composition of all the Elementals we harbor and express.

Now in studying the nature of our own Elementals, and others, we see that 80% of them are created with mostly emotions as feelings and desires. They can receive so much energy from a person that they gain enough strength to crush their personality. Psychology calls these kinds; phobias, fixed ideas and obsessive-compulsive disorders (OCDs). Psychiatrists and drug manufactures give these afflictions names without knowing their nature or how to really deal with them. In today's world, pharmaceutical companies identify an ever-expanding number of these kinds of disorders. In their advertisements, they offer an ever-expanding number of drugs to treat but not cure the disorders they identify. All this sets precedence in the people's minds to seek pharmaceuticals for maintaining control of psychological afflictions most of which could be better resolved by the methods Daskalos taught. Most of these legal drugs come with a list of potential side effects as long as your arm, many of which are far worse than the problem the drug is designed to treat. Recently, another pill has been identified to treat, an increasing modern dya problem. It is a drug for the Shopaholic, people who shop excessively and cannot seem to stop. These kinds of psychological afflictions are driven by the Elementals which are not dissolved and eliminated by a drug; their effects are only dampened by the drug and can immediately return when the person stops taking the drug.

Unfortunately, too many of the Elementals created are the human in nature demons that are destructive, misleading or illusionary. About 20% of all the created Elementals are the human in nature Angels. This is because most of the Elementals are created out of human weaknesses as desires and attachments. This is the reason behind Buddha's Nobel Truths. Buddha's first noble truth is that all life is suffering. The second noble truth is that the cause of our suffering is our own attachments. That is true and we can see that our own personal attachments are to our strongest desires. Our strongest attachments are enslaving us to desires for property, money, people, places, things, and experiences, which cause suffering. Even if you manage to get all the objects of your desire, you will still end up suffering to some degree. Because all those desire objects belong to the constantly changing Worlds of Existence and so in time, they too will pass away. So the enlightened Buddha rightly gave the top priority to detachment as a means of reducing our suffering.

Now the Elementals work in two distinct ways. Regardless of an Elemental's normal size, it starts as a mass no bigger that a grain of course salt. It gets projected out of a man or woman from the area of the third eye; then gets its normal size, does its work, and then returns back to the one who projected it. Now it again assumes the size of a grain of salt and it re-enters that person, bringing along seven other Elementals similar to its nature. This reveals that we are infected and influenced by the Elementals we create and project, but it also means we can be infected and influenced by Elementals of a similar nature as our own Elementals that come from the environment around us.

One way Elementals can influence us is directly. Directly means the Elemental can stimulate us to think and take direct action on how to accomplish the specific desire for which the Elemental was created. The second way they can influence us is indirectly. Indirectly they command power and can bring about circumstances that will deliver your desire – if you leave them alone to do their work. Sooner or later all desires tend to be fulfilled.

You hear this all the time and may have noticed it yourself; that when someone has an ardent desire for something and broods over it for months and months it seldom comes to them. When you have forgotten about the object of your desire, became interested in something else, then the desire tends to be fulfilled – karma permitting. So therein rests a secret. People have the feeling that when they stop wanting something, it is then that it comes to them. That is true because "stop wanting" means they leave the Elemental time to do its work. However, if you keep on thinking about and desiring it, you pull that Elemental back to you over and over by remembering it again. So for a good constructive Elemental to be successful you must stop thinking about your Elemental once you have created it, so it will have time to accomplish its work. Remember, an Elemental can live much longer than a person's lifetime. We create so many desire type Elementals that it is not possible to fulfill them all in a single lifetime. So over the course of lifetimes we can see that many such Elementals created in past lifetimes are being fulfilled in future lifetimes.

Now here is the real problem with that process. When you start to consciously develop yourself spiritually, you may no longer be interested in your desires from previous lifetimes. You may outgrow certain old desires as you unfold spiritually. Moreover, the strongest unfulfilled desire of a previous lifetime may well be the strongest obstacle to your spiritual progress in your current lifetime. You may rightly think that you would be better off without this desire in this lifetime. It was you who created that strong desire in the past. This is one of the most common reasons why people are, rich, poor, healthy, unhealthy, happy or unhappy in their current lifetime. It is a direct outcome of the Elementals that comprised their personality in past and current incarnations.

We have talked about incarnation, dis-incarnation and reincarnation – but who is it that gets re-incarnated. Is it your personality that is reincarnating? For example, if you were named John in a past incarnation and in the next incarnation you are born in a different country with the name Marco. Does that mean John re-incarnated as Marco? Is your personality from this incarnation, going to incarnate again in a different country, under different circumstances and be called a new name? In other words, is that new personality in a future lifetime the same personality you are today?

If in this incarnation you can raise your consciousness to that of the Spirit-Soul in full Self-Realization, then yes those past incarnations are yours and future incarnations are yours. Not yours as a personality but yours as a Spirit-Soul. Incarnations can be compared to chapters in a book. The first chapter in a book is not second, third or any other chapter in the book. Yet the book itself can say all the chapters are mine. In the same way we, as a Spirit-Soul, can rightly claim that all the incarnations are ours. The personality in one lifetime cannot rightly claim to be another personality in a different lifetime. So what happens to all our personalities from past lifetimes?

They have become like living holographic records forever in

the Cosmic Consciousness. Also in the East there is a mistaken belief that a human can reincarnate as an animal and an animal can reincarnate as a human. This notion is wrong; for sure there is no transmigration of a Soul between animals and humans. This is because there is a completely different course of development for man than there is for animals. So these are the main differences between the Researchers of Truth's understandings and experiences of reincarnation compared to the popularized ideas about reincarnation.

What then is the relationship between our past incarnations and our current incarnation? The answer is: Karma. Not in the absolute sense, because in each new lifetime we start with a mostly clean slate. This gives us a chance to lay down past burdens and move forward more freely. However, about 20% of our Karma is carried over from past lifetimes while the other 80%, we create in this lifetime. In any of your lifetimes there is part of your Selfhood that stands between your current personality and the Soul. That in-between thing is what we call the Permanent Personality, which is the Soul in expression in the Worlds of Existence. The Permanent Personality knows everything. It is the expressive part of the Soul but at the same time it contains the correctly distilled essence of all our past incarnations. So it brings forward to each newly incarnated personality the important lessons that have not been learned in past incarnations. This is showing us that what we are calling Karma is not a punishment; Karma is a means of learning, knowing and advancing spiritually.

The reality is that we lived in past lifetimes, we are living now and we will live again in a future lifetime. So why do we not remember the past ones? This is because our personality in this lifetime is focused outside of itself most of the time. The personality is currently centered on its own interests of the current lifetime and so it forgets the past. This loss of past life memory is also the mercy of God, so as not to remember past mistakes and serious wrongs. This gives the current personality the freedom to concentrate on the road ahead and make better steps in their current lifetime. We will start remembering past incarnations when that remembrance, good or bad, will not harm, delay or distract us from our purpose in our current lifetime. That automatically happens when we place our personality in the loving hands of the Spirit-Soul Self. Then past memories will come flooding back in to us. So we must not blame the mercy of God just because we do not remember our past lifetimes. Just because you do not remember past lives does not mean you did not live before. Just because you cannot remember what you had for dinner last Wednesday does not mean you did not eat last Wednesday.

In order to remember, we have to unfold our personality into its real Divine Nature and that is a really big gain. In this you will also gain powers. Now, as a personality you are weak, but as a Spirit-Soul you are a god, and a god is powerful. Your gain is the real Self-Consciousness; you become the master of your emotions, thoughts and life. Now you have reached a much higher vantage point above the personality's self-consciousness. So now, you might even laugh at how before you took the behaviors of your personality as so very real. When Daskalos was a small child he made this statement to his father and he repeated it all his life. It was, "Nothing matters much, and most things do not matter at all." Daskalos said his father was not really able to comprehend him and his abilities as a child. But he did seem to understand this statement, wrote it down and took it to heart.

Now we all have to learn our lessons in life and there are two ways to do that. One way is by reason, to think before we act and then act with reason. The second way Daskalos called the whip of destiny, which is the hard and painful way. Both ways will take you to the same result, but your experience along the way will be totally different depending on which of these ways you get your lesson. With the whip of destiny; when you disturb the balance of the universal laws you suffer, physically, emotionally, mentally or in some combination of the these as these laws are brought back into balance.

Who is it that suffers? Is it your Spirit-Soul? No, your Spirit-Soul Self never suffers for your personality's mistakes. It is always your personality self that pays off the karmic debt by suffering.

In the East they call this way Karma Yoga. Maybe we should call this way, Trial and Error Yoga for that is what it is. Whatever you call it, definitely it is the longest and hardest way to progress in life.

Again it is our own Elementals that are driving this process. Once an Elemental fulfills its purpose it gets de-energized and returns to the Cosmic Consciousness. Or if we ourselves de-energize the Elemental before it fulfills its purpose, it leaves and returns to the Cosmic Consciousness too. However if it is a serious Elemental and we are unable to de-energize it, then sometimes, but very seldom your Guarding Angel will de-energize it for you. In this case, if he does do it, then prepare yourself for a painful sting of consciousness. On rare occasions your Guardian Angel gives you a kind of slap to wake you up to a serious mistake you are committing. He does this out of love, so you will not mindlessly keep repeating the same mistakes and keep reaping the same undesirable consequences time and time again.

Human beings can and should help each other and that is the work of a certain order of Researchers of Truth called the Brothers of Mercy. These compassionate human beings are helping others regain their Divine inheritance. This is the reason all enlightened masters in the past have come; it is why they are here now and why they will always keep coming. Following their great guidance we can understand something of the Common Selfhood of human kind.

It begins to dawn on us that we are in everyone and everyone is in us. If one person on Earth is suffering we all are suffering to a degree. Don't you feel a degree of suffering when you see man's inhumanity to man? When you see the human loss from natural disasters or when you see the pain, injuries and death caused by the world conflicts on the TV news, doesn't a part of you suffer? This is a small indicator pointing to the Common Selfhood of us all. Being a cell in the Common Selfhood of humanity, we should never criticize others because in this regard everyone is us. Please don't look upon difficult people in your life as transgressing sinners. If you feel their transgression is in some way similar as your own, then you are approaching the Common Selfhood of humankind.

Now we have given much information on the Elementals, the good, the bad and the useless. You know the destructive ones in us and others can cause much harm but harmful Elementals can also reside in places and cause trouble there too. There are certain intersections in cities where there are way more accidents than other locations. Sometimes this can be from a poor road design but still, frightening Elementals can become associated with these locations and continue to cause accidents. Also locations where violent crimes have been committed the Elementals of the incident can stay there.

What happens when someone passes through such a place? Do the destructive Elementals attack everyone? If you are a good and loving person with a pure heart you can safely pass through a massive assembly of destructive Elementals and they will not even try to harm you. A clairvoyant will see them part and move away as a strong good-hearted person passes through. Then later after the person is gone, they move right back.

However, if you have similar vibrations as the destructive Elementals or if you quarrel and have ill will and try passing through that area; then those very same Elementals will attack you and can cause an accident. This is because of the principle that evil attacks evils. Of course this is a reason why Christ said: do not resist or fight evil. By complaining against others and fighting, you are also creating poison in your own material body. Harmful Elementals harbored and expressed become part of your personality-self, define your character and delineate your destiny.

So if you have a loving heart and a pure mind, you never need to be concerned about any harmful Elemental. If you are vibrating in similar way as negative Elementals, your own negativity is causing a kind of punishment, a negative consequence, to come to you. So it is our own actions that bring this kind of self-punishment to us. Now keep in mind never will God or any Archangel punish; Archangels do not even know evil, they only know love. Since God is omnipresent, equally present everywhere and in all human beings, if he did punish that would make him a Self-Punishing God – a Supreme masochist. God is not a masochist, God is most merciful.

As we move through our daily environment we travel in a sea of good and bad Elementals. So it is helpful to have a shield guarding us from evil Elementals in the common environment, sent to you by others or coming to you from your own sub-consciousness. What is the best shield of protection? It is a pure and loving heart. We can ask for protection from others, from the Archangels or God and this is good. It is also absolutely vital that we participate in our own protection.

THE PRACTICE: OVERVIEW

We can observe all around us that the Total Wisdom of God has provided protection for all the animal and plant life. If you look at all the different cacti, it is easy to see that it has its own protection. It needs protection from the birds and other animals.

So cacti develop a very effective system of protective thorns. Turtles have their shells for protection, rabbits have their swiftness. Chameleons can change the color of their skin to blend into their environment and that is their protection. In nature every living life form has its own kind of protection. Who decides all that? It is the Total Wisdom of God.

What about the human beings are they as protected as the

other animals? Yes, we have our vital organs protected by our rib cage and a most important organ, the brain, is well protected by our skull. The greatest protection the Total Wisdom has given human beings is the right and ability to use the Mind. In their rudimentary use of the Mind, the first cavemen and cavewomen fashioned clubs and spears to protect themselves from the wild animals all around them. Since that time man has been using the Mind to devise all kinds of protections. Now we come to another way for us to use the Mind to protect ourselves from harmful Elementals. We will not gain any protection from negative and destructive Elementals by being afraid of them. We do gain protection by being clean. No negative Elemental can harm anyone who is not vibrating in a similar way to them. Vibrating similar means a person is harboring or expressing similar negative desires, emotions or thoughts. If we have good clean thoughts and emotions we will not attract harmful Elementals coming from others or from our own Sub Consciousness. In this way we protect ourselves.

So from now on we will learn to send Elementals that work as little guardian Angels and protective servants of good. Once humans learn how to create these kinds of Elementals with Faith, they will have powerful protection. We can also protect ourselves by de-energizing negative Elementals, which is done by completely withdrawing our attention from them. Knowing how to create long lasting shield Elementals; we can protect our family, friends and our self. With this practice we are using the Mind to create our own protection.

Each day we receive Etheric Vitality from breathing, eating and drinking but we can also draw this vitality directly and use it to consciously form it through visualization into a benevolent protective Elemental. You can do this practice every morning or whenever you feel the need. For this we create a protective shield Elemental in the form of a triangle made of pure white light. △

THE PRACTICE: CREATING A PROTECTIVE SHIELD

Relax your material body and feel it is completely calm.

Quiet your emotions and still your thoughts and feel at peace.

Concentrate in your feet and feel that you are in both feet. Move up to your knees. You feel your knees fully.

Now move up to your solar plexus and concentrate your attention in this center.

Breathe deeply and as you inhale see a beautiful sky blue light glow from within your solar plexus. See and feel this energetic light spread throughout your body.

Now move up to your chest. See and feel a radiant rosy light emanating from your Heart Center. You only feel love in your heart, love for yourself and love for all human beings.

Move up to your head and see a luminous golden sun radiating in and around your head. The Etheric Double of your entire body is glistening in pure white light.

Above each shoulder in your Etheric Double there are two powerful centers of energy.

We will use the energy from these two centers to shape a three-dimensional snow-white triangle pointing downward.

The upper horizontal line of the triangle is above the shoulders and extends about six inches off each shoulder and passes through the thyroid gland in your throat.

From the two centers above the shoulder, visualize two lines of pure white light descend downward below the genitals and meet to form an equal sided triangle pointing downward.

The chest and pelvic area are inside the triangle but the hips are outside of the triangle.

See everything three dimensionally. See your shoulders and back inside the triangle of light.

Take deep comfortable breaths filling your chest with Etheric Vitality.

Then as you slowly exhale, feel the air leave your lungs while your body retains the Etheric Vitality. Inhale again and now see the white light of the triangle enter and spread throughout your chest area.

Repeat this part a few times increasing the amount of Etheric Vitality each time. Do not dissolve the triangle; keep it there as a living shield of protection.

At any time you like you can concentrate to see and feel it again. Each time you do this exercise it will become stronger and brighter.

Chapter Nineteen
POSSIBILITIES, PROBABILITIES & THE DIVINE PLAN

The Total Wisdom and the Almightiness govern all manifestations of Life and we understand this by studying the Circles of Possibilities of all living forms. No living form can escape from its Circle of Possibilities and jump to another Circle of Possibilities. This is definite. Any mystic who knows the great law of the Circle of Possibilities from their deep meditation, observation and concentration knows the truth about it. And there is no greater blasphemy than the Darwinian Theory that says we jump from a state of animal life to another state. This is definite. The Divine Absolute Beingness, God, rules His universes in steady laws. Man was always man and will always be a man. He has never been an animal and will never be an animal. So, this theory is dropped. ~ Daskalos

THE TEACHING

Observing everything from a one-celled organism, to a great whale, a solar system or an entire galaxy we find perfect order and balance. Everything has order and balance. We see that all the phenomena of life, all living forms of life, strictly obey the great law of the Circle of Possibilities for its kind of life. We see that no life form can escape its Circle of Possibilities, which contains Divine intelligence as Total Wisdom. It is this Total Wisdom that defines the cycle of existence for any given form of life.

All Circles of Possibilities are governed by the Divine Plan and worked on by the Archangelic Orders. They do this, by working on all the points of a Circle of Possibilities simultaneously. They can work on all the points at the same time because they work on them in the Eternal Now and not in a linear way from the past, to the present and into the future. They also do this great work at the same time for each and every kingdom - the mineral, plant, animal and human kingdoms. This is only possible because of the state of Super Consciousness enjoyed by all the Archangelic Orders.

Although nothing can escape its particular Circle of Possibilities, we do see each living form change in its appearance but it is not changing its nature. An ape is born in the infant form of an ape, and that form changes in its appearance growing into a young ape, an adult ape, an old ape and then the ape's body dies.   So we see a change in the outer form of an ape but not in the nature of the ape. An ape always remains an ape.

This was Darwin's mistake. He saw evidence of what he called evolution within certain species. Darwin saw adaptations in the finches on the Galapagos Islands and then theorized that man and apes could have "evolved" from a common primate ancestor. Even Darwin said his idea could only be considered a theory unless the so-called "missing link" was found that connected man and apes. That missing link has never been found.

Science had long been musing over the idea of biological evolution before Darwin published his famous book "The Origin of Species." In fact, another scientist working in Indonesia named Alfred Wallace had actually come up with the idea independently and before Darwin. He and Darwin exchanged letters about it and then in 1858 Wallace sent his complete theory of evolution to Darwin.

One year later Darwin publishes "his" theory of evolution. Darwin becomes rich and famous, Wallace does not and we end up with the mistaken notion that somehow there has been a transmigration of a human Soul from the body of apes into the body of a human.

What Wallace and Darwin correctly observed was a physical adaptation of animal's bodies to their changing environment, but neither Wallace nor Darwin had knowledge of the changes in the cranial capacity of early hominids or their chronology. Darwin used the term "Natural Selection" to explain his idea that man could have evolved from some common ancestor with the ape. This was a total theoretical jump, to a conclusion that was not based on any actual primate studies or hard evidence. Also, Wallace disagreed with Darwin's notion of Natural Selection to explain the origins of humans. Wallace saw it from a spiritual standpoint. He believed that the "unseen creative Spirit interceded" to initially create the animal life on the Earth and then later interceded to create humans.

Prior to modern man, there were as many as two-dozen species of hominids, sometimes with two or three different species living together in the same place. Hominids are a family of different primates. The theory of evolution proposes that these primordial species lived for something like 6 million years without much change. Then, about 50,000 years ago, their brain abruptly exploded in size and quality producing early man. This cannot be explained by a slow evolutionary development because the brain would have had to triple in size in a short period of time.

Even logically, the theory of man and Apes having a common ancestry does not make a lot of sense. The early hominids were covered in thick mats of hair to protect themselves from the harsh weather and environment. Now the theory of evolution states that all of a sudden, these fury forerunners of man lost virtually all of their protective hair; they grew a big brain and were able to think abstractly. And a brand new gene (FOXP2) appeared that allowed for the development of language. The early primates did not have this language gene. Immediately, these early humans had to start killing animals in order to wear the fur to protect man's hairless body from the cold; so that part sounds more like devolution.

Now all this rapid development of the cranial capacity 50,000 years ago is called the "big bang of the brain," and we are told that it took 40,000 more years before humans starting using stone tools, fire and the wheel. 10,000 years after that, the Printing press was invented. In the last 100 years humankind has gone from the first Model T automobile to a tsunami of high tech innovations that define modern life today, and this is just the beginning of how technology will be impacting our lives; because the amount of technological information now doubles every two years. Based on that exponential growth, can you imagine all the technological changes that will come to shape your way of life in the next twenty years?

No ape has or ever will be able to change their way of life, let alone advance at such an exponential rate. Clearly, man is a separate creation from Apes. If Darwin's theory had been true, we would see at least some evidence of this as primates giving birth to a human or giving birth to a part human part primate. This has never happened and it never will. An ape always gives birth to another ape. A human only begets another human; a lion only gives birth to another lion and so on. Also, apes and all other animals today behave exactly as they have for thousands and thousands of years. We do not see any evolution in the animal's nature or even a change in their behavior in the wild. In captivity we can see that man can train animals to do many things, but if you put a trained animal back in the wild it has been observed that they stop the trained behavior within three months.

In studying the Circle of Possibilities for any form of life we can understand its development. Take, for example, the seed of a giant Sequoia tree, which is similar to a cucumber seed in look and size. The cucumber seed produces a vine that only creeps along the ground and produces cucumbers while living only one summer. A Sequoia seed of similar size produces a tree over 300 feet tall with a 50 foot diameter that contains enough wood to build over 300 houses and it can live for 3500 years. Why do we get such different results from seeds of the same size? The Circle of Possibilities that governs all that is coded into each seed. If you plant an apple tree seed, it will never produce an orange tree. The Circle of Possibilities for any form of life is fixed and immutable.

It is the same for animals; each form of animal life must obey its particular Circle of Possibilities, which is a permanent law. Some duck eggs are so similar to chicken eggs that you cannot tell them apart. If you take a duck egg and put it in the nest of a chicken with chicken eggs, the chicken will keep it warm until it hatches. If it is close to water when it hatches, the baby duck will run towards the water and swim. The baby chickens will stay away from the water. Who taught that baby duck to go to the water and swim? All that information about the life of a duck is encoded within the Circle of Possibilities for a duck. It does not matter if chickens raised the duck or not. A duck will always behave as a duck according to the Circle of Possibilities for its form of life.

What about human beings do we have a seed coded with the Circle of Possibilities for a human being? Yes, to a mystic it is known as the Permanent Atom, which resides at the location of the etheric heart. This contains the coded information concerning the Circle of Possibilities for our incarnation as well as our thoughts, desires, words and actions that have created good and bad karmic influences are stored perfectly in our Permanent Atom. So in each new incarnation we carry the Karma from previous incarnations coded in this Permanent Atom as inclinations, predispositions, talents, and interests both good and bad. These influence the new personality and its life in its next incarnation.

There exists a point in our consciousness, where we can accept or reject these past life influences. In each new lifetime we are given the opportunity to succumb to negative past influences and create more karmic influences of a similar nature and thus we keep encountering the same consequences. Or we can strengthen the preexisting positive influences in us and build a better and better life.

The choice to sow the good seeds or to sow the bad seeds is ours to make and the results are ours to reap. For a human being the Circle of Possibilities starts as a spermatozoon, then conception, then a few cells growing in the womb, doubling and doubling until they become an embryo. The embryo grows in the mother and then is born as a baby boy or girl. The child grows into an adolescent, then a young man or woman then grows old and their material body dies and they, as self-awareness, pass over. The Circle of Possibilities for their material existence in this lifetime comes to an end. Then their life continues at a higher level of existence in the Psychical Worlds.

After completing the Circle of Possibilities for our material life, we continue on fulfilling the Circle of Possibilities for a human being in the Psychical and Noetical Worlds. In these worlds, we continue our life in a Psychical and Noetical Body. Our material body we find readymade for us and it has been built up perfectly by the Archangels, we need to do very little for our body except feed it and wash it. However, our Psychical Body is the body of our emotions, and it is not perfectly made ready for us. What is provided for us is the psychical substance, which we are unknowingly shaping and misshaping all the time by the emotions and desires we harbor and express.

Now this is a point where our Guardian Archangel helps. He is holding for us the perfect archetype of our Psychical and Noetical Body. He holds it as a blueprint we can use to learn to shape our Psychical Body to the perfect model he holds for us. What does that mean? Once you start to become conscious of the dialogue that is already going on between you and your Guardian, you start to learn many important things. He teaches you unconditional love by the way he unconditionally loves and cares for you. Humans think they know what love is but most do not. They mistake love by reflection, which is conditional, to be real love which is unconditional. Love by reflection means you love someone only because they love you.

What happens when that person sees something in you they

do not like? They may criticize you, find faults in you and complain.

When this happens, the all too common response is for the other person to complain and argue back with the faultfinding person and they both polarize against each other. Now their love by reflection has been overshadowed by dislike by reflection. If left to continue in this way it can lead to both people hating each other. What is hatred? As Daskalos explained, "hatred is wounded love." So if you are faced with such an experience and you feel like complaining about it, remember the 4th promise of a Researcher of Truth, "To endure patiently, without complaining, all forms of trials and tribulations the most wise Divine Law may bestow on me."

This promise does not mean we lie down and become a helpless victim to the abuse of other people. This promise does not mean we must stay stuck in unhealthy conditions or that we should not make the effort to improve the situation and in some cases transcend it completely. This promise is about self-mastery. This means we have mastery over our thoughts, words, desires and actions; thereby enabling us to withstand and successfully pass through any kind of difficulty. By applying the sixth and seventh promise we learn this mastery.

This self-mastery is part of the Circle of Possibilities for a human being. At this point in your development, you are not the master of your three bodies: the material body and your actions, the Psychical Body of your emotions, desires and motivations and the Noetical Body of your thoughts and intentions. However, it is in the Divine Plan for us to master our personality in order to assimilate it with the Divine Nature. With the exercises of concentration and meditation we start practicing to become not only the masters of our own mind, but also masters of the Super-Substance of The Mind. This is the possibility of every human being, but every human being must first unfold his or her self within God. No ape can do this. No animal ever considered itself a god or an offspring of God.

Animals do not have a Soul but human beings do. There is absolutely no transmigration of a human Soul into the body of an animal as some eastern schools have imagined. Even though the genetic makeup of a human body is very close to the material body of certain primates, a human being is much, much more than a material body. Our body is ours to live in and express ourselves through. Our body is ours but our body is not us…we are not the material body we inhabit. Christ confirmed this when he said, "Do not fear those who can kill your body, they cannot touch your Soul."

The full Circle of Possibilities for a human being is much longer than the life of the material body. After passing over from our material incarnation we will find ourselves with the same feelings, thoughts and way of living we had just before passing over. All these create a vibration that automatically places us in the exact sub-plane of the Psychical Worlds that we are in harmony with. In the Psychical Planes we continue our Circle of Possibilities in the 4th dimensional worlds.

Eventually we come to the Second Death, as it is called in Revelations and as self-awareness we pass into the 5th dimensional Noetical Worlds. It is our vibrations that place in the exact sub plane of the Noetical Worlds that we are in harmony with. Here we also continue on with the Circle of Possibilities for a human being.

Ultimately, we come to the end of our current incarnation, reaching the point of the Third Death and then pass into the Noetic State. We do not enter into a Noetic bodily form as might be expected; at this level we cannot rightly call it a body. At this level we enter the Archetypal Idea – the Idea of the Heavenly Man, which is to say - our Human Form. Our three bodies, material, Psychical and Noetical are materialized extensions of this Human Form. Neither the Second or Third Death is painful; these deaths are pleasant transitions into higher realms of light. Reaching the Noetic State, we reach what religion calls the everlasting light and science calls the super-light.

Now we will see ourselves clearly in the mirror of Noetic Super-Substance. At this level we will not see ourselves as a personality. Now we see how we really are, have always been and always will be: a Spirit-Soul Self with a vibration, a tone that is uniquely our own. It is this vibrational tone that has characterized our incarnations throughout the past ages and will continue to do so in future incarnations.

Now we know that there is always a Divine Plan that is being followed in the created Worlds of Existence that also governs everything existing in these worlds. That it is totally in our own best interest to cooperate with this Divine Plan. This is the second promise of the Researchers of Truth, "To be ready to serve at all times and in all places the Divine Plan."

Pain and despair exist everywhere in our country and the world. Our planet needs people who have found balance and serve the Divine Plan to help alleviate as much suffering as possible. Christ referred to this point, saying, "The harvest is great, but the harvesters are very few." It is a great honor to serve the Divine Plan; to feel you are a functioning part of the Divine Plan. Serving the Divine Plan can be as simple as giving a smile to a little child or helping a friend. It is not the quantity of service that is important it is the quality that matters most. There is no small service if that service is done with real love in your heart.

The Circle of Possibilities is the Divine Plan in expression. In studying the Circle of Possibilities of any life form, we end up coming to the conclusion that there is a super intelligence behind it all. If we look deeply at any of the living forms around us; from a tiny plant to a great whale, we cannot deny there is a super intelligence actively governing it. What does the word intelligence mean? Does intelligence have a form? We cannot see a form for intelligence, but we can detect it as a force. With Concentration and Meditation we can come to know about this super intelligence we call God. One of the more obvious characteristics of this super intelligence is its Almightiness: nothing is impossible or beyond its power.

The Creative Ether under the operation of this super intelligence and the Archangels builds up and sustains our material body atom by atom. Using the Archetypal Human Idea as a template it forms our material body. It works on this idea in time, space and place to give us the Human Form in all stages of its Circle of Possibilities. All phenomena of life inscribe a specific cycle within the Divine Plan and nothing can get out of this cycle because it is the Total Wisdom of God. This means that whatever is created must remain under the control of God and Its Archangelic emissaries.

When a Researcher of Truth or a mystic studies the Circle of Possibilities for a human being or an animal what do they find? They come to the same conclusion that all the mystics in the past have come to. This means they have caught the same thread of relative truth, which leads to the absolute truth. What they found is the same as what we find and will be the same as what the others who come in the future will find. All find that Life Is and that living beings **are** eternal. Yet they can **exist** in the Worlds of Separation for a time. They also find out about the nature of the material, Psychical and Noetical Worlds.

They all find in the end their Divine Nature as the Spirit Soul. Only people who are willfully blind in their mind cannot see the super intelligence of Life. This is because God is Life, and so we do not need to search for God someplace else. God is Life, we are living and everything around us is living. God is everywhere expressing Itself in all Its creations. God's initial Will-Pleasure to manifest the creation immediately becomes the Divine Plan. This means that everything that is to be created is under a Law-Cause and has its own Circle of Possibilities.

Do human beings have the intelligence to fully understand this Divine Plan? No, it is not possible. Do the Archangels fully understand the Divine Plan? Not even the Archangels can totally comprehend the Divine Plan. There are things unknown to even the Archangels and yet they are perfectly serving the Divine Plan in creation. What we can understand is certain parts of the Divine Plan as it pertains to the Worlds of Existence. If a researcher or a mystic can raise their consciousness to the highest level, then they can understand existence up to the seventh heaven and that is enough for human beings even as gods: as sons and daughters of God.

Our human body is built according to the Divine Plan concerning the Circle of Possibilities for a human being. However, it is not built as a static form like a statute. It is living, growing and changing all the time as is our self-aware personality. According to the Divine Plan, as an eternal Spirit Being Self we are destined to enter in the Circle of Possibilities for a human being, which means to become humanized. A ray of the Spirit-Soul Self then presents a little time and place personality self. The personality is Divine in nature but human in expression. Now our humanized self, can experience and know the mysteries of creation and one day know the Soul in true Self Realization.

First we must get our lessons in the three Worlds of Existence. We were not just born on Earth as a whim of God; there is a great reason behind it called the Divine Plan. Each of us is placed in a certain country, locality, community and family by the law of destiny.

That did not happen by chance or coincidence it can only happen by virtue of the Divine Plan. Nothing happens unless it is the will of God. So we have to accept things as they are and be as good as possible under our current circumstances and then work to make a better life. The lessons contained in ours and other people's circumstances are always the same, which is to use the Mind in a better more reasonable way to create a happier and healthier life.

We all follow the Circle of Possibility and also many Circles of Probabilities to express ourselves as a personality and also as a Soul. Aside from our personality's interests and expressions we can express a will. Our real will power comes from the Soul and is not to be confused with obstinacy that comes from a personality's egoism, which masquerades as our real will power.

So now we start studying the Circles of Probabilities, which is a law. We study it by studying all the forms of life around us. In our study of the Circles of Probabilities for any kind of life, we see the Law of Cause and Effect in action. We see the total power appropriately expressed in each form of life. A great whale can dive two miles deep into the ocean and hold its breath for two hours. It has the total power for its form of life. A tiny ant can lift 400 times its own body weight, which is the total power for its form of life.

The Circles of Possibilities are few but there are many, many Circles of Probabilities within a Circle Possibilities. These are the laws of the Worlds of Existence. Every form of life in these worlds is under the changeless Circle of Possibilities and at the same time under many Circles of Probability. All of which is overseen by the good judgment of the Holy Archangels of the elements and the mercy of God. It is specifically Archangel Uriel that coordinates balances and puts in order all this work; which means that it is Uriel who is ruling all this.

The Circles of Probabilities allows for the halting of development of life at any stage of development. For example, if you plant a seed, it might not sprout. Or a young tree may wither and die before it reaches maturity. A young child's material life may be cut short and they pass over. On Earth each form of life has these two; the Circle of Possibilities and the Circles of Probabilities. The Circles of Probabilities can terminate a life form at any point of its material development. The Circle of Possibilities cannot be terminated, because it is immutable. Both circles are visible and understandable on Earth.

If we make the effort to study the Circles of Possibilities and Probabilities we can gain the right understanding of nature and the living forms all around us. We also gain a right understanding of what is going on in our personality, with all its strengths and weaknesses. We make this effort both as a personality and as the Inner Self, which makes it sound like we are double. We are not really double, but we are dual in one. We have two natures; our Divine Nature and our human nature but only one Selfhood. It is like a coin. A coin is one thing but it has two sides. One side represents our Divine Nature – our real value. The other side represents our personality. The problem is that everyone tends to pay attention only to the one side of the coin; their personality. So from now on, we should try to see and feel as both sides of this coin of our Selfhood.

As we said before the Circle of Possibilities for a human starts as a sperm, conception, and birth continuing all the way to the death of the material body. This is just one phase of our Circle of Possibilities. Death of our material body does not end the path of a human being; instead it reveals a much larger range of the Circle of Possibilities for us that include our life in the higher planes of existence, reincarnation and an expansion of consciousness.

Now, if the life of a child is cut short by the Circles of Probabilities and passes over at the age of seven and we meet them in the Psychical Worlds five years later we would see that the child is now the age of twelve. In these kinds of cases children will keep on growing and continue their Circle of Possibilities in the Psychical and Noetical Worlds in a very similarly way as they would have on Earth. Whatever we have started on Earth must follow its evolution in the Psychical and Noetical Worlds. This is what Christ was teaching when he said, "Whatever you bind on Earth will be bound in heaven, and whatever you loose on Earth will be loosed in heaven."

So this is telling us that the good and bad habits, ways of thinking and ways of feeling we have on Earth will transfer with us when we pass over. What about our future in this lifetime, can we know our future? The future is not ours to see, the future is ours to live. This is because, what we call the future is nothing more than a world of probabilities: probable outcomes based on our behavior in the past and the present.

The Circles of Possibilities and Probabilities are valuable maps of knowledge about our journey in the past, in the present and on into the future. Our past thoughts, desires, words and actions influence our present and future incarnations. Even as a personality we are free to change and make better choices in the present, which will alter the probable outcomes in the future. This is to say, that it is with our own free will we can choose to speed up our spiritual development; or we can leave it to unfold slowly. It is necessary to study the Circle of Possibilities for a human being in order to find our current place in that cycle. Then using the Mind, we can develop our personality to one day be able to reach that great milestone of Possibility - Self-Realization.

There is a key in our heart that God has placed there. The

key is our Heart Center of love. This master key can open the gates to the heavenly mysteries as well as the glory of Earth life. If we want we can use this key to open the door to see the worlds beyond Earth. We can only do this in Spirit because our material body cannot tolerate the highest vibrations of Divine Love. The Divine Law of Love governs the worlds of Spirit. When we break our identification with our little personality we transfer it to the real Soul-Self, and attain universal harmony. Then we consciously become one with the Holy vibrations of the Archangels and God.

At this state, our Spirit-Soul-Self will clearly shine through our personality self. Now the personality knows the truth and is liberated. As soon as we are able to reach that center of our Beingness, we have reached the very heart of life. Now we know without a doubt the true way to express ourselves is to love.

THE PRACTICE: OVERVIEW

The Logos, the Holy Spirit and it emissaries, the Archangels, originate and develop each form of life by acting on the Circle of Possibilities for that form. The Circle of Possibilities is an Archetypal Principle that defines an array of potential experiences for each and every living form. For the Human Form, the Circle of Possibilities outlines the entire cycle of expression starting from our decent from the Divine, through the process of incarnation and back home to the Divine again. In other words, our Circle of Possibilities is the journey of the Prodigal Son. This is a complete cycle that intertwines all our successive incarnations together as our consciousness undergoes its expansion and purification. Each individual incarnation is like a small cycle within the full and complete Circle of Possibilities for a human being. Even so, there are still a vast number of Circles of Probabilities that allow for the interruption and withdrawal of that Circle at the material level and yet that only happens within the providence of the Divine Plan.

In simpler times and cultures, people were more in tune with the natural rhythm of life than today; because they lived more in harmony with the cycles in the natural world. Today as we seek to raise our consciousness to higher and higher levels it is necessary to become conscious of these great Circles of Possibilities and Probabilities. Life forms like a flower, a bush or a tree have a simple Circle of Possibilities and are easier to trace. So in our practice we start our meditations on this kind of Circle of Possibilities. Here is an example of an exercise to expand our awareness of how the Circle of Possibilities works over time. You can do this with a wheat seed, a corn seed or any kind of seed. It may be helpful for you to hold and look at a physical seed before you start this exercise.

THE PRACTICE: WHEAT SEED MEDITATION

First relax your body, your mind and emotions. Let the concerns of the day gently drift away.

Now with your eyes closed visualize yourself sitting at the edge of a big field on a beautiful warm sunny day.

The field has just been plowed and the aroma of the fresh Earth fills you as you breathe.

Using creative thought; see yourself with a seed of wheat in the palm of your etheric hand. See that seed in your etheric hand and feel that seed as solid.

We are using concentration and also the 4th dimensional Aesthetic Ether to feel that seed. Feel the seed as solid. Now we start a creative thought type of meditation.

See the rich fertile soil, and you are digging a small hole for the seed with your hand. See you are putting the seed in the soil and cover it with dirt.

Now see you are giving that little seed water and the sunlight is warming the soil and the little seed. Sit there with it and start to see it grow, first see it in the soil sending little white roots into the Earth. Then see the seed sending a small green shoot up through the soil and bursting into the sunlight.

This is a concentration meditation so you must not allow other thoughts and images to come in to your mind.

See the green shoots growing very slowly -don't be in a hurry. See the little tiny plant gradually growing bigger and bigger.

The small plant is growing in to a stalk of wheat and the golden head is coming ripe for harvest.

See it being harvested. Take a wheat seed from this harvest and put it in your hand, touch it and feel it as solid.

Now stop the meditation.

It is possible for a person who never saw wheat grow physically to do this exercise and by attunement enter in to the nature of the seed and see it correctly go through the successive stages of growth. This is real creative meditation.

Chapter Twenty
YOUR BROTHER LIVES AGAIN

We must try to understand the various levels of Selfhood and see where we really are standing now. All people are not standing on the seventh step of the ladder of evolution. Why are not all human beings on the same level? They are not because they don't want to be! If they want to, they can be. This is because God, as the Lord of Selfhood, is giving us the Mind in abundance to use. And by using the Mind we have to develop in our Selfhood the various kinds of consciousness. Now, by observation what do we see? This consciousness is not only to serve the Selfhood, but also to serve all the other phenomena of life all around us. Now try to understand what I will say. We are Gods as a Spirit-Soul-Self (our individuality). And we are just casting an immortal ray of our Spirit-Soul Self into existence presenting a mortal personality self. But as a Spirit-Soul-Self we have never departed from the Absolute Infinite Beingness - God. Have that in your mind. ~ Daskalos

THE TEACHING

We are here in the Worlds of Existence on an adventurous journey, an extended trip into time, space and place. From our home in Beingness we as a Spirit-Soul, project a luminous Ray in to the Worlds of Existence in order to experience the full extent of God's creation. Fortunately we all have a round trip ticket, which means that one day we are destined to return back to our real home, our Divine Nature in the Eternal Now.

While on this journey, we as personalities, have a temporary subsistence here in these Worlds of Existence. Yet, as Spirit-Beings, we are, have always been, and always will be in Beingness. This projected ray of Spirit Life-Light is the core of our existence as a personality but it is only a projection of a single radiant ray of the Spirit-Soul-Self into existence. In existence, we dress this Spirit-Soul ray with our emotions, desires, thoughts and behaviors thus creating a transient self-awareness we call our personality. The quality of the character of this self-awareness is determined by the quality of the emotions and thoughts we harbor and express in this lifetime.

So we have two states, the changing relative reality of the Worlds of Existence and the permanent Absolute Reality of Beingness. Existence has a definite beginning and end. However, Beingness is Eternal. It has no beginning. It has no end. Incarnated in the material world of existence we find ourselves here in a certain space-place, at a certain moment in time but in a few hours' time we may be in another space-place. Beingness is not like that. In Beingness it is always now – the Eternal Present.

Our Selfhood partakes and enjoys both of these states of reality – the changing states of temporary Existence and the unchanging realm of Eternal Beingness. We as Spirit-Soul Beings are eternal but we also have a temporary expression as personality. Likewise, Life is eternal but Life also expresses a temporary existence in all the forms of life on Earth and in the higher worlds. Now, all forms of life are under constant change.

The forms expressing Life may come and go but the Life animating these forms cannot be destroyed. Life may pass beyond our ability to perceive it but that does not mean it ceases.

To trace our Selfhood from its lowest expressions of our human nature here in the Worlds of Existence to its Eternal source in Beingness, the image of a line is given. The analogy of the line represents our Selfhood as a point extending itself into a line. With any line there are three distinguishable points – one on each end of the line and an invisible point in the middle of the line. If we envision a line running left to right, we can call the point from the middle to the right, our self as a temporary, present-day personality in time, space and place. The section of the line from the middle to the left represents our Self as Spirit. The point in the middle is the Self as Soul/Permanent Personality.

In the illustration that follows, from the mid-point to the left end of the line is a ray of the immortal Spirit-Self, bright luminous and unchanging. From the mid-point to the right end of the line is a ray of our Spirit-Soul Self but now dressed in a mortal personality self and seen as a line with three gradations. These three segments represent our material body, Psychical Body, and Noetical Body. In expression, this personality self is but a reflection of our real Self, cast in the time, space and place Worlds of Existence. The personality's expression in these three worlds may be that of a saint, a sinner or something in between. Yet at the core of all personalities the pure ray of the Spirit-Soul remains untainted.

In the illustration that follows, the left upper side of the line represents our Individuality, our real identity, and the right lower side is our personality associated with our current lifetime. This present-day personality is composed of all our human expressions, our thoughts, emotions and behaviors - good or bad. It is this transient personality that we mistake as our real Self. This personality has three bodies, each of which corresponds with one of the three Worlds of Existence. The material body belongs to the three dimensional material plane. Our Psychical Body belongs to the Psychical Worlds of the fourth dimension and our Noetical Body belongs to the Noetical Worlds of the fifth dimension.

The midpoint of the line represents the Soul/Permanent Personality, which contains all of the experiences from all past incarnations perfectly recorded. Some call the Permanent Personality or the Soul Personality. Others call it the feet of the Soul or the seat of the Soul. Whatever you call it, it is this expressive part of the Soul that projects a ray of itself into the Worlds of Existence reincarnating again and again.

This ray is seen as the symbolic backbone of each new incarnation. It is on this ray as a backbone, we build the character of our personality by our unique ways of thinking, feeling and behaving. In each new incarnation there is a continuation, a carryover from the previous incarnations. We bring into each new incarnation the lessons learned and not learned from our previous life times. In each incarnation we pick up where we left off in previous incarnations and continue on with our lessons and interests. Just like how chapters in a book continue the story line of the book. A single incarnation is the extension of the Permanent Personality into the Worlds of Existence, manifesting a unique personality and then withdrawing back again.

OUR SELFHOOD

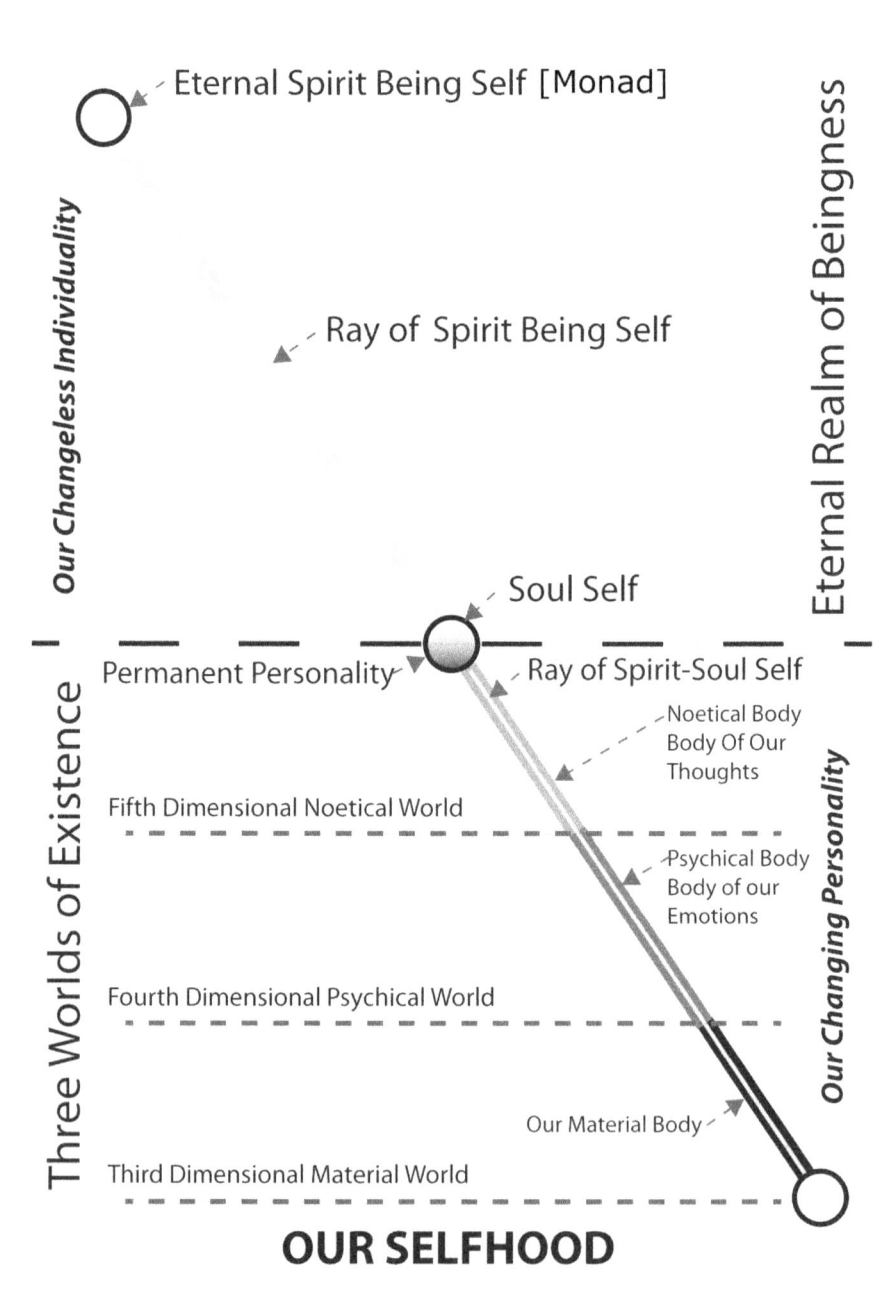

- Eternal Spirit Being Self [Monad]
- Ray of Spirit Being Self
- Soul Self
- Permanent Personality
- Ray of Spirit-Soul Self
- Noetical Body — Body Of Our Thoughts
- Fifth Dimensional Noetical World
- Psychical Body — Body of our Emotions
- Fourth Dimensional Psychical World
- Our Material Body
- Third Dimensional Material World

Our Changeless Individuality

Eternal Realm of Beingness

Three Worlds of Existence

Our Changing Personality

Now we should not imagine a rigid separation between our

Spirit-Soul Self and its projections/incarnations into the world of matter. Likewise, we should not consider Spirit and Matter as two disconnected and diametrically opposed states. Consider three-dimensional material substances as the densest manifestation of Mind. Consider the fourth dimensional psychical substance as a less dense manifestation of the Mind. Consider the fifth-dimensional Noetical substance an even finer manifestation of the Mind. The Mind is the means by which Spirit (God) and His Archangelic emissaries manifest the material, Psychical and Noetical Worlds of Existence. In the above illustration it is not possible to draw the real relationship between our three bodies or the three Worlds of Existence.

Unfortunately, this simple line drawing may give the false idea that these three worlds and three bodies are absolutely separated, which is and is not the case. They are definitely separated in terms of vibration and yet the material world is interpenetrated and surrounded by the Psychical Worlds and by the Noetical Worlds. Likewise our material body is interpenetrated and surrounded by the Psychical Body and by the Noetical Body. For our material body to be alive it must have within it the Psychical and Noetical Bodies. In the case of the death of our material body, our self-awareness transfers fully into its Psychical Body; this body remains interpenetrated and surrounded by the Noetical Body. For our Psychical Body to live it must have the Noetical Body with it. When the Psychical Body is aborted in the second death, the self-aware personality can live independently within in its Noetical Body without having any need for the material or Psychical Bodies.

It is the Etheric Doubles of our three bodies that serve as the connecting links between the bodies. In the same way it is the Etheric Worlds that serve as the connecting links between the three Worlds of Existence. Of course the above two-dimensional illustration, is not capable of adequately depicting the third, fourth, fifth dimensional worlds and beyond. It can serve as a symbolic reference to our Selfhood and the Worlds of Existence we travel through during our incarnations.

After many, many incarnations and the countless life-lessons learned we might begin to seek liberation from our suffering. We may then seek to return back home to our real nature in the unity with God the father, but this journey back home is not measured in terms of time and distance. It is a journey from illusion to truth, from shadows to light, from mortality to immortality. When we tire sufficiently of feeling separated from the Love, Wisdom and Power of our own Divine Nature we long to reunite with it. We eventually recognize our predicament and begin to make earnest efforts to come out of our pain, confusion and sufferings.

Nowhere is this human sojourn of going out and returning home more perfectly explained than in Christ's parable of the Prodigal Son (Lost Son). This parable contains great truths concerning humankind and the conditions we all face in life. This story of the Lost Son is a cornerstone of the teachings of the Researchers of Truth.

This parable tells us:

There was a man who had two sons. The younger son said to

his father, "Father, give me my inheritance." So the father divided his property between his two sons.

"Not long after that, the younger son got together all he had, set off for a distant country and there squandered his entire inheritance on wild living. After he had spent everything, there was a severe famine in that country, and the boy began to starve. So he went and hired himself out to a citizen of that country, who sent him to his fields to feed his pigs. He was so hungry that even the husks he fed to the pigs began to look good to him. Soon he came to his senses, and began to reason saying, "In my father's house even the servants have food to spare, and here I am starving to death! I will go back to my father and ask him to hire me as his servant." So he got up and set off to his father.

While he was still a long way off, his father saw him coming and was filled with compassion for him; he ran to his son, threw his arms around him and kissed him.

The son said to him, "Father, I have sinned against heaven and against you. I am no longer worthy to be called your son.

The father said to his servants, "Quick! Bring the best robe and put it on him. Put a ring on his finger and sandals on his feet. Bring a fattened calf and kill it. Let's have a feast and celebrate. For this son of mine was dead and is alive again." So they began to celebrate.

Meanwhile, the older son was in the field. When he came near the house, he heard music and dancing. So he called one of the servants and asked him what was going on. "Your brother has come home," he replied, "and your father has killed the fattened calf to celebrate his return."

"The older brother became angry and refused to go in. So his father went out and pleaded with him, but he would not listen and complained to his father, "Look! All these years I've been slaving for you and never disobeyed your orders. Yet you never gave me even a young goat so I could celebrate with my friends. When this son of yours who has squandered your property with prostitutes comes home, you kill the fattened calf for him!"

"Please," said the father, "please try to understand, you are always with me, and everything I have is yours. It is right we celebrate your brother's return, because your brother was dead but lives again; he was lost and now is found."

This story beautifully sketches the entire Circle of Possibilities for a human being revealing the great truth. Of course the father in the story represents God our heavenly father. The elder son symbolizes the Archangels who have never left their unity with God. The younger son represents each eternal Spirit Being destined to become humanized and enter the cycles of incarnation. The father's property given to the younger son is the Mind and the right to use it. This means the son has complete freedom. Freedom is the first gift that God gives. The elder brother also has his share of the father's property, which means the Archangels are using the Mind too.

Christ's account shows the true relationship between man and the Archangels, which is brotherhood. The Archangels are our true brothers. They know us as their brothers but we have yet to realize our near and dear relationship with the Archangels.

The younger brother takes his inheritance and goes to a distant country, which means incarnation on Earth. Now the younger son is in the Worlds of Existence spending his inheritance on reckless living and getting lessons from those experiences.

The Worlds of Existence are worlds of duality and so the conditions in this world changed when the famine came and then the boy began to suffer. Now the Lords of Separation had him as their slave forcing him to serve matter by sending him to tend the pigs.

The pigs are the emotion and thought forms, the lower nature Elementals that the younger son had created by riotous living.

It says the boy had to be content with eating the pig's food. This is a reference to filthy emotions and thoughts that pollute our hearts and minds; or what Christ called "unclean spirits."

Now the lost son takes a step forward. The parable says: "soon the boy came to his senses and began to reason," and so he decides to return back home to his father. Now this is a very important teaching on the way to come out of our suffering and that way is by reason.

The boy sits down and starts to reason his way out of his predicament and then make his plans to leave that poor condition for a better one. He thinks, "what am I doing eating the food of pigs that does not satisfy me." This is the question we must ask ourselves when we seek to be free when we are suffering, "What are all these troubling thoughts, emotions and behaviors actually doing for me? Do they really satisfy me?" Now, in the story the boy comes to the truth and decides to leave his unsatisfying condition. So he sets off to return back to his father. While the boy was still a long way off, the father sees him coming and runs to him embracing and kissing him.

What does this mean? Today we would say it this way, "If

you make one step towards God, he will make nine steps towards you."

Another important teaching in this parable is that after the boy has taken some steps to return the father sees him. This means the father is watching and waiting for his return just like God is watching and waiting for our return. When the father reaches the son, the boy says, "I am unworthy to be your son." Nevertheless, the father does not see it like that and claims him as his son, then has him dressed in his best robe. By doing so, the father restored him to his original princely condition, which means to his original Divine Nature. Now he is dressed like his elder brothers the Archangels. In a similar way upon our return to our Divine Nature in Self Realization, we gain what we never really lost: our original status as an offspring of God. We may have lost our awareness of our Divine Nature, but a child of God is always a child of God, even when they behave like a naughty child.

So undergoing the suffering inherent with incarnation we lose nothing. In fact there is a gain, the gain of the golden ring the father puts on his finger. The ring is a symbol for eternity, because if you move around the circumference of a ring, there is no beginning and no end so it gives the sense of eternity. It is movement without any end. With this sense of eternity plus the experiences in the time, space and place; the younger son has a distinct advantage that the Archangels do not have. Because of his outward journey and return home, the younger son now understands both time and the Eternal Now. The Archangels do not understand time they only understand the Eternal Now. Daskalos knew the language of the Archangels and had asked them more than once, "What is time?" The only reply they can give is, "Now! We are in the Eternal Now." They have always been and will always be in the Eternal Now. What time is, does not concern them, what interests them is their work in expressing their nature in the Eternal Now.

Look at your past and you will not be able to find a beginning of it in time. There is an eternity behind us we call past, just as there is an eternity ahead of us in what we call the future. When you think of the past all you do is draw up memories of what once were present moments. It does not matter if the past you remember was only twenty minutes ago, twenty years ago or twenty lifetimes ago, all you are doing in your remembrance is drawing up stored memories. Even if you have forgotten periods in the past of this lifetime or events in past lifetimes; there are ways to remember but it takes training. To authentically remember past lives we must be able to raise our self-consciousness to the level of our Spirit-Soul Self and not be totally focused in our personality self all the time, which is a reason why we do not remember past incarnations.

When you think about the future you just draw upon projected possible outcomes, shadows of things to come, which are more ephemeral as past memories. All we really know is this present moment, and this is the reality for us. That we are living in the present moment is the one and only reality for us. Living is a reality. How can reality exist between the two illusions called past and future? How is it that we find ourselves existing now in the reality of the present moment? If we study this seriously, we will realize there was always a "now" for each of us. All those past experiences were in the "now" at that past time. Those experiences we will have in the future will also occur in the "now." There will always be a now for us, sandwiched between the eternities of past and future.

For a Researcher of Truth, the thing that interests us the most is in knowing who and what we are. Who we are as a personality has constantly changed over the course of our life. So we need not be afraid of changes because we as a personality have never stopped changing and never will. All those changes are in what we call the past; in previous years and decades of this incarnation. What about in previous centuries and in past incarnations? If we start this line of investigation we see an eternity behind us in time. All we really know is the present moment; we know for sure we exist now. How is it possible that we appear in this lifetime if we have not existed before? What will we be in the future? Will we enter a state of nothingness and cease to exist? If so, then how is it that today we are living in the present moment? What if someone asked you that question in 1500 AD? It would be exactly the same. You would know for sure you were living in the present moment in 1500 AD, but you could not imagine yourself or your way of life today in the high tech 21st Century. You might even wonder what you had been in those past 500 years. Were you just like a leaf blown here and there by the winds of Karma, not knowing who you are or your purpose in life? Yes as a personality but as a Spirit-Soul, definitely not! The parable also tells us that when the prodigal son returns home, the father kills a fatted calf, which symbolized the son's material body. The material body has to be sacrificed to enter the heavens; as it is written, "Flesh and blood can never inherit the kingdom of the heavens." Now the elder brother in the parable never left the Eternal Now and entered into a material existence, he never incarnated with a material body and so he was never in need of a calf or a goat to be sacrificed in order to be set free. The Archangels never misused the Mind like the human beings are using it to create and send negative Elementals. The errors of the prodigal son, the errors of human beings set the stage for us to get the very lessons we need to eventually come out of their illusion and return back home to God and our Divine Nature as Spirit-Soul. With these lessons learned the prodigal son eventually returns to God with the full understanding and acceptance of his Divinity.

So we see in this parable the great truth concerning the journey of humankind undergoing a sense of separation from God here in the Worlds of Existence and then returning back home again. We are all prodigal sons/daughters, though some live more prodigally than others. Yet, if we study our own conditions in life deeply, we will find ourselves at some point in this common journey. Some may still find themselves seeking meaning or happiness in a prodigal life. Others may be reaching the turning point in their sojourn where they "come to their senses" and decide to leave their self-created suffering and illusions to return home to their father God. Others may have already turned and felt the embrace and kiss of God welcoming them as they approach. And there are also great ones who have gone before us and already completed their return!

THE PRACTICE: OVERVIEW

Whether we want it or not, it is in the Divine Plan for the

prodigal son to return home. Sooner or later all of us are destined to complete the journey of the prodigal son and return to our Divine Nature. If we want to speed that process up, we have to work on it.

We have inherited the Mind Vitality as Psychical substance, Noetical substance. What have we done with it? We have misused the Mind creating many negative emotions and thoughts that are producing selfish love, jealousies and fighting. We have created these negative Elementals, which have become part of the composition of our personality and we suffer because of that.

So what to do? We must start using the Mind properly to create positive, healthy emotions and thoughts; to unfold our self-consciousness and become the master of our emotions and thoughts. Unfolding who we are as a personality self-consciousness we will one day reach the level of knowing what we are as a Spirit-Soul Self. In this true Self Realization, we can manifest our latent powers of attunement and At-One-Ment with the Divine. We then find that we are all gods, sons and daughters of God the father. So we need to find out what we really are, not just in this moment, but also always.

PRACTICE: ESSENE MEDITATION

This meditation was given by Joshua Emmanuel the Christ, in the synagogue of the Essene Brotherhood, to His disciples before sending them into the world to work as teachers and healers. It had been lost in time but reintroduced by Daskalos to his students.

Before starting, relax completely, breathe deeply and comfortably but most of all consciously.

Visualize Joshua Emmanuel the Christ standing before you,

dressed in His snow-white robe.

As you sit peacefully, ready to listen, Joshua reaches out His arms, blessing us.

In perfect At-One-Ment with His Divine Self, the Logos, and attuned with each and every human being, Joshua speaks to us.

"My beloved ones, all of you are offspring of mine, Spirit-Soul-Egos, immortal Gods, Ego-Selves, in my Infinite Selfhood.

I am the Lord, your God in you. I am your Ego-Being-Self.

I am the Lord, your God in every other human being.

I am the Eternal Being-Self of all human beings.

I am the Creator of everything, and I am in everything existing. Beloved ones, be still, be calm, and listen to me.

I am the everlasting Life, the Life in every living being and in every living thing in my Omnipresence.

Listen to me. I will speak to you in your mind also, by intuition.

Listen to me and understand.

I, together with the Holy Archangels, have given you a material body, and we are sustaining it continuously for you to live in.

I have given you bodies to be my Image and Likeness.

I have given you the Divine Light Body, (in its violet light,) to give you the Wisdom in my world of other Dimensions.

I have given you the body of sensations and emotions; do not allow the Evil Ones to contaminate it with illusions and darkness

I have given you in your material body the Etheric Double. Find it, and use it well. Cooperate in it with the Archangels in your body in their creative work.

Feel your Etheric Double and fill it with my Mind-Light-

Vitality.

Be still. Be calm and listen to me.

I have given you in your material body a human heart. I am in the pulse of your heart.

Hear me in the pulse of your heart.

In the pulse of your heart is my love for you. Clean your heart.

Make it a crystal clear mirror to reflect my love – your love – to every human being, my offspring.

Find me and listen to me. I am Life in your heart.

I have given you two eyes, well protected in their sockets.

You can see the material light and in this light you can see everything material in the material world. Feel me in my Omnipresence.

I have given you in your chest two lungs to breathe my air and my Life-giving Vitality. Breathe deeply and feel the air you are breathing in your lungs.

You can feel me there and you can hear me in your breath.

I am in your breath.

Beloved offspring, all of you,

I am the Life in your bodies. I am the Life everywhere.

I am the everlasting Life.

I am the Omnipresent, Omniscient and Omnipotent Infinite Selfhood.

All of you are my Self-conscious Ego, Spirit-Soul-Beings, and immortal Gods.

Be still. Be calm. Listen to me.

I have given you the Mind to use, that you may understand who you are. I am the Lord God. I am God, your Divine Father.

I am the Lord of Hosts.

I am God the Logos and God the Holy Spirit. See me in the Life-Love-Light in you.

I am in the inextinguishable Mind-Light in the everlasting Wisdom. I am the light emanating from the material sun.

Feel me and see me in the strength and Power of Nature.

See me and hear me in the storm. Hear me in the wind.

See me and hear me in the thunder and lightning. Hear me and see me in the raging sea.

See me as the beauty of the trees in blossom.

See me as the symmetry in all forms. See me in the blossoming flowers.

Feel me in their sweet fragrance and see me in their lovely hues.

I am the everlasting Life in your immortal Spirit-Soul-Ego-Self in my infinite Selfhood. The death is not a reality, but an illusion.

The reality is everlasting life.

Your ever-changing bodies are not you.

Your Self-conscious Ego-Being is an immortal Spirit-Soul-Being. I am not the God of the dead.

I am the God of everlasting, immortal, Self-conscious Gods, beloved offspring of mine."

Chapter Twenty-One
ASCENDING THE LADDER OF RELATIVE TRUTH

The Researcher of Truth gets as close to the truth as possible, but why as much as possible? Because, within the world of time and space we can only have knowledge of the relative truth - not the Absolute Truth. The Absolute Truth cannot be known before we have the whole of the relative truth and see it from all angles.

In the gross material world, the world of three dimensions we now live in, the relative truth is ample for now. Now you come to the point of analyzing. "What am I? Who am I?" Just try to find out who you are. This is the aim of the Researchers after the Truth, of our Circles -serious research to find the Truth. But, you cannot approach the Truth unless you ascend the ladder of the relative truth. It is not so easy to pierce the real meaning of the Truth.

Now, how shall we start working to find the Truth? What is the Truth? Of course, we know the relative truth. We know the relative truth of things in time and place-space by comparison. This is the relative truth about things and conditions in life where you say that this or that isn't true. This is the relative truth. In the research of truth there is need for rationalism, concentration and work in all areas, to correct our views and impressions. This is an important point to remember. We are continually moving on, we don't stop at one point. Now, this is rather difficult to understand, but, try to understand it. The relative truth is so much of the absolute Truth according to the distance and the quality of the things you are studying. Are we in very deep waters now? Maybe. Yet, they are necessary. ~Daskalos

THE TEACHING

As personalities living in the worlds of illusion, it is not possible to jump directly to Absolute Truth. Rather ascending the ladder of relative truth makes our approach to Absolute Truth. We start our ascent the moment we sincerely seek to understand the truth about our real Self, its Source or the true nature of reality.

First let us describe what we mean by relative truth. We can say that relative truth is a portion of Absolute Truth, and that Absolute Truth is unchangeable. It cannot be improved or lessened by anything. A relative truth can be expanded upon, increased and changed; therefore it is not absolute. An example of relative truth from the material world would be gravity. In the material world gravity is a fixed law, a truth no one can deny. This law binds all people and material things. Yet this truth is relative not absolute, because by applying higher laws such as the Laws of Aerodynamics man has learned to build airplanes, fly them, and temporarily rise above the pull of gravity. Or by using other laws of physics, rocket science has allowed man to escape the confines of Earth transcending the relative truth of Earth's gravity. So gravity is but a relative truth within the material three-dimensional universe.

Similarly the law of Karma, the law of cause and effect, is a truth found in all the Worlds of Existence – the material, Psychical and Noetical Worlds. All enlightened teachers from all cultures and times taught the truth of this law. Christ spoke of it as, "You reap what you sow." Yet Christ was able to neutralize the effects of this exacting law with the higher law of forgiveness. As he approached the afflicted he would say "Your sins are forgiven you," and remove the body/mind/emotional afflictions that resulted from their transgressions (i.e. he removed the negative effects and imbalances that are the consequences of transgressing the Divine Laws). In a lesser degree this is what a compassionate confessor in a church or an insightful psychotherapist does with those who confess their wrong doings. As personalities, we are not able to forgive sin as completely as Christ did. However, we can and should forgive all transgressions against us for everyone's sake. What does "forgiveness" really mean? What is the difference between forgiving a transgression and forgiving the transgressor? Forgiveness does not mean forgetting, condoning wrongs or putting up with abuse. Forgiveness does not require us to go on ignoring the hurtful actions of others and pretending things are other than they really are.

Why should we forgive others? One obvious reason is that we want to be forgiven, so how can we ask to be forgiven if we do not forgive others? We will be forgiven by the very same measure by which we forgive others. In our prayer we ask God to, "Forgive us our transgression **as** we forgive those who transgress against us." This is an exact mathematical equation that we will be forgiven to the same degree **as** we forgive others. To forgive someone really means to love someone unconditionally. When you really love there is no need for you to forgive. What about when we make a mistake and cause a problem for someone else, should we ask him or her to forgive us? Sometimes yes, if it necessary and if it is done purely. But asking for forgiveness can sometimes be too egoistic. So in some cases it is better just ask God to forgive you, and send that person love and good will, and God will bless that person. It is 100 percent in your best interest to forgive others and not to allow your heart and mind to entertain bad thoughts and negative feelings. Hatred, animosity and the like produce dangerous poisons in our personality, and cause toxins in our body, which can eventually create physical illnesses like ulcers. An example of this mind/emotional/body connection was proven by medical science when they analyzed the chemistry of tears. They found that tears of sorrow have a distinctively different chemical composition from tears of joy and contain much greater quantities of certain hormones. This proves that strong emotions directly affect our body. So it is vital to remove any negative thoughts and feelings from our personality and keep it clean.

Nobel Peace Prize recipient and past chairman of South Africa's Truth and Reconciliation Commission, Bishop Desmond Tutu explained, "The process of forgiveness requires acknowledgement on the part of the perpetrator that they have committed an offense. We cannot be facile and say bygones will be bygones, because they will not be bygones and will return to haunt us. True reconciliation is never cheap, for it is based on forgiveness, which is costly. Forgiveness in turn depends on repentance, which has to be based on an acknowledgement of what was done wrong and therefore on disclosure of the truth."

There was a disagreeable couple living in Daskalos' neighborhood on Cyprus; they were all the time blaming others and causing trouble. Also they were poor and in need of money for food from time to time. Daskalos became aware of this and would anonymously put money in an envelope and slip it under the family's front door. One time, they started claiming someone stole from them, and blamed Daskalos. The police were eventually called and came along with the accusers to Daskalos' home laying the charges at Daskalos' feet. Daskalos explained that not only did he not steal from them, but also when they were starving, he was the one who had been putting money under their door and named the dates when he did so. This was a great shock to his accusers and with the police they went away. Later they returned feeling guilty that their wrong accusations had wounded Daskalos. They hadn't because, as Daskalos said, he had already killed his own egoism and never felt wounded.

Still, they knelt down before him and said, "Forgive us." "No need," he replied, "I love you."

"They said, "We love you too,"

"I love you," he said again, "But please no more contact between us."

When Daskalos recounted this story, he went on to say that we have the right to end such a connection. Christ has also stated this in his teaching. Daskalos added, "You can forget such people, but have no ill will toward them. To forget them is good, to forgive them is not necessary if you love them." This is mercy. Christ said, "I want mercy, not sacrifice." Mercy means love. After you kill your own egoism, you will not feel the need for someone to ask you to forgive him or her even if they feel the need to be forgiven. Of course you will tell them you forgive them for their sake, but if you want others to come to you and ask for your forgiveness, then it not driven by mercy or love.

In truth, we all belong to one race: the human race. This family called the human race all live together in a common home: the planet Earth. So we should always make the effort to love all our family members. An egoistic person does not know how to love others properly. It is a great principle that the truth sets us free; likewise it is also a great principle that it is our love that protects us. So a pure heart is the best protection from those who consciously or subconsciously wish us harm. If we can raise our standard of love from that of egoistic personal love to real unconditional love, we can be protected from the damage and mischief of someone who considers us their enemy. Researchers of Truth are not allowed to have enemies but, as you probably have noticed, it is easier to make enemies and takes more effort to make friends.

Buddha taught that hatred does not cease hatred at any time. Hatred only ceases by love. In other words we cannot extinguish fire with more fire, we extinguish fire with water. Similarly, harsh words to others arouse anger in both people, but gentle words calms anger in both people. It is so obvious that loving someone who loves us is a natural human response that is common to all of us, but to hate someone who loves you is devilish and to love someone who hates you is Divine. We can also notice that what we call evil attacks good and sometimes it attacks other evil, but real goodness only strengthens the good and never attacks evil. Good tries to redeem evil. So it is up to us to choose which way we will follow.

Even if those who are transgressing against us feel fully justified and unrepentant in their actions, we can still accept the lesson contained in the experience, forgive the transgression, love the transgressor and apply the Fifth Promise of the Researchers of Truth, "I promise to myself, to love and serve my fellow human beings from the depths of my heart and Soul, no matter what their behavior is to me." The sincere application of the Fifth Promise is our best response as it will unlock the chain binding us to wrongs so that healing may occur; freeing us to make another step up the ladder of relative truth.

Now what we consider a relative truth of one dimension can be completely obliterated by a relative truth of a higher dimension. For example, space as measurable distance between objects or places is a relative truth associated with the three dimensional material plane. However, in the fourth-dimensional psychical planes, measurable space as known on Earth is completely gone and replaced with the concept of place. On the psychical planes of existence, many unique localities and things can occupy the same place without being mixed up. It is similar to the way on Earth how programs that are broadcast from many television stations exist all around us simultaneously without mixing up. If you tune your television to the frequency of channel four, you will become aware of that program only. Change the tuning of your television to channel six and for you, channel four stopped existing and you are only aware of the existence of the program broadcast on channel six. In this example no physical movement occurred, just a tuning from one frequency to another. Similarly "traveling" from one psychical place to another can be accomplished by attuning, and coordinating yourself to the vibration of the frequencies of the place you want to be.

In the fifth-dimensional Noetical planes, the concept of time as measured on Earth completely disappears. In the Noetical planes of existence there is a sense of passing events but not time as we designate it on Earth. In the Noetical Worlds 100 Earth years might seem as a single day. The truth of measurable time and space is only relative and not absolute. The more we study, observe and meditate on the relative truth the more we approach the Absolute Truth.

This means that we cannot approach the Absolute Truth unless we scale the ladder of relative truth. We make our ascent up the ladder of relative truth from exactly the place we find ourselves right now. So we first study the relative truth about the current things and conditions in our life.

Unfortunately, the average person does not live their life like a thinking individual, but more of a feeling person living within their own dreams and illusions. Most of the time it is their illusions that create the disappointment and sense of hopelessness experienced in some lives. However, a Researcher of Truth seeks to come as close to the Absolute Truth as possible, because as a personality living in the three Worlds of Existence, the Absolute Truth cannot be understood before fully examining the relative truth. That is all right, because in the Words of Existence the perceptible relative truth is a result of the Absolute Truth. We will never stop our ascent up the ladder of relative truth. We are continually moving from the relative truth towards the Absolute Truth.

Albert Einstein said, "Problems cannot be solved by the same level of thinking that created them." This is telling us that when we are faced with a troubling problem we should make the effort to rise about the level of the problem and see it from a higher perspective in order to find the best solution. Daskalos told me once that when he had a difficult problem he was trying to sort out, he preferred to leave his material body in Exosomatosis to solve it. Of course we are not all able to make an out of body experience when dealing with our problems. We all can make an effort to climb to a higher rung on the ladder of relative truth and see the problem from a higher perspective.

The method needed to make our way up the ladder of relative truth is the method of Comparison. So we compare relative things to conclude the relative truth of them compared to other relative things. Relative truth belongs to the worlds of duality. The only way to understand relative truth is by using the method of comparison. In these dualistic worlds, we must compare two points, two conditions, two teachings, two people, or two events in order to come to a solid understanding of the relative truth of them. We learn by comparison and we teach by comparison. For example, the average person is living, which is a reality, but while living they are dreaming all the time and a dream is not a reality. Yet dreaming can be transformed in to reasonable thinking, which is a reality. Now, as we seek to know the relative truth, we have two points of comparison – dreaming and clear thinking. As we progress in this study of the relative truth we will advance to being able to compare three, four or more points.

So we can study what the reality is and what the illusions are by comparison. This study reveals that there can be no illusion unless there is a reality behind it. In our study we move from the illusion and enter the reality behind the illusion. Even when we pass over after the death of our material body we still will gain knowledge by comparison. This is the method used by the "Invisible Helpers", the light workers, in the Psycho-Noetical planes of existence to assist those who get caught in their shell-hells and can't escape. In these higher worlds, they can help people see things better and create in them a desire to come out of their self-imposed hell. To do this, an invisible helper can safely enter the shell-hell of a person in the Psycho-Noetical Worlds, temporarily take them out of it and show them a much better condition. The Invisible Helper cannot make that person choose the better way, but he can show them a better way. Then it is up to the person to choose.

Nothing can prevent a person from leaving their conditional hell if they have the un-conflicted desire and firm decision to come out of it. However, in the multilayered Psycho-Noetical Worlds of gradated light, one person's hell can be another person's paradise and what is a paradise to one person is a hell to another. As we ascend the ladder of relative truth, it is helpful to notice that our approach to the light of truth has four obvious phases.

SEEING THE LIGHT OF TRUTH

The first phase begins with seeking to see the light of truth. We are encouraged to, "Seek" and we are promised that if we do seek, "…we will find." We are all free to seek and find the truth of anything, such as: The truth of why we suffer; the truth of who we are and what we are, where we have come from, where we are going and our purpose in this life. These are important questions not just for the Researchers of Truth but also for any sincere seeker from any spiritual system or religion. In seeking the truth about the constantly changing phenomena of life all around us we will one day find the truth concerning the changeless Eternal Life that lies behind all the these temporary forms of life.

During this first phase of seeking, the light of truth seems as something outside of us. At times we can rightly say, "I see the light." At first we see the light of truth as something external to be searched for in books, teachers and life experiences. So we begin devouring spiritual writings, attending spiritual workshops or maybe we embark on the "guru hunt" to find a master to help us in our quest. These things can help show us the way and illuminate our spiritual path. But only we can make our own movement along this path and up the ladder of relative truth. Finding a true and selfless master is a great, great benefit but they will not walk your path for you. You must make this effort yourselves to reach the light of truth.

IN THE LIGHT OF TRUTH

When we make the effort to find a greater measure of truth we are transformed by it. When this happens we can rightly say, "I am in the light of truth." Now we feel the light of truth is shining on us; we bask in it, savoring its harmony and beauty. When we find such a clear stream of truth it is natural to want to follow it to its source, to know greater and greater measures of this truth. "Know the truth and the truth will set you free." This gentle persuasion urges us to experience the truth for ourselves. It does not suggest that we blindly follow what others say the truth is. It advises us to make our own effort to know truth directly.

Finding truth and comprehending it intellectually is one thing, but to really know the truth means to understand it experientially beyond ordinary, limited thinking. To penetrate deep into truth, to grasp real meaning, requires: Introspection, Observation and Meditation. These are the prime tools of the Researcher of Truth, which leads deeper and deeper into the light of truth.

THE LIGHT OF TRUTH WITHIN

As we continue onward we will eventually experience a new perspective on the issue. The light of truth we first sought outside of ourselves is now revealed inside. In this third phase, we see and know this radiant light of truth as something within us. This light of truth is not coming from the personality but from something much, much higher. It arises from that Divine part of us which is virtually incomprehensible to our personality. It comes from within and this magnificent light illumines our personality. We begin to experience increasing measures of the liberating truth that resides within us all. Then we can rightly say, "The light of truth is within me."

I AM THE LIGHT OF TRUTH

Up to this point, our experiences of the light of truth have been necessarily dualistic. In each of the previous phases, our approach to truth has had a subject and object orientation. We are the subject, and truth has been the object of our search. This is a dualistic condition. However, Absolute Truth is not dualistic. When we begin to experience the higher states of Truth, we soon realize that the seeker is actually what is being sought and that the light of truth sought for is, was, and will always be the seeker's Divine Nature. However, with virtually all our attention focused through our five senses on the outer world and not the inner, we miss this fundamental fact.

In scaling the ladder of relative truth concerning our self-awareness where should we start? We start with what we know for sure and that is that we are living in a material body. No one doubts this, and so our body is our starting point, which is like one end of a line that extends all the way back to our origin as an Eternal Spirit Being. We begin our life in a male or female material body with a name. Our name is not us; our name is just given to us by the notion of our parents. Continuing our investigation to trace this line of our Selfhood back to its source we see that this first part of the line represents our personality and is multicolored. The colors are not the same in all personalities, because no two personalities are the exactly the same. So the coloring of this part of the line represents the quality of our personality, our character. In other words, this line is colored by the quality of the thoughts, desires, words and actions we express.

Unfortunately, within all these colors there exists a confused mixture of shades, which our conflicting thoughts, desires, feelings and interests have created. At the core of this line of many colors there is that steady, pure and luminous ray of the Spirit-Soul. It is all the mixture of colors and shades created by our emotions, feelings, thoughts and interests that cover this perfect ray of the Spirit-Soul Self. This bright ray absorbs whatever good is present in the shell of our multicolored thoughts and emotions. This means that the Inner Self, our Permanent Personality, distils, absorbs and accurately records our endless variety of experiences in time, space and place. Our Permanent Personality is that part of the Spirit-Soul Self that projects its ray into the Worlds of Existence to be incarnated. It is the personality's acceptance of different qualities of thoughts and emotions that causes the continual change within our temporary personality.

For example, we can imagine that we put a thin glove on our hand and then a bigger glove over the first one and move our fingers we will see the fingers of the outer glove move. The outer glove represents our mortal material body, the inner finer glove represents our temporary personality and the hand inside both gloves is the immortal Soul Self. When we move the fingers of our hand we can clearly see the fingers of the outer glove move but we are not able to see the fingers of the hand move, which is what is actually causing the fingers of the glove to move. We cannot see the inner glove move either.

So when we see the phenomena of movement in the gloves we know it is our hand that is making this movement. The gloves cannot move without the hand in them. If we take off both gloves from our hand they become completely lifeless. Put our hand back in the gloves and they take on the warmth and movement of the hand again. In a similar way when we see movement/life in our material body and movement/life in our personality we are seeing results of our eternal nature, which is Life. In other words, without the Inner Self within our personality and body, they would be as lifeless as the gloves without the hand in them.

The Inner Self is the ultimate reality and not our personality or body. Life and movement are not coming from our material body or our personality self-awareness. Life is the immortal Soul-Self. When you manage to find that steady fixed point in you that is receiving and distilling the experiences of your temporary personality self, you will have found the Inner Self. In the beginning you may not even recognize it, but with the practices of Observation and Introspection you will be able to distinguish it quite well.

This is very beautiful to find your real "I-ness" and discover you are not who you thought you were: just a frail creature with strengths and weaknesses that sometimes feels unsure, hurt, and offended. We can only reach this level of awareness after we calm down the emotions and thoughts gushing through our personality all the time. This means we must learn to be the master of our own home. Now we will find our body and personality will become more powerful. You can never achieve this level of self-mastery as long as you misidentify your real Self with your personality and body.

At this very moment we are both our temporary personality and our Permanent Personality. To understand this better we need to separate these two and see the difference. How do we do this? It is again by comparison. Observing our temporary personality we can see that it is always in a state of flux. It constantly changes over the course of our life from cradle to grave. What changes are our fluctuating sets of thoughts, desires, feelings and interests.

Our personality is like an instrument, like a Stradivarius violin. Our fine instrument is constantly being influenced by circumstances in our environments and it can succumb to these influences and go out of tune. For example, sometimes a slight provocation around us creates annoyance in our personality and produces the unhealthy condition of an irritated egoism. Sadly, we are mistaking this inharmonious egoism to be our Self.

At times we may have this experience; but there is always a point within our personality where we can stop and say no to our egoist reactions. If we introspect on our egoistic reactions, we will find that these reactions are a product of past influences.

This reveals that it is only egoism that reacts in anger, gets annoyed and taking matters in its own hands much to your detriment. Now we can say no, "In the future I will not react egoistically; I will be the master of the situation." When provoked by others I will smile and turn away. Or I will try deeply to understand this provoking behavior; why that person thinks the way they do and how I am being affected by it. Now as a real researcher we are studying human behavior (ours and theirs).

From now on when someone criticizes and characterizes you in an undesirable way, you will be able to research the matter yourself to see to what degree they may be right or wrong. Ask yourself: why has this person come to this assumption about me, but be careful when coming to a conclusion, because your own cunning egoism will start to instantly condemn the other person and exonerate its own negative reactions by making excuses for it. When this happens you can be sure that this is not the true Self. This is a precious moment to catch and disable your own egoism. At this moment you have found your personality wearing an egoistic mask made of hurt feelings and thoughts of offense. Now is the moment to take a hold of it firmly so it cannot squirm and get away. Now you declare that you are not your egoism and will find that you can control it. This reveals that you are the Inner Self that has power to govern your egoism. This is a great, great step forward in your spiritual advancement.

When we begin examination of our personality our intent is not to kill our personality or punish it but to transform it. This is the point. As we find undesirable thoughts, feelings and desires in our personality we gradually stop these things the true Self does not need. As we remove these unnecessary habits, the true Self can now express itself through the personality in a much, much better way. Now our personality becomes brighter, lighter and happier.

It is like having a cloth over a light bulb. If the cloth is dark and dirty not much light will be seen, but if you make that cloth, cleaner and lighter in color then lighter from the bulb can radiate through. Nothing has happened to the light bulb, it did not increase its intensity; but now more light comes through the cloth. Similarly, in cleaning our personality, we are not losing anything important we just gain more of the light. The light did not change; the light was always there brilliant and luminous, just waiting to be uncovered.

So we gain strength in our personality by leaving behind egoistic thoughts and feelings; and we find the Inner Self. Which means that you do not need to make a herculean effort to find the true Self because it is you!

The practice of Introspection requires comparison. This is not a difficult thing to do when you feel you are the Permanent Personality, but it does have dangers. The dangers are in being convinced by the false arguments that come from your own egoism. In introspecting on a disagreement with another person, your egoism will present itself as you saying in essence that the other person was wrong, you are right and that you should intervene, stand up for yourself and show the other person they are wrong.

In virtually all-serious arguments, whether you intervene and argue back or not, it will not make much difference. If you do argue, it will just be more words against a relentless stream of words coming from the other person, which create negative Elementals that sow discord and confusion in and around us. So the fewer Elementals created under these conditions the better. Typically no matter what you do or how hard you try to explain something to a person you are in an argument with, you will not change their mind. You will be either attacked or ignored and so it becomes futile. However, this is still a great opportunity to teach yourself to remain calm and observe how the other person thinks. This requires mastery of your thoughts and emotions, which is really a Concentration and Observation exercise.

Each day we get hundreds and hundreds of opportunities to learn like this and the most valuable part is to be able to carry out a detached self-examination of our own behavior. Let's say someone's behavior to us is off and they act very disagreeable towards us. The common person's response is to feel they are being mistreated and maybe offended or wounded. So when you have the thought or hear a voice rise up from your sub-consciousness saying that, "I am being mistreated," or "You are being mistreated," and that you should speak up…please don't. This is where your strength lies. Keep quiet and silence that voice from your sub-consciousness. What will happen if you do that? If you research conditions and study them in this way, much to your amazement you will eventually realize that you are not who you thought you were. You will discover you are not the wounded or offended egoism who feels mistreated, you are something much, much greater and more beautiful than all that.

You may also find that your Sub Conscious mind is like an untamed wilderness full of harsh emotional beasts as well as beautiful songbirds. Both find expression in your conscious mind. We should consciously choose which of these we give expression to. It may not seem obvious at the moment, but really the only one that can mistreat us is our own egoism. Egoism is the only one who is feeling mistreated and screams at others. It is the egoism that is mistreating your Inner Self and sometimes other people in your life. We can see this in others too; in how victimizers so often cry that they are the victims of other people. When you see this kind of behavior in others, and in yourself, do not judge just calm down. The egoism in you and in others sometimes behaves like a temperamental child, but if you blame and slap it will not help at all. No matter how bad tempered yours or any personality becomes; conflict is not the answer, love and calmness are needed. By reason and correct suggestions from the Inner Self we can succeed to improve the situation. The personality often behaves like a child, but like a child, when it is calm it will accept suggestions.

THE PRACTICE: OVERVIEW

Practicing Introspection using comparison is a scientific approach in which we discern the Inner Self from its shadow, our personality. Our personality is subject to time, space and place and has its own consciousness and sub-consciousness. On the positive side, the calm aligned personality likes to feel that it is this Inner Self. In full attunement - it is. On the negative side our personal egoism likes to deceive and masquerade as the Inner Self.

So when we do our research with the practice of Introspection, we must be careful not to allow our own egoism to distort the truth and deceive us. When we begin, we must be clear as to which one is the egoism and which one is the Inner Self. It will be the personality, which is under the examination of the Inner Self during introspection. So we need to separate our identification of the Inner Self from the personality, which is its reflection in time and place.

This separation is important in order to be able to compare the two. When you are able to make this separation, you find you are not a stressful, suffering being but a rational being with love, wisdom and strength that can make real progress in life.

When the personality starts to split, a clash occurs. This clash is only a conflict within the personality. The Inner Self does not struggle and rebuke its projection, the personality. On the contrary, the Inner Self acts like a loving mother who advises and corrects the personality in order to one day be able to assimilate with it. Do not make the mistake to think the practice of introspection is just studying your desires and interests in life that please your personality and then continue to live in your usual manner. This is not Introspection but self-deception, self-delusion. Real Introspection is positive, logical and produces noticeable results. Not everyone is practicing Introspection in exactly the same way because the environment and circumstances of their life are not the same for everyone. The problems are similar but the specific details are different for different people. The problems of getting hurt, feeling offended and carrying guilt is a common experience to all. What it is that specifically makes someone feel wounded, offended and guilty differs from person to person.

Our aim in understanding this dynamic in us is to be free from our misconception that our personality self is the real Self. To do this we must take action in researching our heart, mind and in improving our behaviors within our current circumstances. Again, this requires that we be able to make the distinction between our own personality-self from the Inner Self, otherwise we will not change and make much progress. The method that really makes any person change is that of comparison. To help others we can only use the method of comparison; to show them a better way and conditions so that one may freely choose. Unfortunately, as visible and Invisible Helpers learn, only about twenty percent of the people will take this help and make a real change.

Again, we cannot know the Absolute Truth but we can know the relative truth and how much of it corresponds to the Absolute Truth. We learn the relative truth by the comparison between two things, two people or two conditions. There is no other way.

PRACTICE: INTROSPECTION BY COMPARISON

Breathe deeply and feel you are completely in your material body.

While feeling your material body, ask yourself the question: Who am I now, concentrating and feeling my material body?

Try to find your real Self, your "I-ness" and not the personality self that bears your name.

Breathe deeply and feel that you are in your material body.

Love your material body.

Simply feel you are inside your body and completely relaxed.

Every muscle should be relaxed.

Now, you have to make two thoughts and compare. What is this material body that I can feel and who am I, who can feel and move my material body?

Now start your comparison between you and your body

Your body is not you. Your body is yours to live in. Your material body is your temporary home.

The Holy Spirit is caring for it and keeping it in good order, circulating the blood, providing it with warmth and vitality.

That is not you as a personality doing this work.

Now compare your body with the heart of your personality – the Inner Self.

That sense of I-ness you are now. That sense of I-ness you have always been. Your body is yours.

Your personality is your creation. And you are you.

But what are you?

Try to understand what you are.

What you are is a god but this god is living in a bodily form.

Just compare these two, enter deeply in the meaning of it and ascend the ladder of relative truth.

Chapter Twenty-Two
THE TRUTH ABOUT MYTHS

We have said that in the class of Elementals called desire thought forms, which range from the most unclean and nightmarish to the most foolish, harmless and innocent. We will study them and see that we create quite a lot of them; we project them and place them in our subconscious daily. I won't ask you to dissolve them all at once, it is not necessary. But we must do away with the harmful ones. We will start dissolving them, particularly those which give us unhealthy feelings in that great Elemental called Egoism, which are; anger, aggression, the feeling of being offended, the feeling of being wounded, lying, blaming and backbiting. We must study all these and each one of you, with honesty to start going within yourselves to research in that labyrinth (maze) and find that frightening Minotaur. And like Thesus, it is your duty to kill the Minotaur.

Believe me, you have within you a horrifying beast (minotaur) which you gave birth to and you are obliged to kill him before you move on. Other Elementals seem like playthings in front of this Minotaur, a most frightful Elemental that we must overpower, and neutralize. And then we will see what good Elementals we have created within us because you must not despair, you have built good Elementals too, but you need to develop them further. We must learn how, through creative thought, which is: to project an Elemental of thought desire form. To project consciously powerful images with which we can build a better world. It is our obligation to build a better world. ~Daskalos

THE TEACHING

The first caveman who began to wonder, "Who am I and

where am I," was researching the truth. At that time the first humans were living in caves behaving in a mostly instinctual way expressing strong emotions. They had a rudimentary form of self-consciousness but they were not behaving much differently than all the animals around them. However, mankind had a distinct advantage over the animals because they had the possibility of using the Mind and developing their self-consciousness. The animals only have the Mind as instinct.

Mankind slowly began to use the Mind and develop a primitive self-consciousness, which in time evolved into the range of self-consciousness we see in our society today. Since animals cannot use the Mind directly their consciousness has not changed at all. A bear today is behaving as all the bear from the past behaved. Although we do see some adaption of bodily forms in certain species, their changing environment and not an evolution in their consciousness drove this. An ape is behaving in the same way today as they did a hundred thousand years ago.

However, mankind at this time, even in its embryonic state of self-consciousness, was able to use the Mind to increase its level of awareness and become more and more self-conscious. During this period, humans and animal lived in a very dangerous world. When we look at the animal life we see that the Divine Intelligences gave different types of protection to different animals. A lion has physical strength, teeth and claws, a rabbit has its incredible swiftness, and a turtle has its shell and so on. What about mankind? What did God give to mankind to protect it? The Mind! Mankind has the ability to use the mind as reason and intelligence to protect itself.

Living precariously in this hostile environment with very little resources, the cavemen felt the need to create gods to protect them and believed they helped them. They were right in the belief that those gods were protecting them. What they did not realize was that they themselves were the ones creating these gods. In reality these gods were Elementals and the cavemen created them subconsciously. These Elemental gods became more powerful than the people who created them, because they were strengthened over long periods of time by the energy of all the people who worshiped them. This gave these created gods their own existence and life. The gods of the past, that still exist today, did help their creators.

They still exist today in the Cosmic Consciousness, but they are inactive because people stopped worshiping and energizing them. At the time they were active but now they are no longer in use, and yet they are still traceable as inactive Elementals in the cosmic memory (which is everywhere). They can still be contacted and their nature studied if one is able to raise his consciousness to the level of Self-Super-Consciousness. They are recorded permanently in the cosmic consciousness, which is really just the memory of God. Those gods of the past were manmade. This is what materialists say and they are right.

Daskalos once had this conversation with some atheists who were visiting him from Russia. When he agreed with them that man made these anthropomorphic gods of the past, he then asked them but who made man and his thinking personality?

They replied, "Circumstances, coincidences and matter". He said, "That is not good enough".

They argued saying, "But matter has made all the animals, trees, living forms of life and human beings".

Daskalos explained that a human being is the offspring of God and as such is a god. They replied, "The Hindus say that and the Christians are claiming that too". Daskalos retorted in his usual witty way asking them, "Do you think all these people were claiming something stupid and now you are the only wise one?"

Because the people created the gods they tended to ascribe their own faults, vices and weaknesses to their created gods. Yet, any god ever created still exists in the Absolute Beingness. These gods were created by Mind and continue to reside within the cosmic memory of Absolute Beingness. This means that when primitive cultures anywhere in the world kneel down and pray to a crude, ugly wooden form of a god, they are still worshiping Absolute Beingness without understanding it.

When people from modern so-called civilized societies see this, they call such people idolaters. This is wrong since everything is of God and from God, whether they know that or not. The people still need to believe they have the protection of intelligences and powers higher than themselves. That was a necessity of mankind since the time of the caveman.

Christians consider themselves as Non-Idolaters and yet in the Roman Catholic and Orthodox services they pray to the saints and display icons of them. You can see people in the Orthodox Church kiss these icons as part of their worship of the saints. Then, in the 16th century the so-called reformers, in a reaction to the rituals of the church doctrines, protested and thus became known as the

Protestants. They protested and criticized the church for its devotion to Mother Mary, the Christian saints and removed them from their newly formed Protestant religion. From this point Christianity became increasingly fractured and splintered until today we have over 250 different man made Christian factions.

It was a mistake to remove the devotion to the saints and Mother Mary because this form of worship benefited people. Mother Mary is the Earthly mother of Joshua Immanuel the Christ. The person Mary reflected the true nature of motherhood, which was a principle even before the birth of the Virgin Mary who gave birth to Christ. In her purity she perfectly reflected this Mother-principle that is the universal, Absolute Femininity of the Holy Spirit. Now the cavemen, who out of necessity and fear of the natural world created with their thought, superior beings to protect themselves. Man can do this because he can use the Mind directly, but no animal ever created a god to protect them. The conditions on Earth at the time of the caveman were extremely difficult. If we had to live that way, we would perish very quickly.

So the men and women at that time were living in caves and found life in that world harsh and unfriendly. There were many active volcanoes spewing forth red-hot lava and smoke that blocked the light from the sun, which created a choking atmosphere. There were horrific weather patterns, which created violent storms that lasted for very long periods of time. Great and frequent Earthquakes, causing mountains to rise and fall killing people in the process.

The cavemen and cavewomen both had to carry heavy clubs to protect themselves from other cavemen, cannibals and the large carnivorous beast who sought to eat each other and man in order to survive. The caveman's primitive self-consciousness used the Mind only to protect him and satisfy his crude but extremely strong emotions. Threatened by the dangers around him he created gods to muster up the courage needed to live in these hellish environments and so mankind created gods for the sun, moon, fire, water, wind and lightning and all the forces of nature. To these he gave names and sometimes the Human Form and sometimes animal forms.

When many people worshiped these Elemental-type gods over time it gave strength and intelligence to the Elemental. These Elementals could then influence their worshipers producing tangible experiences. Seeking to preserve these experiences early man began to create symbols to record their experiences for themselves and future generations in the form of the early cave paintings showing symbols and pictographs from the distant past. Then later these symbols and pictographs were carved in stone like in ancient Egyptian and Mayan cultures.

The benefit of symbols was that they allowed the meaning of ideas and events to be preserved, then remembered and passed down to future generations. By combining the symbols early man was able to express his beliefs in a succession of thoughts. The first symbols were: straight lines, lines in congruence with other lines, intersecting lines, triangles, curves and circles. These symbols were also creating Elementals and were the forerunner of the early alphabetical languages, which evolved into other languages. For example the ancient mid-eastern Aramaic language came from the Egyptian hieroglyphic writings. The Hebrew and Arabic languages came from the Aramaic language.

Soon early man began to consider their relationship with the animals all around them. They admired them for their abilities and powers and began to worship them as gods. The bear was one of the first gods formally worshiped by the primitive people, because it was the most powerful thing in their world. This kind of animal worship continued over many thousands of years. The ancient Greeks, Hindus and Egyptians also developed a vast collection of gods. We see that from the very beginning mankind developed multi god systems of worship. These polytheistic systems continued unchallenged until around 1350 BC. Then an Egyptian pharaoh named Amemophis IV had an ecstatic, direct experience of God. The pharaoh immediately disassociated himself and his rule from the multi-god system and established the first monotheistic system worshiping one God. He called the one supreme God: Aton, which means the incomprehensible. Amemophis IV and his followers believed in one God – the God of Infinite Life. They used the sun to represent this. They did not worship the material sun that made life on Earth possible, but the giver of life itself for which the sun was a symbol.

After his experience the pharaoh changed his name to Ankh-en-Aton, which means the servant of the God Aton. He changed the name of his wife, Nefertiti to Merit Aton and the names of his nephew Khor Amon to Khor Aton. Later pharaoh Akhenaton adopted the infant son of his cousin and named him Tut-Ankh-Aton. Akhenaton and his hierophants started a new system for the worship of the one omnipresent God - The giver of all life. Unfortunately,

Pharaoh Akhenaton was ahead of his time. The existing thousand year old, multi-god religion of Egypt was not ready for such a profound change. The leaders of the 42-god system were not ready to give up their lucrative jobs as priests in the old system. So these priests conspired to put an end to Akhenaton and his one God system. They killed his nephew Khor Aton by stabbing him and they killed Akhenaton by poisoning. His wife, who was also a high Hierophant in the system, had to escape to the south of Egypt to save her life.

    The cunning leaders of this plot temporarily enthroned Tut Ankh Aton, the remaining rightful heir to the kingdom, and changed his name to Tut-ankh-amen. Today he is most commonly known as King Tut. Then possibly as new evidence suggest, they soon disposed of the 19-year-old boy king and the conspirators put themselves in power. Then they got to work, and went all through Egypt eradicating the names of Akhenaton and King Tut from public record. They were so effective that the long line of succeeding Egyptian pharaohs, as well as history in general, had no idea Akhenaton and his adopted son King Tut even existed. It was not until 1922 with the discovery of King Tut's tomb that knowledge of his existence came to light. Akhenaton's murder, like Socrates and Christ's is often the reward to those who bring the light of truth into a dark world of ignorance. This is also a reason why enlightened people in the past hid the truth in stories, parables and myths.

    The truth about the myths used in the ancient mystery schools is that they used myth as a metaphor. A metaphor is a kind of figurative language. It is not meant as an exact literal account. A metaphor is a symbolic representation of some higher truth or some deeper meaning. Today myth is generally considered to be a fictional story. Mythology is one thing and fiction is another. In the myths used in the mystery schools we see both. In the fictional aspect of these stories you can see things that really did not take place but do convey a symbolic meaning. In other parts of the myths we find descriptions of real events. Together they are allegories intended to convey spiritual truth and guidance.

So as researchers we can study the ancient myths for guidance and instruction on our spiritual journey. As students of any spiritual system, we initially seek to comprehend the theoretical framework of the spiritual teaching itself with some degree of understanding of that teaching we seek to put it into practice. In doing so, we soon discover that our spiritual unfoldment comes from the practice and integration of the teachings in our life, rather than just knowing the teachings intellectually. When attempting to integrate spiritual teachings in our life we inevitably encounter difficulties. Myths that are understood as spiritual metaphors provide vivid archetypal imagery depicting the predictable obstacles on the path of Self-Realization. Their dramatic and colorful narratives imprint their meaning and guidance deep into the mind of the student, which can be recalled to guide them during their own difficulties and tribulations.

One of the classic Christian Myths is the Arthurian legend of the Quest for the Holy Grail. The Holy Grail is the cup Christ drank from at the Last Supper, in which according to legend; Joseph of Arimathea collected Christ's blood after the crucifixion. From that point on, the Grail was believed to have miraculous properties.

Joseph of Arimathea is the one who gave his tomb for Christ's burial and purportedly brought the Holy Grail with Christianity to Britain.

The Quest for the Holy Grail story begins in Britain in the twelfth century with King Arthur and his Knights of the Round Table. After numerous adventures and great accomplishments, the knights were getting a little bored and decided they should embark on a new adventure. Being brave heroic knights they chose the ultimate quest of all: the search for the life-giving Holy Grail. According to their creed, a true knight had to find his own way on his journey and could not follow the path of another. It would have been a disgrace for one of these knights to try and follow in the exact steps of another knight on such an important quest. Metaphorically, this is an important point for those seeking Self-Realization.

Ultimately we must make our own journey toward our goal. Masters, teachers, brother guides and books can light the way to Self-Realization. But in order to succeed in our quest, we must follow our own unique path. The destination is the same for all of us but our journey to get there will be uniquely our own. In this story, only one of the knights actually finds the Holy Grail. The others lose their way, become distracted, leave the search, or are killed. The one who finds the Grail, in most versions of this myth, is the knight called Percival. His name, Percival, means the "one who pierces the valley." A valley is a place in between two opposite mountains. So metaphorically the person, who can succeed in reaching Christ's cup of life, is the one who can penetrate between the extremes of duality and go beyond the domain of conceptual good and evil.

This Metaphor instructs the seeker of truth to take the middle path and not swing back and forth between the diametric poles such as aversions and longings. Or as Christ put it, "If therefore your eye be single, your whole body shall be full of light". Duality belongs to the temporary Worlds of Existence (material, Psychical and Noetical).

Our source and ultimate destination is, was and will always be in the non-dual realm of Beingness. Beingness is beyond duality with its twin expressions of relative good and evil, light and dark. For a seeker of truth the Grail Cup story is an inspiring and practical Myth that provides guidance for us on many levels. Historically, teachers and religions have always used stories and parables to convey their teachings to the often-uneducated masses. In Biblical Palestine, Joshua Immanuel the Christ used parables to veil his teachings from those opposing it while revealing it to those with, "Ears to Hear."

In the ancient Mystery Schools of Greece and Egypt, spiritual candidates were given myths as metaphors to meditate on in order to accelerate their spiritual unfoldment. These Myth/Metaphors serve as practical guidance during the process of spiritual unfoldment or what is called the Hero's Journey. In past times, spiritual candidates were often removed from the world, cloistered in a monastery and concentrated primarily on their spiritual life. This was done in part to isolate the aspirant from the coarser vibrations of the world so that they could more easily become aware of and attune to more refined spiritual vibrations. Today, however, most spiritual seekers are still engaged in worldly efforts and family activities while trying to tread the spiritual path. In this condition, worldly and spiritual vibrations can become mixed and cause confusion. In addition, today's seeker has an over-abundance of material to study and consider. When haphazardly done, this too can cause confusion and a kind of theoretical congestion. Yet, when rightly understood classical spiritual myths dispel confusion and serve as a reliable guide for the seekers of truth today.

Another such story used in the Greek Mystery Schools was that of the Cretan Minotaur. The Minotaur was a raging monster with the head of a bull, the teeth of a lion and the body of a man. It represented uncontrollable lusts and powerful egoistic expressions in humankind. The Minotaur was the offspring of Poseidon's Bull and King Mino's wife. The offspring of that union was so hideous King Minos built a huge and complicated underground labyrinth-prison for the deadly monster to dwell in. This maze of chambers was so complex that it was impossible to navigate it without help. To satisfy the beast's ravenous appetite, King Minos would release seven girls and seven boys into the maze for the monster to devour.

At this time the hero of our story, Theseus, hears about the sacrifice of the seven boys and seven girls went to Crete and volunteered to take the place of one of the boys in hopes of slaying the Minotaur and saving future generations of children. Prior to entering the labyrinth, the hero Theseus, meets and falls in love with Ariadne, the daughter of king Minos. Because of her love for Theseus, she shows him a map of the maze and gives him a ball of twine to tie to the entrance of the labyrinth so he can find his way back out. So the next day, Theseus unrolled the ball of string as he entered the gloomy darkness of the Minotaur's maze. Theseus made his way over the bones of the previous victims, found the Minotaur, killed it, and escorted the other sacrificial youths out of the maze by following the string back to the entrance.

This Myth metaphorically represents the essential task of any spiritual seeker who enters into the maze of their own sub-consciousness. There they will find their destructive egoism that has been consuming the Etheric Vitality of their own seven energy centers (Chakras). The seven youths, symbolize the seven prime Chakras. Like Theseus, we need help if we are to be successful in completely eliminating our own egoism. This help can come from spiritual teachings; or it can come from a brother guide who loves us and is willing to lead us. This help, symbolized by the princess Ariadne, can and does come from our own Guardian Angel, who stands ready to show us the way out of the maze of our own confusion and into the light of Truth. The Minotaur of our own egoism continuously tries to lead us away from the light and into the darkness of its convoluted lair where it has the advantage. Our own hero's journey requires that we neutralize this inner adversary and find our way back out of the labyrinth and into the light.

A similar western myth that addresses this same fundamental challenge is Saint George and the Dragon. This and other legends have different versions and levels of interpretation. To the seeker of truth, this myth depicts the internal struggle to overcome his or her egoism. Here the dragon represents uncontrolled egocentric desires and unbridled emotions. In this image there is a lake of water and a woman that is held hostage by the dragon. Saint George is shown riding a white horse and killing the dragon with a spear. So unless you believe there were real dragons in Christian history, then this myth is a metaphor with symbolic meaning. In this story, Saint George represents our inner Self-Aware Soul. The woman, who Saint George saves from the dragon, represents our personality, which has been enslaved by the dragon of egoism. The horse represents our material body; while the spear represents the proper use of Mind as reason, intelligence and will-power. It is by using Mind as reasonable thought that we put an end to wild emotions and endless desires. It is through the use of our mind that our emotions are calmed, cleaned and mastered.

Now we come to our teaching on the Symbol of Life. The symbol of life as a means and methodology; has been used by spiritual seekers for many, many thousands of years. It charts a way of progressing from material mindedness of the three-dimensional world, to the fourth dimensional Psychical Worlds, on to the fifth dimensional Noetical Worlds and beyond. As a methodology, the old Greek myth of the twelve labors of Hercules is initially used to help the seeker make his first steps. The practice is to visualize each of the twelve labors many times in order to help us understand and overcome certain elements in our personality-self that are serious obstacles blocking our way. It is a simple and effective way to learn about and conquer weaknesses found in every personality. The first two labors are very important for any spiritual seeker if they expect to see significant results. The first labor is to kill the lion of Nemea, which represents anger and wrath. Every person should be on the watch for anger to rise up and present itself. We are expected not only to kill it, but find the causes which create it and exterminate the causes.

I knew a woman who was sure she did not have any anger in

her. Then she had children. Her life circumstances changed and placed new demands on her patience and tolerance. Then she discovered that she did have anger but it had been slumbering in her Sub Consciousness and awakened under new challenges in her life. So we must kill this monster in us. We ourselves must use our real will power to strangle the lion of our anger. Which is to say that no matter what the provocation, the seeker of truth must not let anger be expressed through his or her personality.

One afternoon, several hours after a Stoa lesson I was sitting with Daskalos and he told me that a new person came to the lecture that day. After the lesson he came and told Daskalos that he made mistakes and should have said this and that. Daskalos advised me that, "People coming to you will wrongly criticize what you are doing and you may just feel the urge to react and maybe slap them, but you must not; instead just say thank you." Daskalos said categorically: "A Researcher of Truth is not allowed to have anger for anyone, even those that treat us like their enemy."

Now in this myth Hercules strangles the lion to death and then cuts its head off and places it on his head. The symbolic reason for this action is that cunning people must not know that a seeker of truth is harmless. This is because there are opportunists around us that might try to take advantage of our harmlessness. In this case it is ok to raise the tone of your voice but under no conditions should we lose control of our emotions.

The Buddhists teach this in their own symbolic story about a vicious snake that terrorized a village. The people were afraid to go even close to where this snake lived because it would aggressively attack and bite them.   One day the villagers sought the help of a monk. They told him the story and he said he would try to help.

So he went to the snake and began to explain that man was really a brother to the snake. How the snake must never bite man who is his brother. This was no ordinary snake and it understood the monk's teaching and promised never to bite anyone again. A week later the monk was passing by where the snake lived and found the snake beaten, bleeding and near death. The monk rushed to the snake and asked what had happened. The snake said, "I never should have listened to you because when the people found out I would no longer bite; they threw rocks and beat me with sticks". To which the monk replied, "I told you not to bite but I didn't say you could not hiss."

So in our meditation on the first labor we examine and know what causes the feelings of anger in people and especially in our self. Some of these causes arise when we feel that something we want is taken from us. Or when something we do not want is forced on us.

The most common and most dangerous catalysts for anger are the feeling of being offended by people and its twin spirit, the feeling of being hurt by people. Now we should contemplate what happens after a lion of anger becomes active in someone. Just think what a ferocious lion can do. What can a person who is under the influence of wrathful anger do? In the myth it says weapons were useless against this lion. The weapons are a symbol of helpful Elementals we might try to use to stop this lion of anger. Even good Elementals cannot kill anger in us. Instead our hero, Hercules, must get a hold of the lion and strangle it to death. This is showing that it is only the real willpower that can suffocate and kill anger in the personality; it cannot be eliminated in any other way.

So the hero Hercules must come forth and kill it, only then can he can cut the skin and head off, clean it and put it on his own head. Then Hercules goes back to the king's palace wearing the lion head and skin and everyone was terrified and hid under tables or ran away.

This part means that after we kill anger in us we have to sometimes dress in the skin and head of the lion so that others will not take advantage of the quiet mind and loving heart of a seeker of truth. When we put on the skin and head, others can see the teeth of the dead lion but the head of a dead lion cannot bite others. This is the point.

So we find great teachings and practical guidance hidden in myths. The purpose of those who created the twelve labors of Hercules myth was to show the way towards enlightenment and Self-Realization and not just to invent children's bedtime stories.

THE PRACTICE OVERVIEW

When we do the mystery school meditations on the twelve labors of Hercules we are working in our Noetical workshop in our mind, which is represented by center number ten on the Symbol of Life. Before we begin we sit or recline in a comfortable place, feeling completely relaxed mentally, emotionally and physically. We inhale and exhale in a steady, comfortable rhythmical pattern as described before. Then in our mind's eye we will construct the environment in which the labor will take place. Visualize the entire labor in great detail and observe the scene unfold. Then we contemplate how the symbolic elements of the labors play out in us and in our life.

THE PRACTICE: SLAYING THE HYDRA OF DESIRE

This and other long practices can be recorded and played back to yourself, or read by a friend as you visualize each of the steps in the meditations. Each meditation should be done a number of times to be able to see the details clearly and be able to enter deeply into its meaning.

In the second labor of Hercules, he is ordered to locate and kill the Lernaean Hydra, which was a large fat serpent with nine heads that lived in a foul smelling marsh. The Hydra was devastating the farmer's crops and livestock near the town of Lerna. It was such a foul poisonous creature that its breath could kill. So Hercules took his cousin, Iolaus with him to hunt down and destroy the Hydra.

For this practice, we visualize the putrid swamp in a forest, and Hercules as a strong man of action, with his cousin Iolaus as a handsome young man. In your Noetical workshop, you will create this whole scene in rich detail. Start by seeing Hercules forcing the Hydra from its home in the swamp by shooting flaming arrows into the marsh.

As the beast emerges from the swamp on to the dry land in the forest, visualize Hercules drawing his razor sharp dagger and plunging it deep into the neck of the nine-headed Hydra. The huge serpent writhes in agony shrieking a hideous cry as Hercules completely severs one of the heads from its massive body. The moment the Hydra's head is cut off; two more heads emerges from the open wound and it was cured. Upon seeing this, Hercules' companion, Iolaus, set the forest on fire and begins to hand Hercules red-hot flaming brands each time Hercules cut off another head. Hercules continued to sever the heads, burning the open wound with Iolaus' flaming brands before more heads can appear, and thus Hercules kills the monster. Now see Iolaus and Hercules digging a deep hole in the ground and burying the dead Hydra and its severed heads thus completing the second labor.

The Hydra represents our lower uncontrolled desires. Its multiple heads represent the multifaceted kinds of desires we all have.

The swamp symbolizes our Sub Consciousness where the serpent of our desires hides. Hercules represents our Soul Self and Iolaus represents our Guardian Angel who helps in this labor. The flaming brands given by Iolaus is the Mind fashioned as reasonable thoughts, which can put an end to uncontrolled emotional desires.

The dagger used to cut off uncontrolled desires is our will power. When a head was cut off of the Hydra two more would appear and this is the heart of the teaching of this labor. A desire is just like the Hydra's head. If you cut off one desire, two other desires will appear unless the mind-fire of reason is used to cauterize it preventing more desires to grow in its place. Now the practice requires us to contemplate on the causes of our desires; to meditate deeply on the unquenchable thirst for possessing things. Of course desires for the necessary things in life are not bad, but to be slaves of our desires just in order to possess more and more is not necessary or good.

In deep meditation we visualize these scenes and the real life situational causes that activate desires in us. Then we visualize other people under the control of strong unbridled desires. A person controlled by passionate desires is capable of lying, cheating, stealing, attacking people and even killing them to get what they want. So we repeat this visualization exercise many times to find all the cases by which people become enslaved to their desires. By mastering unnecessary desires with reasonable thoughts we can become free from any ardent unfulfilled desires that will not leave us in peace, but continually rise from our Sub Consciousness. Even if a desire is fulfilled, it loses its power on us but is so quickly replaced by other desires. So we analyses our unfulfilled desires in this light; to see if what they seem to offer us is really worth all the trouble and cost needed for their fulfillment. In this practice we come to understand what desires really are and what the fulfillment of our desires really offer us.

Like in the Myth, when a Researcher of Truth decides to kill the Hydra of their lower desires, his or her own Guardian Angel comes to their aid offering the fire of reason to burn up uncontrolled desires in their personality. At first you may not notice this help, but later you will consciously realize the Guardian's relationship and powerful help. So we make the first step to cut off unnecessary desires and then the Guardian will come forward with his help. After completing this labor the Researcher of Truth well be stronger and in a better position to do greater work.

Chapter Twenty-Three
THE DEAD AND THE SLEEPING

Are all people really living consciously now? I am telling you 90% of the people are living subconsciously and they think that they are living consciously. Now, as human beings are today, they are living, I say -subconsciously. They don't know it, because, they cannot meditate -they cannot use self-consciously the Mind. What was Joshua the Christ calling these common people all around us, even in the so-called civilized countries? The Dead. Let the dead bury their own dead! So, for Joshua the Christ the common people all around then were considered dead and not really living, just as they are today. What I am telling you, is that today, most people do not live and they only think they do. They do not know who they are - for if they knew who they were everything would be very different. The world, the gross material world, which although is the lowest world, is beautiful and could be turned into a paradise, if human beings knew who they were. They do not know.

And when a Researcher of the Truth decides to join the research they do not say, Lord wait till I bury my father and then I will follow you. Because he or she will hear, "You follow me and let the dead bury their own dead." "Follow me", what does this mean? To leave everything: our concerns, duties, and our family? Of course not. A deserter returns to the place he or she has deserted. Each one is where he/she belongs according to the Divine Laws of cause and effect, in order to take his or her consequent lessons. Again, I suggest that each one should have a New Testament as his or her best friend and enter into the great, great meanings, especially of the sayings of Joshua the Christ. ~ Daskalos

THE TEACHING

"The child is not dead but asleep", Joshua Immanuel the Christ declared to Jairus and his family as they cried loudly over the death of his daughter. When they heard Joshua's pronouncement, "…they all laughed him to scorn for they knew she was dead." Joshua excused the crowd of doubting friends and family allowing only the departed girl's mother, father, and three of his closest companion disciples to stay. He took her by the hand and said to her in Aramaic, "Talitha koum!" (Which means: Little girl, I say to you, get up). "Immediately the twelve year old girl stood up and walked around. At this they all were completely astonished." It is interesting to note that in this biblical account, when Joshua went to Jairus' home to restore Life to the little girl's dead body, he would not allow all of his companion disciples to come, just John, James & Peter. The reason for this is that when doing healing work on a person it can be helpful to have loving friends present who wish to cooperate in the healing of that person. In healing work, if you have someone present who doubts, his or her doubting thoughts (Elementals) may negatively influence the healing work.

In the story of raising Lazarus from the dead, Joshua again refers to someone whose material body had really died, as not dead but only sleeping. He told his disciples, "Our friend Lazarus has fallen asleep; but I am going there to wake him up." Joshua's metaphor was so convincing that the disciples thought he was talking about natural sleep. So the disciples replied, "…if he sleeps then he will get better." Seeing that his disciples completely missed the point, Joshua had to plainly say, "Lazarus is dead, and for your sake I am glad I was not there, so that you may believe. But let us go to him."

Lazarus was only fifteen years old at this time and had already been cured of Epilepsy by Christ. He lived in Bethany with his two sisters, Mary and Martha. By the time Joshua and the disciples reached Bethany Lazarus had been dead for four days, his body entombed in a cave and sealed by a large stone. As requested by Joshua the people removed the large stone sealing the cave/tomb of Lazarus. Once it was removed, Joshua gave thanks to his Heavenly Father for hearing his prayers. Then in a loud voice Joshua called, "Lazarus, come out!" Lazarus emerged from the grave, his hands and feet wrapped and bound in strips of linen with his face covered with a cloth. Joshua said, "Loose him and let him go."

Taken from an exoteric historical perspective this is an important event in the short material life of Joshua in Palestine some 2000 years ago. This miracle was visible proof of the truth of Joshua's oral teachings and demonstrated that he was sent by God, but the underlying aim of this miracle was not just to reanimate a perishable body but also to inspire Faith in the people and show the mercy of God in an undeniable way. Like his crucifixion and resurrection Christ was proving the truth of his teachings that we are not just a mortal body, but also an immortal Soul that cannot be harmed or killed. We would miss much of the deeper meanings if we consider this to be only a historical record of a physical miracle. Just before raising Lazarus, Christ pointed to the esoteric meaning when he told Martha, the sister of Lazarus, "I am the resurrection and the life. He who believes in me will live, even though he dies; and whoever lives and believes in me will never die." Taken from an esoteric perspective, this account has deep hidden meanings.

Broadly speaking the meaning of this account is that of a true spiritual awakening – the resurrection of humankind's Divine Nature. Even the details of this event have great meaning to a Researcher of Truth today. First let us look at the meaning of the name Lazarus. Lazarus is considered to be a form of Eleazer, which means, "Whom God has helped." Lazarus symbolizes a personality that had become wrapped up, entangled in materiality, unable to help himself that slumbers in the tomb of its own sub-consciousness as if dead. It takes the Divine Self, to awaken one's personality from its own symbolic death.

Awakening a personality living an imprisoned life, enmeshed in materiality and buried in deep sleep, is not an easy endeavor. It takes a strong will and power to do this. Symbolically this is stated in the story that Jesus called in a loud voice, "Lazarus come out." This loud voice represents the powerful vibration of our own Divine Will Power calling and drawing our present-day personality into higher states of consciousness leading to full Self-Consciousness (Self-Realization). When Lazarus came out as commanded he was still tied up, his hands and feet bound with linen strips. These represent entanglements, which ensnare our personality during our Earthly lives, and if left unchecked they can ultimately induce a kind of spiritual coma. There is nothing wrong in having material things especially when we use them for good. However, being too wrapped up in material things is to become their slave and that can put our spiritual life into deep, deep sleep.

Joshua had the people remove the large stone that was sealing

Lazarus in his cave and called him to come out. Those who live their life strictly through a materially oriented consciousness have unwittingly placed themselves in a grave-like shell while others of like mind help seal them in with the stone of materiality. An overly worldly life always places heavy burdens of materiality on a man or a woman, which tends to suffocate their spiritual life. Today, this worldly weight seems to increase in quantity and complexity daily. A person living only in this way can be considered spiritually dead; and yet they can be resurrected to real life by the call of the Divine within them. Now upon seeing Lazarus coming from his tomb still wrapped in his grave clothes, Joshua said, "Loose him and let him go." This represents the release of the personality from its material bondage and suffering, with the restoration of its freedom to express its life anew. Notice how in both cases Joshua calls to the people present (Lazarus' worldly companions) to remove the stone of materiality and the wrappings of entanglements. These were the same people who wrapped Lazarus in these bonds and sealed his tomb with the massive stone. Sometimes worldly companions help bind and hold us to materiality. Once a personality has heard, understood and truly answered the call from its Divine Nature, no material thing can bind them.

The part of this story about the sisters of Lazarus, Martha and Mary, also contains a valuable teaching. Martha's personality was an overly busy and outwardly focused. Martha symbolizes an outwardly focused, material consciousness. Conversely, Mary's approach to life symbolizes a spiritual consciousness with a more inwardly contemplative focus.

The account says, "She [Martha] had a sister called Mary, who sat at the Lord's feet listening to what he said. Martha was distracted by all the preparations that had to be made. She came to him and asked, "Lord, don't you care that my sister has left me to do the work by myself? Tell her to help me!"

"Martha, Martha," Joshua answered, "you are worried and upset about many things, but only one thing is needed. Mary has chosen what is better and it will not be taken away from her." Both the "Martha" and "Mary" types of expressions are necessary. Without outward work nothing gets done. Without inner devotion, and spiritual receptivity; outward work alone becomes a dry, mechanical chore. The message in the above quote is to be careful not to over value outer, worldly activities to the detriment of an inner spiritual life.

Then again at Lazarus' tomb we see Martha expressing the material view. When Joshua asked that the stone which had sealed Lazarus' in his tomb for days be removed, the practical Martha immediately saw a problem and pointed it out by saying to Joshua, "Lord, by this time he stinks: for he hath been dead four days." Joshua replied, "Said I not unto thee, that, if thou would believe, thou should see the glory of God?" Here, the worldly mind as expressed by Martha could only perceive the perishable, the corrupting material body of her brother. Joshua, on the other hand, saw beyond the perishable material body, all the way to the incorruptible, imperishable Soul and called it back.

The historical account of this event ends with the high Jewish priests deciding to have Lazarus killed before word of Lazarus' resurrection spread throughout Israel and strengthened Joshua's following. Fortunately, Joshua persuaded Lazarus, Martha and Mary to make a quick escape to Cyprus before that happened. Later in the town of Larnaca, Cyprus Saints Barnabas and the disciple Mark appoint Lazarus Bishop. Here Lazarus lives for another 30 years. In Larnaca there is a ninth century Baroque style church dedicated to Lazarus that was restored in the seventeenth century. It is built over Lazarus' final resting place. If you go into the church's crypt beneath the sanctuary, you will find Lazarus sarcophagus. Bones reportedly from Lazarus body are on display and people come to touch them for inspiration in remembrance of Lazarus' resurrection.

The meaning of this story transcends all religions. It is not limited to Christianity but is a universal experience of the human condition. This call from Christ to Lazarus in the grave is symbolic of the clarion call by everyone's Spirit-Soul to his or her personality. This call is, was and will always be sounded. However, it is up to us to be ready at all times and in all places to hear that call and answer. Even in the brief history of psychology, we see leaders such as Carl Jung (1875-1961) describes this higher call as the Transformational Impulse within the human psyche. When we quiet our thoughts, still our emotions we can hear this call from home and tangibly feel something very high within us drawing us back to our Divine Nature.

Now we come to a bit of a paradox. In the previous stories, we see Christ referring to those whose material bodies had died, as not dead but only sleeping. In this next account Joshua calls those whose bodies are still alive "The Dead". When a man approached Christ and said to Him, "I want to follow you, but my father and mother are living. I will wait until the pass over and then I will follow you." Christ replied to him saying, "Follow me now and let the dead bury their own dead." When Christ said, "Let the dead bury their own dead," he meant that when we hear the call to follow God; we should not hesitate or postpone answering it because of our Earthly relationships. Christ said, "Anyone who loves his father or mother more than me is not worthy of me; anyone who loves his son or daughter more than me is not worthy of me." Of course Joshua was not making an egoistic statement here. He was not saying that we shouldn't love our family very dearly; he was making an important point that we should not place Earthly relationships ahead of our own relationship to God. Too many people live a subconscious, mundane life loitering about on Earth often like sleepwalkers. They do not lift their eyes up from their habitual material patterns to seek something higher. These are the ones Joshua refers to as, The Dead (spiritually dead at this time).

Relationships with the dead should not be given exclusive priority over cultivating our own spiritual life – this is the point. It is the same today as it was in Christ's time. The majority of people today are not really living. They don't know the higher Self, but the research of truth reveals this knowledge of Self and in finding that, we gain everything else. The Kingdom of God, the Kingdom of the Heavens is in the Inner, Divine Nature of each one of us. Find that and everything else will be ours. This was Christ's advice, "Seek first the kingdom of God, and his righteousness; and all these things shall be added unto you." Without true knowledge of the Self, knowledge about the world will never satisfy you.

In the Lord's Prayer we say, "Thy Kingdom come." We should not wait passively for that to happen, we must try and bring this Kingdom to Earth, but where exactly? It is not to be located in a certain place on Earth, but in each of us. We have a valuable system for researching the truth, which have given us bona fide saints, and Self Realized masters that reached the high level of Self-Super-Consciousness. Engaging in the System for the Research of Truth we have definite aims and objectives. The first is to get to know who we are as a personality through experience, Introspection and Observation. The second is to find what we are as a Soul and as Life. Thirdly we advance in our understanding of God, the Logos and the Holy Spirit. Gaining knowledge of the Soul Self also gives you knowledge of God. Knowledge of God also gives you knowledge of the Soul Self. As we progress over time this knowledge unfolds into wisdom.

We gain knowledge when we concentrate on a particular subject and we begin a sequence of thoughts. When we focus on something we actually are casting Noetical Light, mental light on it and that gives us information and impressions, which when analyzed yields knowledge about that object. Wisdom is different than knowledge, but knowledge leads to wisdom. Wisdom is what each object of our study has to offer us and through assimilation with it, we become the wisdom of it. With knowledge we are in duality, there are two distinct points: you and the object of your attention and focus: it and I. With wisdom, there is only one point: I am it.

In the early stages we get to know about God through the keys of Meditation and Concentration, then later through assimilation.

Similarly we first get to know about our Inner Self by study and then by assimilating our personality with the Inner Self. Through Introspection we come to identify and compare these two; the personality and the Inner Self. We find the common point between them, which is awareness: the personality self-awareness and the Inner Self-Awareness. So first we get knowledge and then wisdom. Once we advance to this point no one can take wisdom away from us. Our knowledge can be taken away by a persuasive argument contrary to the knowledge we have acquired.

In reaching Self-Realization, who are we? Clearly we are not just a personality with strengths and weaknesses that often is in confusion. In Self Realization we find what we are now and always have been - the Soul. To unfold yourself and feel being the Soul, you are not losing your personality self. Unfolding yourself within you, means you are gaining and not losing anything. You still remain you even as a personality with its name, but now your expressions in life will be different since you will no longer be guided by weaknesses, fears and lower desires. Even if you want to remember shadowy experiences from before you can, but who would want to? Once you see the light, no one will want to go back into the mental darkness of illusions. It is like being ill with the flu, once you recover you do not want to go back and feel ill again.

We can remain asleep to the greater reality of life and pass from this world and the next like a sleepwalker living habitually. We can continue this way for lifetimes, but not forever. Sooner or later we begin to awaken; slowly at first and then we start to live more and more consciously in our daily life. What happens during the night when our material body is sound asleep on our bed? What is sleep? Each night our personality withdraws from its material body and enters its Pyscho-Noetical Body for a number of hours. During this period the Holy Spirit rejuvenates the material body through the Creative Ether and makes repairs for our benefit.

Where do we, as self-awareness, go during this time when we are not in our material body? You could be just ten feet away, in terms of locality, dreaming in your Psychical Body. The average person has not developed their Psychical Body to the point of being able to use it independently to consciously express itself as self-awareness in the Psychical Worlds. Since most people do not try to strengthen and develop their Psychical Body by using their mental body (Noetical Body), they are like a sleepwalker in the Psychical Worlds too. Because of this, their Psychical Body does not become active. So this is our work, to activate the functioning of our Psychical and Noetical Bodies. If we did not use our material body it would atrophy and not function properly. It is the same with the Psychical and Noetical Bodies. Human beings are given these three bodies and are meant to use them. Of course we all know how to develop and use our material body through healthy living and exercise. We have specific meditation exercises that we can use to develop our Psychical and Noetical Bodies. As we become more alert and conscious during our daily life we automatically become more conscious in the Psychical Worlds. You will find that you will start to wake up in the Psychical Worlds during your dreams and realize you are dreaming. This is a beginning.

The Kingdom of the Heavens are worlds within worlds that we

should become conscious of, and live consciously in. Some people say they dream others say they do not dream. Some dreams are frightful nightmares, some dreams are illogical, other dreams are logical and still others can be prophetic. The problem is that we do not know the way to bring back the full experience and store it properly in our material brain as memory. The memories of our dreams can be disconnected, fragmented and jumbled together.

So this is why most people's dreams seem incoherent and illogical. It is not that all your dreams are incoherent; it is that the memory of the experience does not get imprinted correctly on your material brain. Daskalos explained how this happens with an example of an old-fashioned film-type camera, the kind you had to turn the film each time you wanted to take a picture in order to advance to the next frame so that each photo was imprinted separately. He said, "Let us say, if our material brain was like a film in a camera and we take one picture after another without turning the film. What will we see when we develop that film? The pictures we took are there, but the way they are imprinted is wrong. Therefore, we don't have clear pictures. So, the reason for the confused dreams is the wrong imprinting of experiences. Also there are many Researchers of Truth who are already working fully in the Psychical Worlds with their teachers but the next morning they do not remember much. Of course is not necessary to remember everything at first. They can work like this for years until they wake up and then they will remember all their experiences."

The meditations and practices Daskalos taught provide the means for creating an "etheric bridge" between the material brain and the Psychical Body, which will allow the memory of their Psychical experiences to be recorded in the material brain. Currently your memory of your nightly experiences in the Psychical Worlds is just a very tiny portion of all of your experiences there. You have forgotten most of them by the time you awake in the morning. Initially, to remember these experiences, takes practice to connect the etheric counterparts of the material, Psychical and Noetical Bodies so that memory can be transferred from one body to the other. Much later when we reach the higher states of full Self-Awareness we will not have to rely on this memory transfer.

With training a Researcher of Truth will be able to differentiate, know and work on his or her three bodies consciously. With further development over time the researcher as a self - awareness will no longer sleep at night. Of course the material body will sleep but the personality will simply withdraw from the material body not to dream but to live consciously within the Psychical World in a similar way as they were in the material world. With still further advancement a researcher if they wish can become an Invisible Helper and come to the aid of others in the Psychical and Noetical Planes.

Spiritual unfoldment is accelerated by service to others. So once we answer the spiritual call and begin to follow it we can become empowered by our progress and often feel the desire to help other people around us. Here we must use caution and distinguish between the dead and the sleeping. Christ's teachings never advise people to proselytize or press their beliefs on others. If we try to share the teachings and our good efforts are not welcomed, the advice is to wipe the dust from our feet and leave – don't force it. So in trying to help others, before we speak we must try to discern between those who are the unresponsive spiritually dead (at this point in time) and those who are only sleeping. If we want to help wake up a spiritually sleeping person we must go slowly. Firstly they should request your help before you try; we do not have the right to interfere with the free will of others. Each personality is different, so before we try to help, we must come to an understanding of who to tell what, how much to tell, and when to tell it. We will not be successful if we go rushing to a spiritually sleeping person and tell them, "Wake up. I found the truth and you must accept it now!" That will have about the same effect as rushing in to a person sleeping in their bedroom, turning on the lights and shouting, "Wake up, you must wake up now. Get out of bed!" This approach will only produce a most undesirable reaction. Instead let the loving vibration of our approach to help others gently say, "Wake up my Love."

THE PRACTICE OVERVIEW

In your effort to awaken spiritually, you first have to develop your ability to concentrate and meditate using certain exercises. Then a second step is to start to consider what your material body is. You know that your material body is not moving itself independently of your will. You know that it is you that moves your body here and there according to your will. Ask yourself, "Who am I that can move my body?" In the morning after sleeping all night your eyes open and you can now say I am awake, I get out of bed, I dress my body and move it throughout the day. Who are you that can do all this? This leads you to say, "I am" a personality and you know that as a personality you have varying combinations of strengths, weaknesses, thoughts and feelings. What is this I am?

This is a harder line of investigation –Who am I? What about all the people around you, your friends and family; who are they? Certainly their material bodies are similar to your own, but definitely their personalities are very different than yours. So who are you as a personality? Every night while sleeping you go into dream states, but during eighty percent of your sleep you enter into a dreamless state, a condition which seems like a state of non-existence to you. Yet each morning you awaken, recomposed as the identical personality you were before falling asleep the night before, with the same likes, dislikes and interests in life. Where were you during that dreamless sleep? If, during that time, you really were non-existent, how is it you awoke in the morning as the same personality?

So we practice this line of research in two ways. How and why we feel and behave the way we do; and how and others feel and behave as they do. This is due to the fact that there is a cause for all this that is common to you and to everyone else. That common cause is desire. Desire is the feeling of wanting something that catches your interest; you want to know more about it, maybe want to own it and call it yours. Why do you feel that way about certain things but not about other things? Likewise, why do certain things cause you to be upset and behave in an angry negative way, when other things inspire you and result in positive behaviors? If you take up this line of study you will come to realize that you thought you knew yourself as a personality, but now you realize that you are much, much more than what you thought before.

Now an even more serious investigations starts when you ask, "What am I?" You know you are a male or female but what is common to both sexes? Who you are as a male or female body and personality is different from one another, but as a male or female what you are is not different. Both males and females are Eternal Spirit Beings - no difference and both are on the same journey towards Self-Realization. What any man can do in this regard, any woman can do and all human beings have the same rights in life and the same ultimate destination of Self-Realization.

THE PRACTICE: WHO AM I? WHAT AM I? CONTEMPLATION

Relax your body and breathe deeply and comfortably. Breathe in as your heart beats four times.

Breathe out as your heart beats four times.

Continue breathing in this rhythm for a few minutes. Quiet your emotions and slow your thinking way down.

Forget your name; forget your gender, because as a Soul you are neither.

Then start this line of questioning, "Who am I? I am living, I am alive but Who am I." Continue to breathe deeply, rhythmically and comfortably.

Now ask, "What am I? What am I as a Soul-Self?" Don't be in a hurry. "What is the relationship between what I am as a Soul-Self to who I am as a personality self, with my strengths and weaknesses, my ways of feeling and thinking?"

Ask, "Who am I? What am I?" These are two distinctly different questions because in the Worlds of Existence we are dual, everything is dual.

You are living but ask yourself, "What am I as Life?

It is that "I am" that interests me and I want to know.

I am belongs to the realms of Beingness beyond the three Worlds of Existence.

Again ask, "Who am I? What am I?"

Expect the answer to these two questions to come in time from within, from your Guardian Archangel who is unified with you both as a Soul-Self and a personality-self. The result will be that you experience and know who and what you are. You can be sure you are on the correct way by the strengths you will gain. These Divine strengths are not given to the egoism of your little personality self. They are not given at all, they are latent within us all, we just have to find and learn to find and express them. In finding your Soul-Self you find your Divine strengths. If you do this contemplation every night before falling asleep, you will get the answer from your Guardian Archangel at a time when you are most ready to hear it.

Chapter Twenty-Four
DIVINE LOVE ~ HUMAN LOVE

What did Christ, the Godman, teach? Love! But, now we have to see things from a different point of view, not just from the angle of our personal interest. Because measuring things from our personal interest with that egoistic measure of our personality, we distort the meaning of everything -Distorting love in relationships, in the family, in the community -everywhere. A man claims to love his wife very much but maybe he kills her. Why? A woman loves her husband and her children very much, yet, torturing them. How does that woman love them? If you ask her do you really love them? She would say "Of course I love them." But you are torturing them. She would say, "They don't obey me. They don't listen to what I say. They don't do what I want them to do." Then, you don't love them if you torture them and punish them, because they don't do what you want them to do.

What do I mean? Human beings love by reflection. They love what satisfies their egoism and their way of thinking. Is that Love? This is the love certain people are expressing and, this kind of love is giving pain and agony! Now, analyze in yourselves the love you have towards your own people, the people you say you love; parents, wife, husband or children. Is that really Love? Or is it just an expression of your egoism? ~ Daskalos

THE TEACHING

Of course it is not possible to adequately describe Divine Love using words. What we can say is something about the characteristics of Divine Love and the various colored reflections of human love. Divine Love, is pure, perfect and self-sufficient. Divine

Love is non-dual. It is without the polarity of subject and object distinctions. Divine Love simply IS. It does not come or go. It does not decrease or increase. It has no reason or season. Divine Love is unconditional and everlasting because it is the very nature of God.

Beyond the oscillations of human love found in the three Worlds of Existence, we will find this unwavering Divine Love in the realm of Beingness and at the center of our Beingness, and all these Worlds of Existence are suspended within Divine Love. They are a creation of Divine Love. We, and the other inhabitants of these Worlds of Existence are embodiments of Divine Love - obscured to a lesser or greater degree by our self-created shells. It is the quality our own emotion/thought forms (the Elementals), which determine the degree of transparency of our personality's shell. Thus it is the composition of this shell that we must cleanse and make translucent to allow the radiance of this Love to shine forth, light our way and help others. Divine Love is the eternal nature of God and as a Spirit-Soul; it is also our eternal nature. Total Love is the prime expression of the Logos. Ultimately, Divine Love is the irresistible force that will claim us all one day.

In the Worlds of Existence we have the spectrum of human love with its vast range of expressions in varying degrees of purity. Love is often identified as an emotion. Real love is not an emotion, but an emotion can carry love. Likewise, noble thoughts and acts of kindness are carriers of love. Love's unifying force is found throughout the three Worlds of Existence (material, Psychical, and Noetical). We can even find it at work in the laws of physics in the material universe. As Daskalos often noted, "The scientific laws of cohesion and attraction are Love at the material plane."

In our prayer to God we say, "Clean our hearts to reflect Your Love towards You, and all other human beings." As a personality we can reflect Divine Love, but as a Spirit-Soul we emanate Divine Love directly from our own being. Divine Love is whole and everlasting. It never changes; it is uncontaminated and without any degrees of purity. As a personality we also express what we call human love, which has a wide range of purity that fluctuates over the course of time. At one end of the human love spectrum there is what is known as "selfish love." When human love between two people becomes contaminated with selfishness; then manipulation and domination over the so-called "loved one" can enter and damage or destroy the relationship. We all know about this kind of love At the other end of the human love spectrum is the luminous selfless love, which brings freedom and joy to both the giver and receiver. When we love selflessly we are reflecting Divine love brightly and clearly. Learning to love selflessly is a required course in the school of life.

So what is the difference between selfish love and selfless love since in both cases we are using the same word love? If you light a fire, the wood will crackle and smoke as it burns giving off some light. The smoke can get in your eyes and make you feel pain until tears run down your cheeks. Then we have the light of the Sun. What is the difference between the light of the sun and the dim light of a smoky fire? Both are light but there is a great deal of difference between these two kinds of light. Likewise, there is a great deal of difference between selfish love and selfless love. Selfish love can make you feel pain and agony and make tears run down your cheeks.

Problems in our relationships arise when we mistake love by reflection to be real love. Love by reflection is when someone is satisfying and feeding another person's egoism, which makes him or her think the other person, truly loves him or her. If your beloved starts to go against your desires complaining, blaming and maybe attacking, you might fight back and blame them too. Then the love between you starts to dissolve like a water-color painting in the rain. Maybe you both find out that each of you only loved the other person, when they loved your egoism. So it is this kind of reflected love between the egoism of two personalities, which we must be aware of because it is very dangerous.

For example, let's say a man meets a woman and that woman is very nice or complimentary to the man and it starts to feed his egoism. Immediately his egoism may start to swell and feel: I really like this woman; this lady understands me and appreciates me. So that man starts to "love" the woman by reflection. Now let's say the lady feels the positive attention and appreciation coming from the man and all that starts to make her egoism swell. So now her egoism starts to think I like this guy he really understands who I am and appreciates me – I think I am falling in love. So it builds on this with one person's egoism feeding the other person's egoism. One common aspect of egoism is that it can get totally infatuated with its self, so when another person seems to validate the egoisms view of itself, whatever that might be, the egoism mistakenly thinks this is love. Of course this is not evil – but it is not real love either. Maybe call it immature love, which potentially can mature into real love.

In too many cases what happens? At some point one person

sees something they do not like in the other's personality. When the one egoism realizes the other person does not see them in the same glorious way as it sees itself, that egoism starts reacting. Next comes the complaints, criticisms, judgment and fighting, which in marriages can lead to divorce. What started as two people attracted to each other ends in both people repelling each other. This love was conditional love. I love you because you do something for me that I want and you love me because I do something for you that you want. This type of love is more like a business deal than true love. What happens when one person stops doing that something for the other one?

    I am not saying that a relationship where each person fulfills and provides something to the other is not good or loving. What I am saying is that a relationship that is only based on feeding each other's egoism is dangerous. It is dangerous because sooner or later that way of life becomes unsustainable and then what? The relationship ether has to mature and grow into something better or come undone. Things cannot stay in this condition forever. Look at the life all around you. It is either growing or declining.

    What I am trying to say is that too often what we call human love is really love by reflection. What they really love is what is satisfying their own egoism and their point of view. This is love by reflection that people initially misunderstand and mistake to be real love. In the end this kind of love can cause so much suffering to each person. What kind of love is that? I knew a man who claimed to "love" his wife and yet for years and years told her he would literally kill her if she tried to leave him – and he meant it. He would even tell her how he would kill her and he would show her exactly where he would do it. This was the mother of his children and yet he firmly claimed he loved her but would kill her if she left. What kind of love is this?

So we have to see love from a higher perspective and not just from the vantage point of our own personal interests. If we allow our egoism to measure things based on its personal interests it will distort the love with our partner, with our family and fellow human beings. So this brings us back to the importance of the practices of Introspection and Observation. We need these tools to analyze what kind of love we have for our parents, our spouse and our children in order to weed egoistic love out of our garden.

Of course marriage should be something positive and it will be when it has the proper foundation. Let's look at marriage, or just call it a union between two people on Earth. Is it sacred? Is it binding? Of course to God, the physical union of a man and woman united in real love to become co-creators with God in creating a material body for newly incarnating Souls is sacred, but man and woman are more than just material bodies. So a good marriage of two people is more than just a loving physical union. What kind of union is created if there is not a union on higher planes too? This means the psychical and the Noetical; the marriage of the heart, mind and body is seen as the best foundation for a lasting marriage. Man is a trinity; even at the personality level we have the trinity – mental body, emotional body and material body. So without a harmonious union between all three bodies, a couple can be legally married, live together for many, many years and be very, very far apart.

One time in Cyprus, a German couple came to see Daskalos. All the time they were fighting and they had created a hellish condition in their marriage and in their home. Both had had it with each other and came to Daskalos for advice. They asked him, "Should we separate?" Daskalos retorted with irony, "You are already separated!"

People are attracted to each other and join in marriage and there are always lessons to be learned in any marriage. So now we have another point of view on marriage - the many lessons to be learned from marriage or marriage-like relationships. Of course the main lesson is to learn to love not in an egoistic way but in a pure and selfless way. This means that both partners learn how to enter into the oneness of each other. This is the symbol in the marriage ceremony were the two candles are joined and the two flames become one.

Unfortunately, some marriages become ill. What starts as two people believing they found their Soul mate can unfortunately turn into two people living like cellmates in a prison of their own making. This is the case when one person wants to dominate over the other or there is so much enmity and fighting that it makes them and their children sick. No one married or not, has the right to make a hell for another person. Also no one can force somebody to stay in a hell if they decide to leave. So in these cases sometimes it is better to divorce than continue torturing each other, building monstrous heart crushing Elementals. So it is not the priest reciting marriage prayers or the required legal language of a civil ceremony that binds the marrying couple. It is their heart and Soul that does the binding.

Indifference, faultfinding and complaints separate people. Love unites them. This is true on Earth, and in the Psychical and Noetical Worlds beyond.

Even the greatest marriage can only last for some years on Earth and then the married partners pass over. Do husbands and wives find each other on the other side in the Psychical Worlds of existence? Yes, if there is real love between them, but if they are not united in heart and mind in the material world they will not be likely to meet in the Psychical or Noetical Worlds.

Married couples come again in subsequent incarnations to learn the lesson they did not learn before. So God is uniting couples again and again until they learn the lessons of love and understanding. Or in some blessed cases a couple can return in harmonious Attunement with each other to share the sacred journey on Earth once again. Or they come again to join forces for a special purpose in life. Daskalos said he had seen couples come to him that had been married in more than ten previous incarnations.

The most powerful force joining two people together is their Soul connection. Then at the personality level, it is love and understanding. When you have real love, true understanding and a genuine Soul connection that marriage is sacred. When two people first experience love for each other, it is often referred to as "Falling in Love". When that love is true and selfless their actual experience is more like "Rising in Love."   Selfless love lifts the couple on its upwardly expanding currents, higher and higher. It gives the lover and the beloved a glimpse of the Divinity within them both.

Loving those who love us is human, but what should we do

when someone does not love us but hates us? It is said that loving someone who hates you is Divine and hating someone who loves you is devilish. This was Christ's advice, "I say unto you, Love your enemies, bless them that curse you, do good to them that hate you, and pray for them which despitefully use you, and persecute you." Of course we should not consider anyone our enemy, for in truth they are a brother or sister who is suffering under negative illusions, which means they need our love maybe more than our friends do. Others may consider you their enemy but you should not consider anyone your enemy. "If you love your enemies you will have none," Leo Tolstoy once declared.

Daskalos lived and taught on the Greek Island of Cyprus, about 65 miles from the coast of Lebanon where the clash between the different sects of the Muslims and Christians destroyed the city of Beirut and much of its population. Before the conflict erupted in the streets, Daskalos had over 200 students there and at the end of the conflict only two students were still living. In 1974, Muslims from Turkey invaded Cyprus killing and chasing the Greek-Cypriot Christians from their homes on the north side of the island to the south before UN troops halted the invasion.

At one point during this occupation the Greek Christian Cypriots decided to celebrate "National Days" with a parade in the streets on the Greek side next to the neutral zone. In doing so, they stimulated the same nationalistic pride in the Turkish Muslim Cypriots on their side of the neutral zone. Soon the Turkish Muslims started to celebrate their own version of National Days. Before the Christian Greeks started this kind of celebration, the Turkish

Muslims never cared about it or celebrated this. What was occurring was the Greek celebration created and greatly empowered nationalistic group Elementals, which awakened the same feelings in the Turks and so they started celebrating in opposition to the Greek celebration. These kinds of group Elementals are very powerful and can cause much harm. There are group Elementals within families, local communities and entire countries that greatly affect the people. When these groups are negative or have a "them vs. us" mentality human beings can become strongly influenced by these Elementals resulting in conflicts and wars.

Speaking to this Daskalos once said, "What have the Christians and Muslims succeeded to do in Lebanon? They have planned everything and you see how much bloodshed is in Lebanon? Do you think they did not plan to do the same thing in Cyprus? Why didn't they succeed? (Certain people are wondering, even telling me about that.) They did not succeed because we did not allow them to do it. There is a group of the Innermost Circle doing the work, flooding Cyprus with love, with the atmosphere of love. Thoughts have in them much power.

There is not any clash between the Muslims and the Greek Cypriots. Only on two occasions, and that was not on national things but on love affairs. They are wondering about this on both sides, but we take out the fuse from these bombs all the time, but how do we succeed to do that? If those fellows in the group, I call them Invisible Helpers, had in them the least trace of hatred, they would not succeed to do that. The life and blood of the Turkish and the life and blood of the Greeks are for us sacred in the same way. Now, we try to create Cypriot consciousness, for both of us, Christians and Muslims.

You in Switzerland, you have succeeded in it, you have created the Swiss consciousness, and no matter if you are German-speaking, French-speaking or Italian-speaking, you are Swiss. This is what we try to do in Cyprus now. To create Cypriot consciousness, Turkish-speaking or Greek-speaking, Cypriots are Cypriots, brothers. They must live together and they, I hope will succeed in the end. Love all, without exception. We cannot have enemies. Shall we have friends? Neither enemies nor friends - have brothers and sisters, fathers and mothers belonging to the same family, the human family. Now, I say that nationalism is a very bad thing. You ask me what nationality I am. I am a human. What is my country? It is the planet. What are the nations? They are rooms in the same big construction in which my family lives, and my family is every human being!"

Every human being is receiving the same sunlight, the same common substance of air that gives vitality and oxygen, not just to some but also to all. By that fact alone, we should be able to understand that all people have the same right to live and no one is to be considered an enemy. Look how often people who are slaves to their own egoism, start relationships as friends that turn into enemies. They start nice friendships but if they are victims of their own personal egoism, the friendship can become spoiled and they become enemies in the end. Yet, for the one who can reflect real unselfish love in his or her heart towards all, the elderly become like mothers and fathers, their peers become brothers and sisters and younger people become their children.

Loving others like that does not mean we love our blood related children, brothers, sisters or parents any less, it means we love more. You are not depriving your kin of love by loving other human beings unselfishly. If we learn to love others unconditionally and not egoistically, we receive protection from those who may wish us harm. So to stop making enemies we must first unseat egoism in us and learn to love properly. An egoistic person does not know how to love properly.

Some of the best teachings on real love can be found in the letters from Saint Paul, which state, "If I speak in the tongues of men and of Angels, but have not love, I am only a resounding gong or a clanging cymbal." (Notice how he is mentioning the language of Angels? This is because he knew the language of the Archangels) "Love is patient, love is kind. It does not envy, it does not boast, it is not proud. It is not rude, it is not self-seeking, it is not easily angered, and it keeps no record of wrongs. Love does not delight in evil but rejoices with the truth. It always protects, always trusts, always hopes, and always perseveres. Love never fails." ~ Saint Paul

So how can we express this kind of love? Who can express such a perfect love? Who is capable of teaching us what it means to really love? There are some who walk the Earth that can teach you about real love because they embody it. There is none nearer or dearer to show us what real love is, than our brother guide, our own Guardian Archangel. He is ready, willing, and able to teach us the miracle of Divine Love.

As we come into contact with our Guardian Archangel we will learn so much. We will learn about the nature of Divine Love by observing how our Guardian loves and cares for us. For our Guardian Archangel has been emanating his perfect love for us uninterrupted from the moment of our humanization and first incarnation. His full unification with us allows him to unerringly know all our intentions, motivations, thoughts, feelings, desires and actions. His charge is to guard and guide our developing personality.

Take note of how he carries out this duty of love:
- He constantly follows our life without interfering in it
- He leads us without coercion
- He shows us our mistakes without judgment or criticism
- He councils without dominating over our free will.
- He serves eternally without expecting a thank you in return

When we allow ourselves to get disturbed and start behaving badly by getting jealous, angry and hating; the Archangels accompanying us take a step back as it were. These types of destructive behaviors are disturbing the Holy Archangels in you, but it disturbs your Guardian Archangel more. Pay attention to this point. When we are disturbed enough to express anger, hatred, jealousy and the like, we are disturbing our Guardian and so our Guardian temporarily takes a step back from us so to speak. When we misuse the Etheric Vitality the Archangels provide us, they do not get angry; they simply withdraw for a time.

Your best spiritual master and guide is your Guardian Archangel, who is attending you, following every action of yours, every thought of yours, and every emotion of yours. Please try to understand that you are never ever alone. Every one of us is lovingly attended by his or her Guardian Archangel. Even when you are sleeping at night, your Present-Day-Personality is either in other planes of existence or sleepily dreaming. Your Guardian is never sleeping; he stays with you behaving just like a tender mother attending her beloved child. His love for you is perfect and uncontaminated. A Guardian Archangel is so closely attuned to a human being that he has sometimes been mistakenly identified as our "Twin Soul" or our "Inner Self." He is not our twin Soul and he is definitely not our Inner Self; although he is in unification with our Inner Self. So he rightfully speaks for the Inner Self, but he is a bit more lenient.

Now, imagine this perfect Eternal Spirit Being, who is complete in its immaculate Love, Wisdom and Power, always watching even your most subtle thoughts, feelings and actions each day, seven days a week, 52 weeks a year, throughout your whole life, on Earth, and in the worlds beyond, lifetime after lifetime. Can you imagine this kind of love? Can you conceive of a love that is capable of witnessing all of our mistakes, all of our crimes of spirit and all of our violations of Divine Law that we have committed over all our many lifetimes? He does this without a single complaint or condemnation. Can you feel his Divine Love for you? What kind of love is this?

Who saw to it that such a great guide and powerful protector as our Guardian Archangel would accompany each and every human being in all their incarnations? What love is so caring that it provides each of us with this Super-Conscious Guardian? It is the love of

God, of course, but it is also the Guardian Archangel's own love that joins his Spirit Ray with our Spirit Ray at the point of our humanization. These Guardians are Archangels, Divine emissaries, and their will is the same as God's will. God's will automatically rise within all the Archangels as their own will. They express God's will according to the classification of their particular Archangelic order. They are so near and dear to God that we could metaphorically consider them as the very breath of God.

When we speak about the Divine Love and the work of the Guardian Archangels, we are not offering you a dusty old theory, mechanically repeated century after century by those without direct experience. We are not presenting some unsubstantiated new-age notion for you to blindly believe. We are revealing our own first hand experiences and that of many, many other seekers of truth past and present. If you are sincere with your approach to the Guardian Archangel, it will be your own self-evident experience too!

THE PRACTICE OVERVIEW

To reflect Divine Love we must make our personality clean and bright. If we have light coming in our home from a window, and we place a piece of black paper in that sunlight, it will not reflect any light in the room. Place a white piece of paper in the sunlight and it will reflect the light very well. Place a crystal clear mirror in that light and it will reflect the sunlight perfectly. In a similar way when we clean our personality of anxiety, fear, animosity, and other negativities, we become brighter and can reflect love to others much better.

So this is our aim, to sincerely make an effort over the course of our life to eliminate any dark thoughts and feelings that will obscure the light of love. The practices of the Researchers of Truth do this and replace any negativity and darkness in our personality with positive life affirming qualities. This creates the conditions that allow an ever-increasing amount of Divine love to be reflected though our personality to others and that also accelerates our own spiritual unfoldment.

THE PRACTICE: REFLECTING DIVINE LOVE CONTEMPLATION

Close your eyes, and relax completely.

Love is the Divine flame uniting all Souls. Why not all personalities? You are already united with everyone as Spirit-Souls in the common Selfhood of God. Why not unite ourselves, our personalities also, in that Divine Love of the Logos? This Love nourishes all of our bodies (our Psychical and our Noetical Body, and the Etheric Doubles) purifying them and uniting us with the Logos, who is everywhere and in us.

Breathe deeply now and ask yourself these questions: What is love? Do I love? Whom do I love and why?"

Now, make your heart a bright sun with golden light, or canary-yellow light, radiating this light around you. Feel that light.

Clean any negativity from your hearts so to be able to reflect God's love clearly.

Clean your heart to radiate this Love towards God and towards all other human beings.

Now, bring in front of you certain people, one by one, with whom you had differences. Now see them happy. See their faces lit from this light of your own heart. Now bring more people around you, people with whom you have differences and whom you love. Fill the space, your Noetical space with people you know. See this light from your heart shine on their faces and send them a wish with this light, "May God always keep you in good health and in His love." This is a most powerful Elemental, purely Noetical Elemental. The only desire in it is your wish to see these people in good health and living happily. Learn to create these most powerful Elementals. They can stop wars! Of course, one has to learn how to love, starting with the individuals and the members of the family first.

Chapter Twenty-Five
INITIATION & PROTECTION

Now, what is the need for initiation? For anyone who has attended three lessons and wishes to continue, you are entitled to ask to become an initiate of the Researchers of Truth. The ones who don't want to be initiated they can still attend the lessons without being initiated. A point to remember is that initiation itself is of no importance. What does initiation symbolize? Does it make any difference for those who are initiated and those who don't want to be initiated, while attending classes and want to continue? No, not for your teachers, and me but it does give the initiates a sense of belonging to a circle of research. It is something that helps them and they gain more confidence and Faith within themselves. It is for their own concern, as those that attend classes get help from their teachers.

So initiation is not necessary, at least in the beginning. Naturally those who will enter the inner and innermost circles must be initiated. But initiation is not necessary for those who want to follow lessons only up to a certain point even if it is quite advanced, up to Exosomatosis. After a certain point is reached where everyone's aim in the group is for the common work within the Divine Plan, then, initiation becomes necessary. On your initiation you make the seven promises. These promises you make to yourself, it is only a promise not an oath. We differ from other systems because we follow Christ's teachings. "Do not take an oath." You will not take an oath and then find that you cannot carry it out. The promise is to yourself that you will try live by the promises You may not be able to do it in the beginning but you can keep on trying. So in actual fact it is an obligation to your Self. ~ Daskalos

On this day, my friend, Mr. Will from New York and I were especially eager to arrive at Daskalos' home as he had agreed to create a unique and very powerful talisman for each of us. This type was no ordinary talisman as it was extremely potent and created a lasting protection for the one it was created for and would go on protecting those related to them for generations to come. During its creation, Daskalos also invoked the assistance of the Archangels who would volunteer to come forward and help lift some of our Karmic burden. Additionally, the procedure would burn off some of our own negative Elementals that were hindrances to our progress. The process took some dedicated time so we arrived early and found him waiting for us in his sitting room. The deeper significance of all this was beyond our understanding at the time, but we did know how great and rare this opportunity was and so we were grateful and willing participants.

Before creating the talismans, Daskalos was to initiate us into the System for the Research of Truth. This initiation was done in the same way as it had always been done in the past centuries in this lineage. For this small ceremony, Daskalos used the un-pointed sword, a replica of the sword broken by the Magi Melchior (Ham El Khior) when he saw the Christ child. Daskalos explained that whoever was to be initiated would see the un-pointed sword that has written on it, "At thine immaculate feet, O Logos be all authority."

Daskalos then asked his daughter, Panayiota, and another member of his inner circle to attend as witnesses to the initiation. The rush of modern cultures towards the future has left the age-old rite of initiation behind. The ritual of initiation in itself is not that important. The importance is in what it symbolizes, the transmission it confers, and also what a mystic has to gain as experience and truth. There are many tests one has to undergo to receive the initiations. There is not just one but many initiations into the wisdom and the teachings, which do entail dangers. In more advanced initiations we face life and death situations. This is why it is important to choose wisely as we approach real initiations. If we not are strong and courageous is better not to proceed, because you will face powerful tests. Over 35,000 years ago, initiations performed in caves marked a major transition, a rite of passage from one stage of life to another. These early ceremonies propelled young males into manhood and the adult life. Others kinds of initiations launched prepared seekers into the great spiritual mysteries. These were not empty rituals as most ceremonies are today. They were full of power actualizing a dramatic psychological shift on the individual.

As I bent to kneel for the initiation, I reflected back on how the lineage of the Researchers of Truth began 2000 years ago as the three Magi knelt before the Christ child. Now Daskalos was initiating us into the same system of mysticism started at that profound moment in history. We made the seven promises and Daskalos asked if we would like to serve in psychotherapy or in social work. We said psychotherapy. Then he made some statements giving us his blessings and finished the initiation by touching us with his replica of the un-pointed sword as we knelt on one knee. Not only did this resemble a ceremonious induction into spiritual knighthood; it had in it the power and purpose of it as well. We rose and he kissed us on the cheeks.

After completing the initiation, Mr. Will and I followed him as he carried the un-pointed sword into his kitchen and prepared to create our talismans. Daskalos did not speak as he assembled the materials needed for his work. He collected two small plates of different size, a candlestick holder with a white candle, a black and a red felt tip marker and set them down on the table next to the sword. Next, he took a small disc of black charcoal the size of a quarter and some white pebble size chunks of floral incense like the type used in the local Greek churches. Then he brought out two pieces of pastel yellow paper about nine inches by nine inches and sat down at the head of the table with us.

Daskalos placed the little nuggets of incense on top of the charcoal disc and set fire to the edge of the disc. As the flame touched charcoal, it began to make a hissing sound. Tiny orange sparks, like miniature fireworks effervesced out in all directions quickly spreading over the entire disc. The charcoal became glowing hot and the heat melted the white incense. It bubbled and turned black as it released streams of sweet smelling smoke into the air. The spiraling smoke and my anticipation rose steadily upward. The smoke billowed outward, mixing with the early morning light coming through the kitchen windows to create a misty sanctuary all around us. Daskalos lit the candle and made a prayer. Sacredness fell over the room. He started by using a plate and a black marker to create a black circle about six inches in diameter. Then using a slightly smaller plate and the red marker, he created a red circle within the black circle. The dry squeak of the felt tipped marker dragging over the paper broke the room's soft silence. Next Daskalos used the un-pointed sword as a straight edge and drew a red, double six-pointed star one within the other; both inside the circles. The double six-pointed star is a most powerful protective symbol as it protects both from negative forces coming from outside us and from those negative influences that arises within our own personality.

    He turned and asked what religion I was, to which I replied "Christian," and he made some marks on his drawing. Then he began combining Indian Sanskrit and Egyptian hieroglyphics into individual symbols. He implanted protective Elementals on these. He also drew and wrote other things within and under the red six-pointed star. All the time he held a strong, unbroken attention on what he was doing. The reason for using all these forms of writing was to insure no one skilled in the black arts could decipher what he wrote and break its protective power. This was not a problem I expected to encounter in rural America; but apparently, it was a problem on Cyprus. This kind of talisman was the kind made by the old Egyptian Hierophants that protected the entire material body as well as the Psychical and Noetical Bodies.

As he completed the drawing, I assumed he was done but he was just beginning. Next, he placed the lit candle over the center of the talisman. The flame burned steadily, its soft glow cast a slight golden light on Daskalos' face. Then he really turned up the power.

He drew a slow deep breath, concentrated very intently and went to work. Daskalos moved his hands mysteriously above and around the drawing for a few minutes. Then his eyes focused on the space between his hands and the flame. He held up his index finger about two feet away from the flame. Then he very slightly moved his index finger about a half-inch towards the candle flame. As he moved his finger, the flame instantly sputtered, flickered and moved simultaneously in the opposite direction of his finger movement. He did it again with the same results all the while intensely staring at the flame. He continued this for about five minutes moving his hand lightly around the candle at the same distance repeatedly tapping his finger towards the flame. The whole process looked as if he was pressing something invisible into the flame. Judging by the flame's instant reaction, he was. Later he explained how in that process he was capturing certain negative Elementals and driving them into the flame, which freed me of their influence. From his first incarnation, Daskalos had always felt an affinity with the fire element and spoke of how much he enjoyed dissolving negative Elementals by driving them into the flame.

At the end of this extraordinary rite he asked the Archangels if any would volunteer to help. Daskalos announced that Michael and

Raphael had come forward and would help me in life. Concluding his work, he turned to me and began revealing specific and very private things about my relationships that no one knew but me. He also revealed hidden dynamics in these relationships that I had not yet discovered but soon would. Daskalos disclosure hinted at things I could do to improve those conditions. When I went back to America I followed these suggestions and these things resolved quickly. That certainly proved to me that he had indeed seen problem areas unknown to me, correctly diagnosed them and offered the proper remedies that did work. Next he did Mr. Will's talisman in the same way. Finally, Daskalos demonstrated to us how to use our hands and fingers on the talisman to call on the Archangels and him when we truly needed help. This too I tried when I returned to America and it produced a fast and significant help for someone.

Then Daskalos did something completely unexpected and touching. He had our talismans mounted and framed at the shop across the street from his home and presented them to us as a gift. All this wisdom and power offered to us so sweetly with love penetrated me to the core. We thanked him heartily; he slightly nodded barely acknowledging our gratitude. Daskalos did not need or want acknowledgement for his service and a thank you was about as much as he would accept.

The sweet floral incense lingered on our clothing as Mr. Will and I stepped out of the sanctuary of Daskalos' humble home and into the brilliant Cyprus sunlight. Our precious time with Daskalos was just about over and our return to America was eminent. I wondered to myself if I would ever return to Daskalos again. The instant I had that thought, the answer arose within me loud and clear, "Many Times!"

Epilogue

THE GREAT SUN

    I am the Great Sun but you do not see me

    I am your husband but you turn away

    I am the captive but you do not free me

    I am the captain you will not obey

    I am the truth but you will not believe me

    I am that city where you will not stay

    I am your wife; your child but you will leave me

    I am that God to whom you will not pray

    I am your council but you do not hear me

    I am your lover that you will betray

    I am your life but if you do not name me

    Seal up your Soul with tears and never blame me

Found on a 16th century Norman crucifix

GLOSSARY OF TERMS

Our System for the Research of Truth employs terms and concepts in a particular fashion. The translators have labored to preserve the eloquence contained in the Greek original. To avoid confusing our language and terminology with that of other schools and other disciplines, and to gain clarity over the material, we appeal to the readers to consult this glossary.

ABSOLUTE BEINGNESS, INFINITE BEINGNESS, GOD, THE FATHER, THE LORD, THE HIGHEST.

These terms are used interchangeably. In spite of the use of masculine pronouns with any of the above terms, Absolute Beingness and any of the other expressions used for God are without gender. God is all and everything.

ARCHANGELS, ANGELS

Archangels are Holy Spiritual Beings assisting in the construction and maintenance of the worlds. They possess Total Wisdom and Absolute Self-awareness (though lacking the self-conscious individuality specific to humans). We speak in praise of the Archangels of the elements, the Orders of Authorities, of Cherubim, of Dominions, of Overlords, of Principalities, of Seraphim and of the Thrones. In our work we speak of seven Orders of Archangels, each composed of billions and billions of Holy Monadic Beings serving Creation. Angels are Elementals of the Archangels.

ARCHANGELIC MAN

Archangelic Man is one of the Ideas (see 'Heavenly Man' and 'Causes, Ideas and Principles' below). The Holy Monadic emanation passes through the Idea of Archangelic Man on its way to the Idea of Heavenly Man, thus the Archangels are the brothers of humanity.

AT-ONE-MENT

The super-conscious state in which a Being is able to merge itself in total oneness with any other Being or existence, and with Absolute Beingness in Theosis, without ever abandoning its Ego.

ATTUNEMENT

Attunement means adjusting our vibrations to the frequency of any other existence or Being to the extent that we can observe and study its nature. Attunement is reached prior to at-one-mint.

BEING and EXISTING

Existing has a beginning and an end and is thus a timed or temporal phenomenon. Being is timeless and eternal, without beginning or end.

CAUSES, IDEAS and PRINCIPLES

The Will-pleasure of Absolute Beingness is the primal Cause, as it is the cause of Creation. It is from within the Will-pleasure of Absolute Beingness, all the Causes spring. Causes then give rise to Ideas. Every Idea holds within it the whole Cycle of Possibility of the form to be created. Archangels work through the Ideas and impart

Total Wisdom to each form. Principles govern the expression of Causes in time and space.

CAUSAL STATE

Above the Noetic State, the causal state is a condition of pure Ideas and Principles. It is also known as the fifth heaven.

CAUSE AND EFFECT, LAW OF

Scientists as well as mystics recognize the Law of Cause and Effect. This Divine Law requires every action to result in a reaction. Yet, whereas Eastern religions often teach a deterministic view of this Law (terming it Karma), we believe that debts can be born for others or transcended through repentance (see below) and reparation. The Law of Cause and Effect operates over several lifetimes as well as within much shorter periods.

CHRIST, CHRIST LOGOS, LOGOS, LOGOI, LOGOIC

The Greek word Logos can be translated as 'word' (as the Authorized Version does in the first chapter of St. John's gospel). Christ, as used here, alone or in conjunction with Logos, refers to the 'Only Begotten Son'. When Jesus, as the incarnation of the Christ Logos, is specifically meant, He is sometimes referred to as 'the Most Beloved Logos'. In our work, we often speak of the Holy Logos and the God-Man Jesus Christ, a full, direct, and pure incarnation of the Logoic expression of Absolute Beingness, synonymously. Logoi is the plural of Logos, Logoic is the adjective.

COSMIC CONSCIOUSNESS, COSMIC MEMORY

Here every event, past and present, in all the worlds is recorded. A mystic can perform research by attuning himself to the Cosmic Consciousness. Contained within the Cosmic Consciousness is the Cosmic Memory. This is the 'heavenly archive' where the impressions, actions, thoughts, emotions and desires of all the Beings are recorded.

CYCLE/CIRCLE OF POSSIBILITIES

The Cycle of Possibility of each form is laid down in Total Wisdom in the Divine Laws and Causes. All forms are continually developing: from seed to tree, from child to adult. Each form changes so that experience may be gathered. In the Eternal Now a form is complete and based on a Principle, with its Cycle of Possibility already established. On entering the Worlds of Existence (material, Psychical and Noetical), the Cycle of Possibility is inscribed on the Permanent Personality, and parameters are set (time and place). No form may escape its Cycle of Possibility, thus ruling out transmigration from one form to any other (humans will always reincarnate as humans).

CYCLE/CIRCLE OF PROBABILITIES

While the cycle of possibilities is the ideal development and is inescapable, the cycle of probabilities allows for the halting of a developing life at any point of its development.

A seed may not grow, a young tree may become diseased and die, or a child may pass over. Within each Cycle of Possibility, we find millions of cycles of probabilities; it is probable that something or someone may stop existing or, conversely, continue to exist. Each Cycle of Possibility, whether fulfilled or interrupted, has great wisdom behind it in serving the Law.

DIVINE

The Word Divine is used only for the Qualities, Causes, Ideas, Laws and Principles, and Beings, which emanate directly from Absolute Beingness.

DIVINE GRACE

It is a gift of Divine Grace that we exist as humans, in our bodies, in the universes.

DIVINE LAWS

The Divine Laws are the basic structure of Creation, governing all worlds and universes, and corresponding to our higher nature. Epitomizing Reason and Love manifested, it is our recognition of, and alignment with, these Laws (e.g., of Cause and Effect, of Harmony, of Order, of Growth of Love), which leads to our balanced and enhanced spiritual development.

DIVINE MEDITATION

Intricately linked to the Will-pleasure of Absolute Beingness to express Itself within Itself. Divine Meditation, for lack of a better term, is believed to be the state prior to the Will-pleasure where Absolute Beingness contemplates expression. Within Divine

Meditation Creation is conceived.

DIVINE MERCY

A little understood, but most compassionate force in Creation, that permits the seeming miraculous to take place. James, in his epistle, wrote, 'and mercy rejoices against judgment' (3:13).

DIVINE PLAN

The Divine Plan is the blueprint of Creation, perfect and complete, accounting for everything and for all occurrences. Attuning our thoughts and actions to the most-wise Divine Plan of Absolute Beingness is the purpose of our existence.

ECSTASY

Real Ecstasy is a going out from oneself into the Kingdom of Heavens through expansion, At-One-Ment and/or Attunement. Ecstasy implies a passing beyond all conceptual thinking of discursive reason.

EGO and EGOISM

Our use of these terms is not to be confused with contemporary psychological terminology. Egoism defiles Mind by the construction of selfish desires, and by the base emotions of greed, malice and envy. The Ego (with a capital E) is the Self as Beingness, the Soul nature, and is reflected through a reasoning and loving personality. While egoism (a weakness of our present personality) is the source of disease throughout the personality, the nation and the world, our Ego nature brings forth love, compassion, reasoned thinking and reasoned action.

ELEMENTALS

Every thought, emotion and desire creates and transmits an Elemental-also called thought-form-that carries on an existence of its own. We create and regenerate two types of Elementals. When an emotion governs a thought, we have created emotional thought-forms, or desire-thoughts. When our ideas, desires and emotions pass through reason and love, we create reasoned thought-forms, or thought-desires. An Elemental can never be destroyed, only dis-energized (by no longer feeding the Elemental with Etheric Vitality). Elementals of a kind collect to form powerful group Elementals. If an individual, or a collection of individuals, are vibrating at the same frequency, they will attract such group Elementals. Archangels also create Elementals: benign and angelic in the service of humanity.

ETERNAL NOW, ETERNAL PRESENT

Beyond the Worlds of Existence is the Eternal Now, the state of Everlasting Life. There, past, present and future collapse into a single present, without time or place.

ETHER, ETHERIC VITALITY

'Our daily bread', Etheric Vitality (Mind) is obtained through breathing, meditation, eating and rest. We swim in a sea of Etheric Vitality which surrounds and permeates the globe, yet, through disharmonious lifestyles; most of us exhaust our portion of Etheric

Vitality and are unable to restore it, leading to physical and psychic distress. All existence, including our bodies, is constructed within a mold of ether (the Etheric Double). We speak of four conditions of ether: creative, sensate, imprint and kinetic.

ETHERIC CENTERS, SACRED DISCS

Centers of energy and activity (Sanskrit: Chakras) located at various points on the Etheric Doubles of our bodies. Each of the three bodies, from the gross material to the more refined, displays these centers, which correspond to organs of the material body. We must exercise care in working with these centers, for while it is necessary for us to develop and awaken certain of them, others are the domain of the Holy Spirit, the Archangels and the Logos (e.g., the 'root' and the heart centers) and we should refrain from any manipulation or direct interference. (For 'Heart Center' see below)

ETHERIC DOUBLES

Each body of every existence, from the simplest to the most complex structures, possesses an Etheric Double centered within the body and extending slightly beyond it. The Etheric Double exists as long as the body (whether material, Psychical or Noetical) is projected. When a material body is withdrawn (passes over) its Etheric Double dissolves. The Etheric Double serves as the mold for the body's construction and in the preservation of the body's health.

EXOSOMATOSIS

Exosomatosis is the Greek equivalent of the English

expression 'out of body experience' (OBE). We all leave our bodies each night, during sleep, and travel to other planes subconsciously. The aim, however, is to live consciously while out of our bodies. We know of first, second and third Exosomatosis.

GUARDIAN ARCHANGEL

At the point of our first incarnation, upon passing through the Human Idea, the Self-aware Soul is protected and guided, throughout its long sojourn into the worlds of separation, by an Archangel. This Archangel, our faithful companion, is from the Archangels of the Thrones.

GROSS MATERIAL WORLD, BODY

This is the lowest vibration of Mind. Mind made solid to compose the material world and the bodies.

FAITH

Not only an individual or theoretical belief in the dogmatic truths of a religion, but an all-embracing relationship, recognition of, and love for Absolute Beingness. As such it involves a complete transformation of a person's personality, whereby we are taken up into the whole the anthropic activity of God in Christ and of man in Christ through which we achieve Theosis. Faith, above all, is an active virtue: 'Faith without works is dead...' (James 3:26). Also see 'Repentance' below.

HEAVENLY MAN/HUMAN IDEA

The Heavenly Man is the Idea of Man or sometimes called the Human Idea. Our bodies are constructed according to the Causal Law of the Heavenly Man – Human Idea – Human Form.

HEART CENTER

Not simply the physical organ but the spiritual center of Mankind's Being. Man made in the image of Absolute Beingness as reason and love, our truest self, our inner sanctum, through which the mystery of the union between the Divine and the mundane is consummated. 'Heart' has thus an all-embracing significance. Prayer of the heart means prayer not just in the emotions and affections, but also of the whole person. We should strive to purify this heart for 'God knoweth your hearts,' writes Luke (16:15).

HOLY

All Creation is Holy, born of the Divine expression. That which is Holy is projected (as opposed to that which is emanated) from the Divine.

HOLY MONAD, HOLY MONADIC SELF

A Holy Monad is one of countless myriads of 'cells' within the Multiplicity of Absolute Beingness - God.

HOLY SPIRIT

The Holy Spirit is the impersonal Super-consciousness that expresses the power of Absolute Beingness and makes possible the creation of the universes. It is the dynamic aspect of the Absolute.

IDEA, DIVINE

See under 'Causes, Ideas and Principles'

INNER SELF

This is a term indicating the Self in its expressions above the present-day personality.

KARMA

See under Cause & Effect, Law of

LOOKING WITHIN

This is the process of Introspection or self-examination, of 'knowing thyself'. This is the core practice of every Researcher of Truth and all those interested in Self Realization.

MIND

The Mind is a Divine emanation of Absolute Beingness to which all existences owe their construction. Imbued with the Divine Wisdom, Love, Power and Purity of its Creator, Mind is not an immortal Being, but is eternally used as the substance of all Creation. Mind is Divine at its source, and Holy in its expression.

NOETIC STATE

The Noetic State is a state of Ideas and unexpressed forms beyond the worlds of separation. This state is where we come to rest in between incarnations and where the Archangels derive the forms into which to breathe life.

NOETICAL IMAGE

A multi-dimensional image of Noetical or Psycho-Noetical substance, fanned by thought by means of Noetic light. Once formed it is everlasting, as are all Elementals.

NOETICAL WORLD, NOETICAL BODY

The Noetical is the worlds of the fifth dimension and the most rarefied of the three worlds of separation. In the Noetical Worlds (home of the Noetical Body), the Total Wisdom of Absolute Beingness first finds expression as form, ranging from universes and galaxies to unicellular organisms. Time and place are attributes of the Noetical World, but not in the sense understood in the psychic and material worlds.

OVER LORDSHIP

In varying degrees, we find over lordship as in a sense of dominion and Divine Authority as ordained from above.

PERMANENT ATOM

That part of the Permanent Personality, which acts as the recorder of the experiences, it has received in the place-time worlds. The Permanent Atom is situated in the etheric heart of each body simultaneously, and registers all the emotions, thoughts, reactions and experiences as they occur in the three worlds.

PERMANENT PERSONALITY

This is the active and expressive part of Soul in Self-awareness within the worlds of separation, which filters knowledge (from the present-day personality) and distils Wisdom.

PRESENT, PRESENT-DAY, TEMPORARY PERSONALITY

A personality developed during each incarnation, whom we call 'George or Mary' or whatever. The present-day personality is a projection of the Permanent Personality into the worlds of separation.

PSYCHIC/PSYCHICAL WORLD, BODY

This is the fourth dimensional world, also known as the 'World of emotions'. The super-sensuous Psychic World is composed of seven planes, each having seven sub-planes. It is to the psychic World that we travel in first Exosomatosis, in our Psychical Body, and to which, on passing over, we first return.

PSYCHO-NOETICAL

The relationship between the psychic World (emotions) and the Noetical World (thoughts) is often so intimate and interwoven that we need to consider them as semi-unified. In a thought there is often emotion, and in every emotion there is a measure of thought.

REPENTANCE

The Greek word for repentance is metanoia, which signifies

primarily a change of 'mind' or 'change of intellect': not only sorrow, contrition or regret, but also more positively and fundamentally the conversion or turning of our whole life towards alignment with Absolute Beingness' Divine Plan. Also see 'Faith' as described above.

SELF-AWARENESS, SELF-AWARE, SELF-CONSCIOUS

These are terms referring to conscious awareness, in varying degrees, of the Self within the Divine Plan.

SELFHOOD

This term refers to the Personality as a unified, Divine, Being. Selfhood encompasses all the expression of the Self from Its apex as the Holy Monadic Spirit-Ego-Being filtered down to the petty present day personality. Within the Selfhood not a single expression is devalued; each is cherished in its own right. Our Spirit-Ego-Being partakes in the Will-Pleasure of Absolute Beingness (to express Itself in Itself) by expressing Itself within its own Selfhood. We mirror God's Good Creation within our own good creation, within our Selfhood.

SELF-REALIZATION

This is the Self-Realization of the Permanent Personality as Individuated Beingness. It is the culmination of the gathering of experiences in the worlds of separation. At the point of Self-Realization, the Permanent Personality reunified with Self-aware Soul is prepared to assimilate with the Spirit-Ego-Being in Theosis.

SELF-SUFFICIENCY

Self-Sufficiency is the primary Nature of Absolute Beingness, in complete Abundance, Blessedness and independence of all needs.

SEPARATION, WORLDS OF EXISTENCE

This phrase covers the three worlds of existence (material, Psychic and Noetical) in which our personalities spend their periods of seeming separation from the Spirit states of At-One-Ment and Beingness

SOUL

A Soul is formed when a ray of a Holy Monad passes through the Idea of Heavenly Man. The Soul is not created; it is a small pearl from the Spirit, which comes to be known as the Self-aware Soul. The Soul is in a formless state as Spirit, and remains formless. When returning to the Godhead, marries the Spirit-Ego-Being, it has become fuller.

SPIRIT-EGO-BEING

This is the Self in its full divinity, eternal, unmovable. Our Spirit-Ego-Being is the Self as Holy Monad; in total At-One-Ment with the Self-sufficiency and Multiplicity of the Godhead. The Will-pleasure of Absolute Beingness to express Itself within Itself is identical with the Will of our Spirit-Ego-Being to express Itself in Its own Selfhood.

SUB CONSCIOUS, SUB CONSCIOUSNESS

Researchers of the Truth understand the triadic nature of Sub Consciousness. One chamber of the subconscious contains all the Elementals composing our personality. A second chamber is the storehouse of Etheric Vitality (sometimes called our 'animal vitality') The third and most valued chamber is that of the Logos and Holy Spirit, for it is through the subconscious that the Holy Spirit and the Logos impart Total Wisdom, Total Power and Total Love.

SUPER-CONSCIOUSNESS

Super-consciousness is total awareness in Beingness.

SYSTEM FOR THE RESEARCH OF TRUTH

Our system of Esoteric Christianity celebrates the eternal truths known to all great religious traditions, while firmly based in the teachings of the God-Man Jesus Christ and the New Testament. Through directed study, exercises and meditations, we seek the balanced evolution and integration of our entire being. Our approach is methodical, safe and self-evident.

TETRAKTYS

(Pronounced tet-ruk-TEES) A group of four. The elements of Earth, Air, Fire and Water compose a tetraktys.

THEOSIS

At-One-Ment with the One God, Absolute Beingness.

TOTAL LOVE, WISDOM and POWER

This is the Primary Natures of Absolute Beingness and Beings. Forming a sacred triangle each Nature is dependent on the other to be expressed properly.

WILL-PLEASURE

The Greek word 'euareskeia' has no exact equivalent in English. It carries a sense of pleasure derived from bountiful giving, as practiced by a warmly generous and wealthy source. Will-Pleasure was used in preference to 'bounty' or 'charity' to avoid misconceptions. We have described euareskeia as 'God's pleasure in creativeness'.